PRANIC

Using Breathing With
Healing Mantras

Dr. L. R. CHOWDHRY

HEALTH 🌳 HARMONY
An imprint of

PRANIC HEALING

First Indian Edition: 1997
5th Impression: 2009

© 1997 by Dr. L. R. Chowdhry

Published by Kuldeep Jain for

HEALTH  **HARMONY**

An imprint of
B. JAIN PUBLISHERS (P) LTD.
An ISO 9001 : 2000 Certified Company
1921/10, Chuna Mandi, Paharganj, New Delhi 110 055 (INDIA)
Tel.: 91-11-2358 0800, 2358 1100, 2358 1300, 2358 3100
Fax: 91-11-2358 0471 • Email: info@bjain.com
Website: www.bjainbooks.com

Printed in India by
J.J. Offset Printers

ISBN: 978-81-319-0107-6

DEDICATION

This Book is dedicated as Commemorative Volume to the Linguists of English language who knew the Power of Healing Words to coin words like IMMUNITY, the utterance of which can boost the immunity of a person. Similarly the word "COMMUNICATE" sets up communication between various sections of our Brain. Also the word HEALING stimulates the healing process in our body, the word IMPROVING helps to improve our health, and the word ILLUMINATE indeed brings about illumination in our eyes and brain. And, above all, the word ENERGY can energize us. Thus, these words have the potentiality to save millions of people suffering from the scourge of Cancer, Aids, Alzheimer's and other chronic diseases.

About the Author

Dr. L.R. Chowdhry M.Sc., Ph.D. has been a Nuclear Physicist by profession, with brilliant academic and research record. He was initiated into Transcendental Meditation in Hyderabad in 1976 and later participated in a Conference on Science and Transcendental Meditation; in which Maharishi Mahesh Yogi was present.

Also, the author came across a very authentic book on Yoga, "The Complete Illustrated Book of Yoga by Swami-Vishnudevananda where-in on page 323 are given the list of words which can give resonant sonic energy to various Astral body Chakras.

Then, he read a very meaningful article in Scientific American, where using Ultrasonic Waves, the entropy of the system was made reversible, a normally irreversible phenomenon like old age. This triggered his imagination. Why not use the power of the sound words to rejuvenate, and thus reverse old age.

And, since 1990, after his retirement, he has applied his keen scientific intellect in studying the effect of each spoken word on various Astral Body Chakras and their healing effect on various gross body ailments. Based on this, he recently read a paper entitled "The Role of Healing Words in Managing Parkinson's and Alzheimer's Diseases"; in First International Conference on Yoga in Daily Life, held in December, 1996 in New Delhi. Since then, many more papers have been read in various International Conferences on Yoga/Alternative Therapy. This work has been acclaimed as a very powerful technique in Self Healing. He is presently Founder Director of Divine Mantra Pranic Healing Institute at 1004, Sector 4, Gurgaon-India-122001.

CONTENTS

Chapter No.	SUBJECT	Page No.
(i)	Preface	8

SECTION-I
MIRACLE OF THE MANTRA

1.	The Power of the Words/Mantra	15
2.	What is Pranic Healing	45

SECTION - II
BLOOM AND BLOSSOM AT ALL AGES

3.	The Fore-Most Mantra - 'AHAÑM'	55
4.	Heal Thyself	60
5.	The King of Mantras	62
6.	The Godly Mantra	64
7.	The Mantra — Pra	69
8.	Develop Wisdom Teeth	72
9.	Rejuvenate Your Heart	74
10.	The Mantra — Imperial - Living	82
11.	Become Taller	84
12.	A Salutation Mantra	86
13.	A Nourishing Mantra for the Mind	88
14.	Invest in your Health	90
15.	The Mantra — I Kindle Life	92
16.	Mantra — I Am Flowering	94
17.	A Meaningful Health Mantra	96
18.	Sky is the Limit	98
19.	A Flourescent Mantra	100
20.	Want to be Wealthy	102
21.	A Beautifying Mantra	104
22.	A Heart Warming Mantra	106

Chapter No.	SUBJECT	Page No.

23. The Mantra — Mingle 106
24. A Great Health Improving Mantra 110
25. The Self Searching Mantra 113
26. A Fragrant Mantra 116
27. Develop Impressive Personality 118
28. Live Eminently 120
29. Become a Lamp 122
30. Star-Dawn/Industry 125
31. Become an Iron Man 129
32. Water - The Major Constituent of Body 131
33. Bloom & Blossom at all Ages 134

SECTION - III
IMPROVE EYESIGHT AND BRAIN POWER

34. Improvement in Eyesight 143
35. Strengthen Brain and Memory 157
36. Enjoy Magnificent Memory 171

SECTION - IV
SLOW DOWN AGEING PROCESS

37. Slow Down Ageing Process 175
38. Experience the Timelessness 179
39. Become Ageless 180
40. Conquer Old Age 183
41. A Song Capsule to Cure all Diseases 189
42. Increase Health - Span 195
43. Re-Ignite Your Body Fire 197
44. Mantra for Liver Improvement 200
45. Prevent Tooth Decay 202
46. Boost Sex Power 204
47. A Life Revival Mantra 213
48. A Mantra to Live Hundred Years 219

Chapter No.	SUBJECT	Page No.

SECTION - V
MANAGEMENT OF CHRONIC AILMENTS

49. Management of Alcoholism 225
50. Cure Obesity 234
51. Remove Constipation 241
52. Cure Bronchial Asthma 244
53. Cure Cervical Spondylitis 245
54. Management of Back Ache 252
55. Cure Diabetes.. 254
56. Management of Parkinson's and
    Alzheimer's Diseases 261
57. Develop Immunity Against Cancer
    and AIDS... 273

SECTION - VI
STRESS MANAGEMENT

58. Stress and its Management 279
59. Say, Yes to Life.. 315
60. I am Interested in Me.. 319
61. The Soul Searching Mantra...................................... 320
62. I am in Equilibrium... 323
63. A Friendly Mantra 326
64. Become an Angel.. 328
65. A Simple Mantra to Reach the Seashore
    of Life Safely.. 330
66. Sleep Inducing Mantra 333
67. Still the Mind 337
68. I am Hopeful 339
69. The Mantra — I Am Brilliant 342
70. The Bhakti Mantra 345
71. The Mantra — I am in Prayer 347

Chapter No.	SUBJECT	Page No.

72. A Zero Gravity Swim 349
73. Wear a Coveted Smile 351
74. Refresh your Body/Mind 352
75. The Mantra — I am in Heaven 354
76. Laughter - The Best Medicine 356
77. Walking - The Best Health Mantra 359
78. A Life Saving Mantra 363
79. Silence - The Great Tranquillizer 366
80. Become Fearless 371
81. I Am Like That - 'SOHAM' 373

SECTION - VII
BECOME A SIDHA / HEALER

82. Remain Energetic and
    BECOME PRANIC/REIKI LIKE HEALER 379
83. A SIDHA MANTRA 'AUM' 385
84. The Parting Song 391

PREFACE

We are on a joyous visit to this Temple of SELF-Healing where God helps those who are ready to help themselves. This is possible by yoking ourselves to the God Almighty-the Super Consciousness, through the medium of breath which enlivens our body. Thus, we can recharge our life battery with pranic life energy and further by breathing with the help of certain healing words called mantra, we can strengthen our total body/brain Endocrine glandular system to boost our immune system against all sorts of body ailments.

Our sages knew the healing power of these words and usually passed on the knowledge to their disciples mostly orally. Thus, it never became a Science of Healing. I am a Nuclear Physicist by profession and since my retirement from Deptt. of Atomic Energy, Govt. of India, at the age of 60 years on 31st May, 1990, I have been working for the last seven years in researching the power of the words to heal us and to make it an open chapter, and a very potent science in healing chronic old age diseases which are so far termed incurable and affect almost 1/5th of the mankind.

For this, I came across a very authentic book on Yoga, "The Complete Illustrated Book of Yoga by Swami-Vishnudevananda published in september 1972 by POCKET BOOKS, NEW YORK, where-in on page 323 are given the list of words which can give resonant sonic vibration to various energy conglomerates in our body, called chakras, known by our Hindu sages through intensive meditation.

Also, I came across a very meaningful article

9

in Scientific American, where using Ultra Sonic Waves, the entropy of the system was made reversible, a normally irreversible phenomenon like old age. This triggered my imagination. Why not use the power of the sound words to rejuvenate myself and reverse old age. I was getting old and having been a workaholic and also having been exposed to lot of harmful Atomic radiations during my 36 years service in the Deptt of ATOMIC Energy, particularly because, we were the first lot of scientific personnel in India to work in this so far unknown field of Atomic Energy and atomic radiations being invisible, I had been exposing myself, inadvertently to these dangerous radiations. Thus at the age of my retirement at 60 years, I was biologically seventy years old person and for me to die afflicted with cancer was the most dreaded thought.

I am not afraid of Death, because I have been face to face with death many times in my adventurous life, but I wanted to die young—walking fit, without being burdened with old age diseases like Parkinson's and Alzhiemer's for which there is as yet no cure found. With this aim, I started coining breathing mantras to see their effect on my body/mind system. The result was very healsome and I started experiencing the on-rush of bio-energy currents in my hands and brain and in between the two eyebrows, giving me a feeling as if my Third Eye of Lord Shiva is going to develop slowly and steadily and I occasionally see the blue diamond glow in the 3rd Eye. This gave me an impetus to continue this journey of searching the power of Healing Words.

Though normally, I do not take more than two pegs of alcoholic drinks at home or in social parties, but on New Year Eve or on my birthday party when hundreds of people have gathered, my friends will make me over-drink offering me drink from their own glasses and waiting to dance with me again and again, as I am supposed to be very good dancer, then, I go gay — gay, drinking & drinking & dancing & dancing for hours together, even now, at my age of 66 years, much to the excitement and astonishment of the audience, with congratulations flowings from many beautiful lips, "you are indeed a good dancer". This boosts my ego further, adding fuel to the fire, and I keep dancing and dancing, but the next morning is spent in hellish aches and I begin to think in self repentance, "Is the end result of all excessive happiness - pain and sorrow, particulary, as we grow old". Then I return to myself with oft repeated saying, "Moderation is the key to happiness and stressfree existence", but off & on I relapse in these spirits of excessive gayness and that is how this life goes on.

But, one very suggestive and healing breathing mantra "want to live" has saved my life from excessive drinking damage to my body by my inhaling rapidly with half mouth open with "WANT" and exhaling with, "TO LIVE", first with the hypnotic power of the mantra that I want to live on, and secondly by replenishing the much needed oxygen and pranic life energy to my body/mind system. How this power of healing words helps in this mantra is given in detail in chapter no 78 in this book. The above life saving mantra strengthened my search which is now appearing in the form of this book.

The breathing mantras given in this book have completely rejuvenated my body/mind system, that my much younger wife aged 40 years recently wrote to her very intimate lady friend, "Though my husband is 66 years old, he looks 56, functionally he is 46, playful like 26 and dances feverishly like 16 year young boy". This is because mantric breathing helps me to rebloom and blossom into a new entity every new day, retuning my body's total endocrine hormonal orchestra daily with mantric breathing and repairing my body cells and opening up new memory branches, called dendrites, in my brain, expanding it to new horizons to learn more and more and I want to share my truthful experiments on rejuvenation with the power of healing words with all of you, through the medium of this book. Each chapter of this book should be well digested before proceeding further, because each breathing healing mantra is a Treasure of Health, without any religious tint. The whole science of designing new healing mantras has been revealed in this book, thus enabling us, not only to heal ourself but heal others also. And I am sure, soon, this book on pranic healing will become the Messiah in Self Healing, expanding our consciousness to bring about enlightentment and restore harmony between the Body, Mind and Soul.

Sd/-
(Dr. L.R. Chowdhry)
M.Sc. Ph.D.
Director, Rejuvenation Centre,
1004, Sector-4, Gurgaon-122001
INDIA
Phone : 8-324498 from Delhi

SECTION - I

MIRACLE OF THE MANTRA

Chapter - 1

THE POWER OF THE WORDS/MANTRA

"THE SOUND OF MUSIC MOVES THE SOUL"

INTRODUCTION : We, human beings, are the privileged species who have been endowed with the power of intelligent speech. and the words which we utter can work wonders in our life. Some words can lull us to sleep, other words can soothe us and some other words can make us laugh and sing. But, some words can also injure our feelings and make us cry and weep. Still other words can move us into acts of bravery and fame. Some proper words from a National Leader can move the whole nation into an act of War or Peace. Thus, each word has its own sonic vibration energy which can resonate with our Being to move us into some form of action, which is another name of life flow. Thus, each word has its subtle effect on our body organism and sometimes a word has such a powerful effect that it reverberates in our body and mind system again and again to cast a shadow of its effect throughout our life.

And Word can effect us deeply is conveyed aptly in the following proverb:

"A bullet, an arrow, and a word of mouth once released, cannot be brought back". Thus, we have to be very cautious in our utterances.

And according to Hindu Sages, the Primordial sound vibration heard by enlightened ones is the

15

all reverberating sound of 'AUM', which the Hindu sages utter to unite with God. And in Bible also, they refer to the Holy Word "In the beginning was the Word and the Word was with God and the Word was God", and Muslims speak the Holy Kalma (words) and the Sonorous Word mentioned in Buddhist Scriptures. And also according to Hindu Sages, Man is a conglomerate of seven energy focal centres which they call Chakra or Wheels of Energy Flow, each Chakra is resonated by one seed word and influenced by other associated words and a list of such words is given on page 323 of "The Complete Illustrated Book of Yoga" by Swami Vishnudevananda published by Pocket Books, New York, Sept., 1972. And I am dedicating this chapter hereby to his memory because he was one of the greatest authority on Yoga.

As per the Hindu Sages, all these Chakras are located in the Astral Body surrounding our gross body and the Astral and the gross body are interconnected with each other, with vital life currents. which impart/exchange energy with our body.

And a human being is a network of energy pathways, thinking, bubbling and kicking, deriving its energy from the charioteer of our body - the soul which we in Hindi language call Atmañ which manifests in our body as Breath. This in turn, derives its motive power from the Earth, the Water, the Solar energy, the Air, the Ether and above all the Super-Conscious Life Energy Field with which we constantly exchange energy through our seven Astral body Chakras. And this exchange of life energy can be enhanced by breathing with a mantra, if designed, to be in consonace with natural breathing. Astral Chakra has a seed word with which it resonates to vibrate and exchange energy with our body to its maximum potential. And mantra is a combination of these seed words and designed to be in phase with the location of the reflected position of these Astral Chakras in our body, otherwise it can harm our body as it happens when we are in Anger and speak all hotch potch, many of the spoken words being out of phase with our natural breathing, thus causing hindrance to the natural flow of breathing. This results in the deficient supply of oxygen/nutrients to the brain/ heart. Then, immediately, sympathetic nervous system in the brain directs to release the hormone adrenalin etc which raises the heart rate and makes the liver to release more glycogen to save the brain/heart from damage. Thus, a properly designed Mantra in consonanc with natural breathing can help to enhance the recharging of our life battery, while a disconsonant mantra can harm our body. Thus, all the mantras given in this book are designed to be in consonance with natural breathing, and all these breathing mantras are to be spoken softly and silently (inwardly) with mouth closed to help augment the exchange of life energy from the Astral Chakras with the focussed power of thought. And in this book, we are concerned with how, breathing with a particular mantra affects our gross body and strengthens its associated, endocrine gland. Therefore, we shall not refer to the Astral body henceforth in this book, except in this introductory chapter.

STIMULATING ASTRAL CHAKRAS WITH THEIR SEED WORDS :

List of various Chakras, their seed words and their reflected location in the physical body and the associated endocrine gland are given below. Also alongwith the seed word, an inhale/exhale

Mantra to stimulate the particular Chakra is also given below :-

I. MOOLADHARA/BASIC SEX CHAKRA :

Seed Word	=	L
Inhale Mantra	=	LAÑM
Exhale Mantra	=	MOOLIL
Associated Words	=	S, SH
Principle	=	EARTH

The basic chakra gives power to the legs and is located between the base of the spine and the genital organ. It strengthens the Sex gland - the procreative gland, hence it is called BASIC or MOOLADHARA, on which the whole life process depends. This Chakra forms the Base of the Kundalini - the Divine Potential Energy, normally lying dormant and in its dormant state, it is compared to a coiled serpent and when the Kundalini energy becomes kindled, it moves up alongwith the breath to other Chakras, through the so called Sushumna opening in the spine to ultimately illuminate our Being. The seed word of Basic Chakra is "L' and its associated words S & SH are able to kindle the Kundalini.

STIMULATING THE BASIC CHAKRA

Inhale with the word LAÑ where Ñ is pronouced like the word N in Long or Song with which we can inhale as deep as we like. Thus word LAÑ yokes us with Infinity-the Super-Conscious Life Energy Field and raises the kundalini energy, so kindled with the power of the word LAÑ, to move up along with the breath through the Sushumna opening in the spine. Then, the breath activates the crown chakra with its seed word M by the inhale mantra LAÑM. Pause for a second and then start exhaling with the mantra 'MOOLIL' upto the location of BASIC CHAKRA, which will set up resonant sonic vibrations in the Basic/Mooladhara Chakra with 'LIL' to stimulate it. Pause for a second or more but convenience is the watch word. Giving a pause at the Chakra while thinking of the Chakra, will kindle the chakra because Thought is the most refined form of pranic energy to stimulate the chakra. Then inhale/exhale as above ten times or so to stimulate this chakra. Similarly, we stimulate all the following chakras individually with their seed words.

It may please be noted here that it is the word LAÑ which opens the sushumna opening in the spine while the word LAN instead takes the breath to the Brow chakra (seed word N) and the left brain through the right nostril which is the energizing breath, called pingala-the Sun Breath while the word LAM takes the breath through the left nostril to the crown chakra/right brain (seed word M) which is cooling and pacifying breath (Ida) called moon breath. But the word LAÑ yokes us with Infinity-the Super Conscious Life Energy field to fulfil our Being, breathing equally through both the nostrils. Thus, it is the transducer of pranic energy. It prefers neither the right brain nor the left brain but permeates and unifies the total brain. It is stressed here that potential kundalini energy is made kinetic with the help of the seed word L (BASIC CHAKRA), S, SH (breath centre) & also with V-the seed word of the following swadhishtana chakra given below. And see the Beauty that the word 'VESSEL' is also constituted of these very words - V, S & L, as if kundalini is the vessel of energy. The mantra - MOVE -VESSEL will help to kindle the divine kundalini and make it move up along with its mirror image inhale mantra - LASSAVAÑM.

II. SWADHISHTANA/OVARY/SACRAL CHAKRA :

Seed word	=	V
Inhale Mantra	=	VAÑM
Exhale Mantra	=	MOOVIV
Associated Words	=	S, SH
Principle	=	WATER

It strengthens the Ovaries, the lower intestines, and the sacral region of the spine.

While the ovaries nurture life and it is in the lower intestines where the digested food gets absorbed into the blood stream for supplying the nutrients to all the cells of our body. This Chakra is located in the spine around the location of the Ovaries and lower intestines about four fingers width below the Navel and about four fingers width above the bottom of the spine.

And see the beauty of the construction of the words - Womb, Water, Move, Love, Live, Voules Vous, Will, all these words contain the word 'V' and alongwith the word 'L' constitute the words LOVE and LIVE which permeate our BEING.

The Swadhishtana Chakra forms the top of the Kundalini.

Besides helping the assimilative process of digested food in the blood, it also helps the elimination processes of waste matter through stool.

III. Manipura/Navel chakra/Solar plexus centre :

Seed Word	=	R
Inhale Mantra	=	RAÑM
Exhale Mantra	=	MIRROR
Principle	=	FIRE

This is a Life Preservation Chakra. The Child is yoked to the mother through the navel for food sustenance. It is located around the Navel region in the spine. As this Chakra represents Fire Principle and as it suggests, it helps to digest the food through all the digestive processes in the abdomen, by releasing proper digestive juices and enzymes, through the proper action of liver and the balanced assimilation of glycogen in the blood through the secretion of hormone 'Insulin' by the Pancreas gland in the abdomen. Thus to correct Liver action, the working of the Pancreas and the digestive problems, and to increase body metabolism, we make use of the word 'R' in the breathing Mantra. This also stimulates the life saving Adrenal glands.

IV. Anahata/Heart Chakra

Seed Word	=	Y
Inhale Mantra	=	YAÑM
Exhale mantra	=	MEEY-YOU
Principle	=	AIR

It strengthens the Heart for proper circulation of blood, to circulate air/oxygen/nutrients to all the cells in the body. It imparts compassion to our Heart to develop the feeling of oneness with all persons — we are all the children of this beautiful world. It activates the Thymus gland. This Chakra stimulates the Heart for all embracing love for Humanity, and it also helps the heart to secrete a powerful peptide hormone called atrial Natriurebo factor (ANF). This hormone has an important role in the regulation of blood pressure and blood volume. It exerts its effect widely on the blood vessels themselves, on the adrenal glands and on the large number of regulator regions in the brain (R-1).

V. Vishudha/Throat Chakra

Seed word	=	H
Inhale Mantra	=	AHAÑM
Exhale Mantra	=	MIHHIEÑ
Principle	=	ETHER

It strengthens the hearing sensation and mouth action/vocal chords and also helps the breathing system. It activates the Thyroid gland which helps to regulate fat and carbohydrates metabolism in our body. It also helps to strengthen the communication between the lower body and the brain and is thus called the 'Watchman' of the body. This Chakra is located around the throat. We make use of its seed word 'H' in the breathing mantra for curing people of Obesity and the Spondylitis in the cervical region of the spine.

VI. Ajna/Brow Chakra

Seed word	=	N
Inhale Mantra	=	PRANNAÑ
Exhale Mantra	=	PROONIN
Principle	=	SIGHT/INSIGHT/ BEHOLDER

This is the chakra of the 3rd Eye of Lord Shiva or the Single Eye mentioned in Bible. This is located between the two eyebrows at slightly higher level. It helps to strengthen the left brain, (Hypothalamus and autonomic nervous system),

Eye-sight and all the sense endings. It also activates the pituitary gland - the master gland which directs the total glandular activity in our body. It also represents clairvoyance – the power of the 3rd eye to foresee what may happen in the future. This chakra helps us to meet the Challenge of Stress, because this is the chakra of energy.

VII.Sahasrara/Crown Chakra

Seed word	=	M
Gland	=	PINEAL
Inhale Mantra	=	PRAMMAÑ
Exhale Mantra	=	PREMIM
Principle	=	RIGHT UPPER BRAIN/MIND

This is located in the crown of our head. It strengthens mind/ right upper brain. It also helps to strengthen the pineal gland, which is called the Transducer of Super-Consciousness Field. This is the ultimate chakra in our head which unifies with the super consciousness to receive commandments from the spiritual-mind, guiding our trueself. When the kundalini energy reaches this centre, our whole Being begins to illuminate like a Lamp unto ourself and to all others. It is the spiritual gateway of our total BEING to attain enlightenment. That is why it is called the chakra of thousand-fold un-foldment and blossoming of our Being. The pineal gland releases the principal hormone - Melatonin which removes depression from the mind.

The word 'PR' has been added to help inhale/ exhale from the Brow and Crown chakras fully to stimulate them properly. The word 'PR' helps to breathe fully from both abdomen (R) and from the lungs (P) as explained later.

VIII. Yoking with Super-consciousness

Breath is life and it is through breath that we are yoked with super-consciousness-the God Almighty and in mantric breathing, we can strengthen our link with super-consciousness by breathing with the seed word AÑ which constitutes the infinity in breathing as in the word "LONG". You can breathe as long as you want, to your maximum capacity. A mantra which yokes us with Infinity is given below :-

Inhale with   ATMAÑ
Exhale with   IMTIEÑ

The word Atmañ in Hindi means Soul. Thus the mantra ATMAÑ Yokes us with the super-soul to draw in as much pranic life energy as possible and thus cure us of all the diseases, dissolving all the stress in the process The word 'T' stands for taste gland in our body and from this it is apparent that the soul resides in our body as long as we continue to cherish the taste of living/Eating.

IX. **Breath Centre** : The seed word for breath centre is S or SH. It is located just below the Swadhistana Chakra and above the Muladhara Chakra and forms the top of Kundalini - the vessel of divine life energy which is activated by the four words L, V & S & SH. Kundalini energy is imagined as both potential (Sleeping) as well as Kinetic. Dormant Kundalini energy is symbolised by the sleeping coiled serpent and the Kinetic Kundalini like the wakeful serpent, and the kindled Kundalini Energy moves alongwith breath upward upto the Crown Chakra through the so-called Sushumna opening in the spine. The movement of Kundalini energy is amplified by the seed words L, S, SH and V of Basic and Sacral Chakras.

Our breath connects the kundalini - the vessel of life force at one end to the continuum of Infinite life energy what we call the super-consciousness at the other end, with the seed Word SAÑ where the word SA signifies inhaling and Ñ signifies the infinity in breathing. Thus, we can inhale with the help of the simplest mantra SAÑ spoken as SAAAÑÑÑ, to get united with the God and exhale with its exactly opposite mirror image mantra-IEÑS where 'IE' signifies exhaling and the mantra helps to exhale breath back to its origin signified by word 'S'. Thus, the simplest science of breathing with mantra is SAÑ-IEÑS. And this breathing mantra is NEUTRAL. It neither prefers left brain nor right brain but stimulates the total Brain/Mind.

A summary of the characteristic features of these Astral Body Chakras is given in Table-I for ready reference and illustrated in Figure - I.

Optimum Breathing :

We are yoked with the God Almighty through the medium of breath, the breathing going on automatically without any conscious effort by us, being controlled by the respiratory centre in the brain but God has endowed human beings with the power to voluntarily control breathing also, as we require to do it during under water swimming and in the conscious control as in pranayam exercises to develop control over our body/mind system. Normally, a person takes about 15 breaths per minute, its frequency as well as the depth of breathing depends to a great extent on the physiological state of our body/mind system. In jogging or running, the rate of respiration increases to meet the additional demand of oxygen by muscles. The tired feeling at the end of running indicating the accumulation of un-metabolised lactic acid which during the proper rest period comes back to normal. Similarly during the situation of anger or stress, the breathing becomes more rapid to help the brain to meet its addtional demand on oxygen. And during illness also, the breath becomes shallow and un-rhythmic, thus indicating a state of imbalance between the Body, Mind and Soul. The breathing mantras given in this book help us to restore the breathing to its natural equilibrium and depth, thus healing us completely, supplemented with balanced nutrition, because diseased state of our body/mind system is the result of blockages in the harmonious flow of pranic life energy and nerve currents, either due to improper breathing or deficiency in the nutrition to supply the proper minerals/protiens/vitamins/fat/carbohydrates input to our body. Because, our health depends upon i.e. what we breathe, what we drink, what we eat and above all what we think - since positive thinking opens up our energy channels while negative thinking impedes the free flow of pranic life energy and nerve currents, thus making us prone to illness. And according to Hindu thought, more rhythmic, and deeper and slower the breathing i.e. less the number of breaths per minute, longer the life span.

Mantra for Abdominal Breathing

The Words which help the lungs to breathe with greater efficiency are Y,J,H,JH, B, BH, P, PH (F) BR (Bronch), PR, Z, etc. and these words will be utilised in the mantras framed in this book to breathe more efficiently. Out of these helpful breathing words, the word BRA or PRA help us to inhale both from the lungs with their seed words B or P and also from the abdomen with its seed word R. That is why the word "BREATHE" helps us to exhale fully from the lungs as well as from the abdomen. Similarly, the word PRANNA fulfills our lungs with P, the abdomen with R and the Brow chakra and the left brain with ANA. The complete breathing mantra for total breathing is however, SA-PRANAM and its exhale mantra is INMPRESS.

And complete abdominal breathing helps to supply oxygen and the pranic life energy to all the cells of our body, thus recharging our life battery fully again to meet the challenge of stress and disease.

Our breathing alongwith blood/water circulation also helps to keep our body at the stable temperature of 98.6^0F, through also the action of breathing alternately through the right nostril called the sun or hot breath and the cooling left nostril breathing called the Moon (Cool) breath.The switch over from hot breath to cold breath occurs every one to two hours depending upon our physiological needs of our body. The right nostril breathing activates the left brain, hypothalamus/pituitary gland etc. while the left nostril breathing stimulates the crown chakra, the right upper brain, the pineal gland and helps us to sleep well by its pacifying action on the brain. Similarly, movement of right hand up first, while standing or sitting opens up the right nostril breathing, stimulates the left brain etc. and the movement of the left hand up first opens up breathing through the left nostril, stimulates the right brain and the crown chakra, thus helping us to communicate with various portions of the brain through breathing.

Similarly, inhale mantra YAHHAN stimulates the left brain/Brow chakra while the inhale mantra YAHHAM stimulates the right brain and the crown chakra. And breathing with the mantra YAHHAÑ- is NEUTRAL, it neither prefers the right brain nor the left brain but fulfills the total brain, unifying the total brains' action.

What is Mantra

Mantra is a combination of words, where its each word has a potent sonic power contained in it. And we have seen how we can resonate with each energy chakra and its associated organ/ gland in our body with its seed word and partially activate it with its associated words. Thus, each word we utter affects one or the other organ in our body, but breathing mantras in this book are so framed to be in harmony with the sequence of natural breathing or location of various energy centres in our body. But, while speaking normally, some words we utter will be in phase/tune with natural breathing depending upon the vowel used in it, while other words will be out of phase/ harmony with the sequence of natural breathing, thus, interfering with our natural breathing and we know how in anger, we speak words rapidly, thus interfering with natural breathing, so much so, we get out of breath, the heart starts pumping rapidly to make the oxygen/nutrients reach the brain to save it. Thus, normal speaking tires us, while breathing with the properly designed mantra will help draw in pranic life energy to rejuvenate our body/mind system.

And Guru Nanak-the founder of Sikh Religion truly said, "O, Great is the Power of the WORD

(MANTRA), but few there be, that know it".

Activating Various Chakras with Single/Two Stage Breathing Mantras

Now, we shall proceed further on this journey of **Self Healing** by coining breathing mantras with these healing words, in consonance with the sequence of natural breathing. The vowel 'A, AU' stand for inhalation and EE, I, and OO stand for Exhalation. Earlier, a breathing mantra is given to stimulate that particular energy chakra only, but now we shall give breathing mantras which encampass or traverse more energy chakras simultaneously to be more useful in the healing process. The exhale/inhale mantras are mirror image of each other. We can also choose existing meaningful words from various languages as breathing mantras, provided these words satisfy the criterion of being in consonance with the sequence of natural breathing.

I) Resonating Basic Sex Chakra with Simple Breathing Mantras Using "L'

The English Word 'Long' spoken as Laang can help us to take a very long breath from the bottom of the spine (L), then it yokes us with infinity - the Superconsciousness with the word AÑ to draw in as much pranic life energy as possible and the breathing mantra ends at the words 'G' which is the seed word for left brain. The word ANG helps to strengthen the nasal cavity hormone-Immuno-globin A to boost our immunity. Because of the property of the word LONG to help us inhale a long and deep breath, I call it a **Longevity mantra.**

1) Thus, inhale with   =   LONG
     Exhale with   =   GLEEÑ

2) Another mantra which helps us to breathe from the bottom of the legs is Alla and reaches the crown chakra with M to illuminate our being, because the word 'L' as said earlier also kindles the divine Kundalini.

| Inhale with | = | ALLAM |
| Exhale with | = | MILLI or ILLUME |

3) The Word 'Healing' is very healsome mantra. Besides, it helps by its suggestive power of continuance of healing process

| Exhale with | = | HEALING |
| Inhale with | = | LAHHANG |

In the above mantra the word 'H' is the seed word for throat chakra, which strengthens the thyroid gland and the communication link in the cervical region of the spine between the body and the brain. The word H also helps in the metabolism of fat/carbohydrates in our body. The action of words L&ANG has already been explained above in the mantra LONG.

4) Another breathing mantra which helps to strengthen the heart's circulation and impart to us the angelic quality of COMPASSION, is by using the word Y/J- the seed words for Heart Chakra.

| Exhale with | = | Angel |
| Inhale with | = | LAJJAÑ |

5) In order to help us breathe to our optimum capacity with our lungs, we make use of the word PH, in the breathing mantra

| Inhale with | = | LAPHAN |
| Exhale with | = | NEEPHIL or NEW-FILL |

This mantra also strengthen the brow chakra with its seed word N, thus helping to strengthen the left brain and the pituitary gland which is director of total glandular activity in our body/ mind system. thus fortifying our body's immune system to keep us healthy and fit. That is why the word 'Laphani' in our Hindi/Urdu language means Immortal. This is thus the simiplest mantra to helps us to become Ageless.

The exhale mantra-New-Fill is very suggestive indeed, as if we are newly filling our body and re-charging our life battery daily to become immortal.

II. Resonating the Ovary/Swadhishtana Chakra with Mantra Using V.

This Chakra vitalises Ovaries and the lower intestines to bolster our body's assimilation and elimination processes. We can use the following mantras :-

1) Exhale with   =   MOVE
   Inhale with   =   VAAM

This is a movement mantra. It also helps to take the kindled Kundalini energy to the crown of the head with M.

2) Exhale with   =   MOVIE
   Inhale with   =   AVVAM

3) Inhale with   =   WARM (VARM)
   Exhale with   =   ME OR MEEVE OR MER

4) Inhale with   =   WARM
   Exhale with   =   MEST

All these three mantras are warmth imparting, because we have included the word "R" which represents Fire principle - the seed word for Solar plexus.

5) Exhale with   =   IMPROVE

Inhale with   =   VAPRAM

This is indeed a health improving mantra. The word PR helps us to breathe from the abdomen (R) as well as from the lungs (P), besides activating the Swadhishtana Chakra (V) and the crown chakra (M). Also this breathing mantra gives the hypnotic influence of suggestion to "improve" our health or state of our Being

III. Resonating the Navel/Manipur Chakra/ Solar Plexus with 'R'

1. Inhale with   =   ARRAN
    Exhale with   =   NOORIE

This breathing Mantra helps to resonate with its sonic energy the solar plexus with its seed word 'R' and the Brow Chakra with its seed word N, thus helping to give fire to our body by strengthening the digestion of food in the abdomen, and help strengthen the left brain and the eyes and the Pituitary gland. This mantra brings about lustre in our eyes by providing the required pranic life energy. And the word Noorie in our Urdu/Hindi language means Lustre-full, true to its action on our body/mind/ eyes system.

2. Inhale with   =   ARRAM
    Exhale with   =   MIRROR

As compared to mantra No. 1 this breathing mantra resonates with the crown chakra with its seed word M, instead of the Brow Chakra. This mantra thus helps to improve our right brain besides improving our metabolism. A separate chapter is devoted to it.

3. Inhale with   =   RAHHA
    Exhale with   =   HOORIE OR HURRAY

It is a joyful mantra (Hurray) and improves our health by invigorating the thyroid gland with its seed word H and the solar plexus with R. This mantra can help obese people to shed their extra fat.

4. Inhale with = RAMMA
    Exhale with = MERE

Its action is the same as mantra No. 2, but it is a Bhakti (Devotional) mantra and a separate chapter is devoted to it. The total mantra-Mere-Rama means-O, My Lord Ram. In this Mantra, one totally surrenders and gets totally submerged into the thought of Lord Ram. Lord Ram flows into the devotee and the Devotee flows into Lord Ram.

All the above four breathing mantras strengthen the Liver, the Pancreas, and the abdominal secretions for proper digestion/assimilation of food to give us the Fire with its seed word R.

IV) Resonating the Heart/Anahata Chakra with Breathing Mantras Using (Y or J)

1. The following mantra helps to strengthen both the heart (Y) and the right brain (M) and the pineal gland

    Inhale with = AYYAM
    Exhale with = ME YOU

2. The following mantra instead strengthens the left brain and the left eye and the pituitary gland with the word N.

    Inhale with = AYYAN
    Exhale with = NEE YOU/NEW

This breathing mantra gives newness to our heart and brain system.

3. Inhale with = RAYYAN
   Exhale with = NEW YEAR

This mantra besides adds fire to the action of mantra No. 2 and improves our digestion (R), heart circulation (Y) and the left brain/eyesight (N).

4. Inhale with = LA-YOUNG
   Spoken as = LA-YAANG
   Exhale with = GLEE-YEEÑ

This is a youthifying mantra, by resonating with basic chakra (L), heart with (Y) and the nasal smell sense endings with ANG, besides yoking us with the superconsciousness with the word AÑ to draw in as much pranic life energy as possible and hence its rejuvenating effect on our body.

5. Another juvenating mantra is given below

Inhale with = JWAN or VAJJAN
Exhale with = JEEVUN or JUVEEN

The youthifying action of the above mantra is because of the action of the word V (ovary chakra), J (Heart Chakra) and N-the brow chakra, to improve assimilition, circulation and also improving the brain, eye- sight and our immune system, by activating the pituitary gland.

V) Resonating The Throat /Vishudha Chakra with Breathing Mantras Using The Word H

This throat chakra imparts Vigour to our being, by strengthening the Thyroid gland which improves the fat/Carbohydrate Metabolism and establishes the link between the body and the brain through the neck.

It is indeed an invigorating chakra.

1. Inhale with = LAHHAM
   Exhale with = HEAL-ME

This mantra resonates with its sonic vibrations with basic chakra with L, throat chakra with H and the crown chakra with M. And this mantra is also suggestive and implores God to Heal-Me. Thus it is indeed a Healsome Mantra.

2. Inhale with = SAHHAM
   Exhale with = MIHHISH

Its action is similar to mantra No. 1. It contains the words S instead of L and both are almost equivalent in action. This mantra helps to cure people of their Cervical Spondylitis.

3. Inhale with = SAHHAN
   Exhale with = NIHHISH

As compared mantra no. 2. it instead resonates with Brow Chakra with N to strengthen the left brain, the eye sight and the pituitary gland, thus strengthening our immune system.

4. Inhale with = RAHHAM
   Exhale with = HEAR-ME or MIHHIR

This mantra helps to improve digestive processes in our body with R, the seed word for solar plexus, besides activating the Thyroid gland with H and the crown chakra with M. This helps to put our health back on the rails.

5. Inhale with = HEALETH
   Exhale with = LAHHANTH

Thus, all the above mantras are health imparting and particularly helpful to cure Cervical Spondylitis.

VI) Resonating with Ajna / Brow Chakra With Breathing Mantras Using Word N.

This chakra strenghtens the left brain, the eye sight and the pituitary gland, the word Ajna itself can form a suitable inhale mantra. to stimulate Itself.

1) Inhale with   =   AJNAÑ/AJNA
   Exhale with   =   ENGIEÑ/ENGINE

This Ajna chakra is like the distributor system in the Engine through Hypothalamus and its pituitary gland which is the master gland controlling the secretions of other glands in our body engine. The Ajna Chakra is thus the beholder of our Body Engine overseeing its proper action. The above mantra includes the seed word J of heart chakra to improve the circulation of blood.

2) Inhale with   =   ASSAN
   Exhae with   =   NEESH

The word Assan in our Urdu/Hindi language means easy and it is one of the easiest and simplest mantra to improve our eye sight with the word N and helps to breathe from the legs with the word 'AS'. Thus, it is a total body breath mantra. This is the first breathing mantra which I suggest to improve the eye-sight and its defects of Myopia and Hypermetropia and it has shown good results in correcting these eye defects, combined with proper supportive nutrition.

3) Another mantra which helps us to breathe fully through our lungs is by using the word PH.

   Inhale with   =   SHAPHAN
   Exhale with   =   NOOFEES

The word Shaphan in our Urdu/Hindi language means Health Imparting which it truly accomplishes by fulfilling our lungs and left brain with pranic life energy.

4) Inhale with   =   SARAN

Exhale with   =   NOORESH

The word Nooresh in our Urdu/Hindi language means full of Lustre, this mantra really imparts sparkle to our eyes and left brain with N, fire to our digestion with word R and ignites the Kundalini energy with S. Thus, it is an illuminating mantra for the body/mind system.

VII) Resonating the Crown Chakra With Breathing Mantras Using The Word M.

In many of the above mantras, we have used the word M to strenghten the crown chakra and the right brain. I shall give only two mantras here using M.

1) Inhale with   =   MINGLE
    Exhale with   =   LAGGANM

This mantra particularly helps us to Mingle our Being with super-conciousness with the word gañ and then ends at M to bathe the crown chakra with divine Kundalini energy so kindled with the word L.

2) Inhale with   =   ASSAM
    Exhale with   =   ME-SHE or MISHSHI

This breathing mantra helps us to breathe completely from the legs to the crown of our head.

VIII) Strengthen The Breath Chakra with Words S & Sh.

Make life a song, for this, make the word song as your inhale breath.

1) Inhale with   =   SONG, SPOKEN AS
                            SAANG
    Exhale with   =   GEESH

The mantra 'Song' is like long and originates a

little above it. Thus, it is also a longevity mantra like long. Thus make your life long and full of happy song.

2) To become smart and smarter every new day, for this

Inhale with   =   SMART
Exhale with   =   TER or TEST

This mantra endows smartness to our body with the word S,R, T & M.

3) Now we shall design mantras to activate various chakras between breath Centre (S) and the Brow Chakra (N) :—

i)   Inhale with   =   SARAN
     Exhale with   =   NOORESH

ii) Inhale with   =   SAJJAN
     Exhale with   =   NEEJJEESH

Because of the word J, it is a heart friendly mantra and the Sajjan in Hindi language means a friend, while mantra no 3(i) is a digestion friendly mantra

iii) Inhale with   =   SAHHAN
     Exhale with   =   NIHHISH

The mantras at 3 i), ii), iii), activate navel chakra for better digestion, heart, chakra for improved circulation and the throat chakra for better thyroid action respectively.

4) Similarly, we shall design breathing mantras to activate various chakras between breath Centre (S) and the crown chakra (M).

i)   Inhale with   =   SARAM
     Exhale with   =   MEEREESH

ii)	Inhale with	=	SAJJAM
	Exhale with	=	MIJJISH
iii)	Inhale with	=	SAHHAM
	Exhale with	=	MIHHISH

This throws light on how we can frame breathing mantras to strengthen various chakras and their associated body organs or glands.

5) Now, we shall design a breathing mantra to strengthen both the left & right brain.

| Inhale with | = | SANNAM |
| Exhale with | = | MUNNEESH |

This mantra helps to take the kindled kundalini energy with the sonic resonant energy of word S to the brow chakra and then to the crown chakra, thus strengthening the left brain, the eye sight and the pituitary gland with the resonant vibration of the seed word N and then the right brain and the pineal gland with the seed word M, thus fortifying our immune system.

Thus, 'SANNAM' is truly a Health-Friendly Mantra-true to its name.

And when we fall ill, our breath becomes shallow and erratic and one or more of the body glands stop functioning properly either due to malnutrition or the pranic life energy is not reaching it fully, thus affecting the harmonious working of our body/mind/soul system and we can restore our body/mind harmony by breathing with properly chosen mantras. Thus, we have seen that Words can work Wonders on our body/mind system.

And while Archimedes said "Give me a lever long enough and a fulcrum strong enough and single handed, I can move the world." And speaking of the power of the Words, Joseph Conrad said "Don't talk to me of your Archimedes lever-Give me the right Word and the right accent and I will move the world."

And those right Healing Words are right here, given in this book to restore the health of the people and rid our World from the agony of stress of various ailments by breathing with the power of Healing Words.

OM-TAT-SAT / AMEEN

R-1;Marc Cantin & Jacques Genest "Heart As An Endocrine Gland, Scientific American, Feb. 1986.

TABLE - 1

MAJOR ASTRAL BODY CHAKRAS WITH RESONANT SEED WORDS AND ASSOCIATED BODY ORGAN/ENDOCRINE GLAND STRENGTHENED.

Sr. No.	Name of Chakra	Location in Gross Body	Seed Word	Endocrine Gland	Body Organs Strengthened
1.	Sahasrara/ Crown	Crown of Head	MA	Pineal	Right Brain, Pacifies the Mind
2.	Ajna/Brow	Between two Eye-brows	NA	Pituitary	Left Brain, Strengthens sympathetic nervous system.
3.	Vishudha/ Throat	Around Throat	HA	Thyroid	Neck, Establishes link between body and brain.
4.	Anahata/ Heart	Around Heart	YA	ANF (R-1) Thymus	Gives Compassion and strength to Heart.
5.	Manipur/ Navel	Around Navel	RA	Pancreas Liver	Assimilation of food in ABDOMEN.
6.	Swadhi-shatana/ Ovary	Midway between navel & Genitals	VA	Gonads and ovary	Strengthens ovaries, and assimilation and elimination process in lower intestines.
7.	Mooladhara/ Basic Sex Chakra	Midway between bottom of spine & Genitals.	LA	Gonads	Gives Power to legs, sex, kindles Kundalini.
8.	Breath Centre Seat of Kundalini	Midway between ovary & basic chakra.	SA	Gonads	Breath origin, moves Kundalini energy upwards with breath.
9.	Super Conscious-field.	Top of Head	SAÑ	Transducer of Super-conscious-field.	Unifies total brain action.

Chapter - 2

WHAT IS PRANIC HEALING

Prana, literally, means flow of life, because the word pran means life and 'A' indicates movement of breath. Thus, Prana is a life sustaining electromotive force.

Is Prana the oxygen only? No, oxygen is part of Prana, but prana is much more than that. It is all that we inhale from air, surcharged with the vitality of Solar Energy, plus high energy ionising Cosmic rays, plus ionising radiations from Uranium, Thorium, Potassium and radon/thoron radio-active gases always present in the Air, plus all those life giving nuclei present in the air, not yet fully understood.

Prana is also contained in the food we take, prana is also present in the water we drink and the surcharged water, besides providing minerals, is also ionised to some extent, charged by total Solar Energy spectrum etc. Similarly, all vegetables, fruits and other food stuff are of different colours and hues thus loaded with vast spectrum of energy which imparts vitality to our body; and also by the Vitamins and Minerals, Carbohydrates and Protiens present in them.

And, as an illustration of the part played by both positively and negatively charged electrons and ions in life processes, it may be noted that it is the negatively charged male sperm which is able to fertilise the female ovum, to create new life.

And to create ionisation in our body, God has

provided potassium as a necesary part of our body cells, and one of the potassium isotopes is K-40, which is radioactive and is thus able to create ions/electrons useful in life processes, besides production of ions in our body by other processes. For example, glucose, in the process of giving metabolic energy to the body gets first converted into pyrovate $(C_3H_3O_6)$ which is negatively charged product of Glucose. This is to cite just one example.

And let us not forget the so much talked about oxidants — the positively charged oxygen molecules, which when let loose, become damaging like a rogue elephant, and we are asked to gulp vitamin C and Vitamin 'E' — the so called anti-oxidants which neutralise these oxidants. Thus, it is seen, that both negatively and positively charged ions play a very significant part in life processes.

Thus, Prana is a dynamic life sustaining force, and throughout the text of this book, we use the word **PRANIC ENERGY** which means Universal Life Force that sustains life.

What is Pranayam

Breath is life and life is breath and cessation of breathing is cessation of life itself. Natural breathing goes on automatically at the average rate of 15 respirations per minute, but when we run, or become angry or fall ill, this respiration rate changes to meet the demands of our body. In order to restore our breathing to normal pattern and to make the breath deep and long at our will, we use the power of the thought to control the breathing and pranic in-take. This knowledge and control of prana in our body is called Pranayam. This, then, gives us the ability to restore the uneven distribution of Prana evenly to all parts of our body/mind system and also to create some reserve of pranic life energy in the Solar Plexus for emergency use. Also by controlling the prana, we can control and calm our restless mind and bring it under our control.

Thus, in Pranayam type of breathing, we control the breathing by our thought process i.e. we can make the breath rise from the bottom of the spine-the basic sex chakra, and then take the breath to our Navel Chakra, Heart Chakra in this spine, then to throat chakra, to Brow Chakra and then ultimately to the Crown Chakra and then at the end of inhalation, we can also give a small pause of a second or so. Then we start exhaling upto the bottom of the spine and again give a pause of one second or so at the end of exhalation. This pause period can be extended from one second to four seconds or more with practice, but this pause in breathing should be practised upto the tolerable biological limits i.e. convenience is the watch word. This pause in breathing both at the end of inhalation and exhalation process is said to give the person control over oneself. Normally, I have myself tried to give pause of no more than a second or so because I never believed in developing extra-sensory powers for myself except to enjoy a perfect health, However, during this pause period due to the fusion of inhale breath current (male breath) and exhale breath (female breath), we experience bliss and since this bliss is so enjoyable, the pause period automatically gets extended because of this bliss-the ultimate aim of our Being.

Also, with Pranayam, we can direct the flow of pranic energy to the ailing part of our body with our thought, thus curing it steadily by supplying it the required pranic life energy. Also with pranayam exercises, we can develop control over our mind to become master of ourselves what we call SWAMI. This is quite possible with pranayam or Mantric Pranayam.

Mantric Pranayam - is to breathe with a Mantra and we can also similarly give a convenient pause in breathing both at the end of inhalation and exhalation. In Mantric breathing, we make the breath arise from a particular organ in our body by making use of its seed word. Thus, with the breathing mantra - Vahanam, we take the breath from the Ovary (V) to the throat chakra (H) and then to the brow chakra with N and ultimately to the Crown Chakra with its seed word M. Similarly, we can exhale with its mirror image Mantra -'Minih - heev' to exhale breath back to the ovary chakra. Thus breathing with a word/mantra makes the breath to arise from a definite organ of our body and reach a definite organ of our body. Also, mantric Pranayam helps us to resonate with various chakras/body organs and their associated endocrine glands with the sonic energy of their resonant words to get them strengthened in the process so as to heal us.

And similarly we can construct a breathing mantra for the breath to arise from the bottom of the spine to activate the basic sex chakra with its seed word L and make it illuminate our mind with the words D,N&M.

Inhale with   =   LAHA - DANAM
Exhale with   =   MIND - i - HEAL

The complete mind gets reverberated with sound energy of seed words H, N, D&M which this breathing mantra achieves. And the Exhale Mantra is very suggestive and by its hypnotic suggestive power, it gives the commandment-O, MIND HEAL and you will surely get healed because Thought is the most refined form of Prana to Heal our Being.

Method of Breathing with a Mantra

Since we know by now, which word emanates from which organ of our body, because our body is like a musical instrument where its location point on the string emanates/resonates with a particular note or the sound frequency. So knowing, we breathe with the healing mantra by speaking its each individual word inwardly, smoothly, deeply and rhythmically and as non-violently as possible to simulate the natural breathing except in the depth of its breathing because we are particularly helping ourself to breathe deep and long with the help of rightly chosen words in mantra. Choose one suitable breathing mantra for each of the eight energy chakras **given before.** Inhale/Exhale 10 times each with each of the mantra, it will take about eight minutes. Also repeat them in the evening selecting a **pollution free environment.** This is a necessary condition for the mantric breathing to be potently effective. We can sit in a convenient chair with spine in an erect position or stand comfortably with spine erect to breathe with these mantras silently. Of course, for the sake of getting used to the mantra we can speak aloud these mantras a few times and then inhale/exhale silently with these mantras and soon within a few days of practice, we will start experiencing the on-rush of blissful life currents in our hands, brow chakra and head showing that **healing process is ON.**

We can also give a convenient pause of a second or so at the end of both inhalation and exhalation with a mantra, so that the eddy currents generated in inhaling and exhaling fuse with each other to impart us the bliss of fusion currents.

Advantages of Breathing with Mantra are Five Fold

i)   It is also a pranayam type of breathing deep in character and we can also give a convenient pause. Most of the inhale mantras start with L, S, Sh, V or R, thus, these mantras help us to breathe deeply from the abdomen and the bottom of the spine to recharge our life battery completely.

ii) Since now we know, which word relates with which organ in our body and the mantras are so designed to be in consonance with the sequence of these organs, we can make our thought also move along with the breath, as it traverses that particular energy centre or body organ, thus bringing in the added advantage of VIPASANA MEDITATION - first advocated by Lord Budha in which thought moves along with the breath, thus dissolving all stressful conditions of the brain/mind.

iii) Most of the breathing mantras chosen in this book are also very suggestive to the process of self healing i.e. juvenating, improving, healing etc. and thus have the hypnotic power of healing by suggestion also, because thought is our Being and life energy moves with the Thought.

iv) And each word in a mantra stimulates its associated body organ and its related endocrine gland by its resonant sonic energy, thus boosting our immune system to accelerate the healing process.

v) This helps us also to yoke with Infinity — the super-consciousness with mantra AÑ to bring about Harmony between the Body, Mind and the Soul to put our Health back on the rails.

WHAT IS PRANIC HEALING

Prana, as already explained, is the Universal Life Energy which sustains life and it is present in the Air. Ether, Water, Sunlight/Fire. Vegetables, fruits, grains and various other earth elements/ minerals, various herbs/ chemicals/medicines- all of those agents which help to sustain life in varying degree; and their excessive use, however, results, in harmful side effects.

Just, to cite an example, sunbathing is useful activity for the proper growth of our body, but the same sunlight can harm our body with long exposure, particularly, in old age; when our capacity to metabolise sunlight diminishes. The same sunlight which nurtures the young plants during their growth period dries them up near their fag end.

Thus, the secret of pranic healing lies in always GROWING through proper inhalation/ exhalation with Resonant mantras as given in the following Chapters of this book, combined with balanced nutrition. And this continuous growing happens because we raise the energy level of our body/mind system through constant attunement of our chakras with the resonant sonic energy of their seed words.

Just, as in a television set, we can control the sound and picture intensity by pressing a switch in the remote control, similarly these seed words of astral chakras are the switches for stimulating them to release life sustaining hormones in the blood stream to boost our immune system to fight any invading disease. Thus we can recharge our life battery continuously with Pranic Energy to propel our life engine efficiently, by properly digesting and utilising the food, and its circulation in the blood stream. Besides, pranic healing with a resonant mantra can expand our consciousness to make us fully enlightened Person, a SIDHA, thus we can become a lamp to ourself and to all others. Thus, surcharged with pranic energy, we become a channel for Universal Life Energy to flow through us abundantly to not only elevate our energy levels to heal us but also empowers us to heal others.

It must be stressed here that the exhale breathing mantra decongests the chakra and sweeps away the disease from the associated body organs, while the inhale mantra fulfills it with pranic life energy, may times more than the conventional pranayam, because of the resonant absorption of sonic energy by the Chakra with its seed word. Such is power of word that Christ declares it in New Testament. "In the beginning was the word and the word was with God and the Word was God".

SECTION - II

BLOOM AND BLOSSOM
AT ALL AGES

Chapter - 3

THE FORE-MOST MANTRA
'AHAÑM'

The whole universe is centred around the Self Evolution 'AHAÑM' which, in Sanskrit Language means SELF or MYSELF. Everyone loves one-self the most. Thus, this mantra focuses attention on self Healing and if we come to realize our own self or our own existence every moment of our life, we can never fall ill.

i) The word 'A in AHAÑM means inhalation in Mantric breathing.

ii) The word 'H' is the seed word of Vishudha/ throat Chakra. It stimulates the Thyroid gland which is the gland of growth, helps in metabolism of fats and carbohydrates. And the word 'AHA' also helps to re-establish the communication between the Body and the Mind through the cervical region of the spine.

iii) The word HAÑ yokes us with Infinity - the super consciousness to draw in as much pranic life energy as possible to fulfill our total BEING and then stimulates the crown chakra with its seed word M.

iv) The word 'M' by its resonant sonic vibrations strengthens the right upper brain and the mind - the Charioteer of our body. The word AHANM is only an inhale mantra. Its exhale counter part is given below:

1. Thus inhale with =   AHHAÑM

Exhale with = MAIÑ HOOÑ or MIHHIEÑ

The exhale mantra MAIÑ HOOÑ also means - I AM (I exist herewith). This is the most meaningful Mantra for ourself. This whole world exists for me as long as I Exist. This mantra helps us to REMEMBER our own existence, to fulfill our BEING totally.

2. Fulfill Your Heart

Inhale with = YA + AHAÑM = YAHHAÑM
Exhale with = MIHIYYIEÑ

This mantra also strengthens the heart and fills our heart with compassion with its seed word Y.

3. Improve Digestion

Let us add 'R' to the above mantra to improve our digestion. The word 'R' is the seed word for Navel chakra, it stimulates the liver, the Pancreas and all abdominal secretions, the spleen and even the Adrenal gland-our emergency life saviour gland.

A. Inhale with = RA + AHAÑM = RAHHAÑM
   Exhale with = I AM HERE or MIHHIR

B. Inhale with = RAJA + AHAÑM =
                 RAJAHHAÑM
   Exhale with = HJOORIE MAIÑ

The inhale mantra 3B means I am the king of myself and the exhale mantra means – I surrrender unto you completely, I have become the valley, ready to be fulfilled. This is indeed a very potent health restoring breathing mantra.

4. Breathe fully from Abdomen and Lungs

Inhale with = BRA + AHAÑM =

		BRAHHAÑM
Exhale with	=	MIHHI - BRIEÑ

This mantra helps us to breathe fully, both from the abdomen with its seed word R and from the lungs with B. Thus, this mantra helps to fulfill Ahañm — our being with Pranic life energy to dissolve our stress, improve our digestion, because total-breathing including abdominal breathing is known to dissolve stress.

And we must not forget that we are Yoked with God through the medium of breath and the whole Universe (BRAHAMAND) is also supposed to breathe, as it expands and contracts.

5.	Thus Inhale with	=	BRAHAMAND
			(This means Universe)
	Exhale with	=	MIHI-BREATHE
			(The word D is
			equivalent to Th)

Thus, love yourself and breathe lovingly with Ahañm and you shall never fall ill. Make Ahanm your breath and you will never exceed your biological limits to cause it stress.

In this connection, I remember my college days, when I was asked to participate alongwith my other two class-mates to speak on the subject, "The dearest person in my life" All three of us were asked to speak for five minutes on our individual dearest person. I spoke thus :-

"Today when I was asked to speak on "Whom I love the most in my life," my thoughts rushed in search of such a person. In my childhood, my mother was the dearest to me, she is a beautiful lady who loved and caressed me the most, but as

I grew upto 7 years old, my first brother was born, then all my mother's attention got shifted to my younger brother. My mother had hardly any time to love and caress me.

Then, as I grew up, my mother and father would spend their spare time in club and ask me to read books all the time and finish my home work and whenever I happened to eat roadside fast food, they will admonish me not to eat such hot stuff, as it will harm my stomach and digestion; but my parents themselves will take the same fast food off & on, with their friends. Thus, my mother fell from the pedestal of idealism in my estimation and I no longer loved my mother as dearly as earlier in my childhood.

Then, as I joined the High School, there I came to love the Captain of our School Hockey Team. He was like a wizard in the game of hockey. He would dribble the hockey ball and take it from one end of the goal to the other side to score a goal, with such speed and dexterity, crossing all opponents on the way. I began to love him the most. He also liked me and taught me how to play hockey correctly. But the boy was quite senior to me, and soon left the School and thus faded out of my memory.

After some time, the lady class teacher of my class captured my imagination. She was indeed a very good teacher and beautiful too. She will exhort me to become a good citizen and also inspire me to score good marks. She was very kind to me and I also began to like her the most; but after some time, she got married and left the school and she also faded from my memory.

Today, when I have entered the 17th year of my life, my mother often compliments me by saying, "you have grown beautiful." My father also compliments by saying, "You have grown smart" and my mother's lady friends also greet me by saying, "You have become charming."

Everyone has started appreciating me - How I walk, How I talk, How I look. And these days when I look up myself in the mirror, I find myself very healthy, smart and beautiful, my cheeks radiating glow and my eyes shining. Thus, these days, "I Like My-Self the Most," but who will be my most loved one in future, this, time and circumstances alone will tell". Thus, I ended my speech and I was awarded the Ist prize for this talk.

And, there is no denying this fact that all we do is ultimately to make ourself happy. Thus, REMEMBER yourself daily by inhaling with 'AHAÑM and exhaling with MAIÑ HOOÑ (which also means I exist) and so doing, you will always remain disease free. Thus, we also come to realize our abilities, and limitations, our true place in this Universe and so knowing, we continue to improve and evolve with the use of these breathing mantras, because these help us to communicate with the Universal LIFE Energy Field continuously and, lead us to the Realization of the Self which is another name of Self Enlightenment.

> *It is not for the sake of the husband, my beloved, that the husband is dear, but for the sake of the Self..... my beloved, the wife is dear, for the sake of the Self. It is not for the sake of the children, my beloved, that the children are dear, but for the sake of the Self.*
>
> **— Brihadaranyaka Upanishad**
> 2.4.4-5

Chapter - 4

HEAL THYSELF

You are thy own Healer. The word HEALTHY is derived from the word HEAL THEE and this is indeed very very True. Make the very suggestive healing mantra "HEAL THEE" as you breath.

1. Exhale with   =   HEAL — THEE
    Inhale with   =   LAHHANTH

This mantra helps us to breathe from the bottom of the spine with L, through the cervical region of the spine with (H), and then yokes us with infinity - the super consciousness with HAÑ and ends at TH - the seed word for taste/teeth and salivary glands. It also stimulates pituitary gland.

i) And the word L generates in us the will power to heal ourself, gives power to the legs and boosts the sex glands, kindles our divine kundalini energy to illuminate our total being.

ii) The word 'H' - the seed word for Vishudha/Throat chakra stimulates the Thyroid - the gland of growth and vitality and re-establishes the communication betweeen the body and the mind. Thus, it is a very HEALSOME mantra. The word HEAL-SOME is also a very potent mantra.

2. Exhale with   =   HEALSOME
    Inhale with   =   LA - SAHAM

This mantra instead stimulates the crown chakra with its seed word M, strengthens the right brain and the pineal gland.

3. The word 'HEALING' suggests the continuous process of healing.

Exhale with   =   I AM HEALING or
                      IMMIH - HEALING.
Inhale with   =   LAHHAM-MANG

In this mantra, the word 'G' stimulates the left brain/pituitary gland and the sense endings of smell, it also stimulates the hormone - immunoglobin A in the nasal cavities to protect against invading bacteria/viruses which are always lurking around to attack us.

4. Similarly Exhale with   =   HEAL - ME
            Inhale with   =   LAHHAM

5. Also Exhale with   =   I AM HEALTHY
                              or IMMIH HEALTHY

            Inhale with   =   LAHAM - MANTH.

6 Similary Exhale with   =   HEAL - WOMB

            Inhale with   =   LAVABHAN

This mantra will help to heal the right womb.

All the above very suggestive breathing mantras, inspite of being very very simple mantras, are indeed very very effective to put us back on the rails of health, supplemented with a balanced nourishing diet. These mantras will also go a long way in healing persons suffering from cervical spondylitis which is a common ailment prevalent amongst the desk workers these days.

*"Look into the depths of your own soul and .....
you will understand why this illness was bound
to come upon you."*

FREUD

Chapter - 5

THE KING OF MANTRAS
'NAM'

The word "NAM" means a word or Holy word - a Mantra given by the Hindu sages to their devotees for daily silent chanting and it is not to be disclosed to anyone else. This is like a secret NAME GIVING from the Guru to the faithful disciple - the 'NAM' to be chanted all day or whenever convenient or stressed to make the disciple lead a stressfree existence.Guru Nanak - the founder of Sikh Religion attaches great sanctity to Holy Word by saying, "Sabda, the Word, is the guru and the mind attuned to the Word is the disciple."

And in our breathing MANTRA Therapy, the Mantra - NAM is used as a suffix to the inhale Mantra and is the king of all mantras because it contains the word N & M, the seed words of Brow chakra and Crown chakra respectively.

The word 'N' by its resonant sonic vibrations strengthens the left brain, the eyes and the pituitary gland - the Director of total endocrine orchestra in our body/mind system and thus plays the most important part in meeting the challenge of stress.

The word 'M' being the seed word for crown chakra, strengthens the upper right brain and the pineal gland and comes to the rescue of left brain whenever necessary, to calm and soothe the mind by releasing melatonin hormone.Thus, the word NAM stimulates the total brain. This is why we call it the king of mantras.

And if we add the word ALL - the seed word of basic chakra, then we are able to inhale deeply from the bottom of the spine.

1. Thus Inhale with =   ALLA - NAM
    Exhale with   =   NEELUM

The word 'Neelam' stands for a precious blue Gemstone in our Urdu/Hindi language. This word when spelled as Neelum helps us to see the blue diamond inbetween the two eye brows at the site of 3rd eye/brow chakra. The inhale mantra - ALLA-NAM-means - all is in the name, though Shakespeare said long back, "What is there in a name, a rose will smell as sweet by whatever name you call it." But here the word 'NAM' is specific and is a miracle mantra to cure various diseases since the word 'NAM' helps to boost our immune system.

Another suggestive mantra with 'NAM' is given below:-

2. And Inhale with =   ALLA - RAJA - NAM
                            (It means the king of all
                            is NAM)

    Exhale with   =   MANAGERIAL

And as we know Manager is the king of the office. And this suggestive breathing mantra rejuvenates our total body/mind system and will thus help us to become good Manager of ourself and in the office.

Another very useful mantra with NAM is given below:-

3. Inhale with   =   SDA - NAM

    Exhale with   =   MEDICINE

This is indeed a very suggestive mantra which will prove a good medicine to cure the ailing person without costing him/her a penny.

Chapter - 6

THE GODLY MANTRA

1. OMNI — NAMMA
2. OMNI — PRESENT

The word OMNI means ALL and its also constitutes all the healing properties, because N is the seed word for Brow Chakra and it strengthens with its sonic resonant vibrations the left brain, the eyes which are the Beholder of our body. Also the word 'N' stimulates the pituitary gland which is the master gland controlling the total endocrine hormonal orchestra in our body, thus strengthening our total body immune system to fight against disease. And word 'M' is the seed word for crown chakra, it strengthens the right brain and the mind and the pineal gland which is the transducer of super-conscious field. The word 'OMNI' is to be used as exhale mantra for which it is to be spoken as "OOMNI' and its inhale mantra is 'NAMMA' which means salutation in our Hindi language. In life, every one salutes the person who is imbibed with all qualities and so the mantra 'OOMNI-NAMMA' means - Salutation to God. And when this mantra OOMNI is combined with PRESENT, it becomes God—OOMNI-PRESENT, who is present every where.

1. Exhale with   =   OOMNI-PRESENT
   Inhale with   =   SA-PRA-NAMMANT

(i) The word SA kindles the divine Kundalini energy to move up alongwith the breath to the

64

crown chakra (M)

(ii) The word 'PRA' helps to breathe totally, from the abdomen with its seed word 'R' to endow the Fire to our body by proper digestion and assimilation of food and the word 'P' helps the cardio - vascular circulation.

(iii) The word MAÑ Yokes us with infinity - the superconsciousness to draw in as much pranic life energy as possible.

(iv) And the inhale mantra ends at the word 'T' which strengthens the salivary glands to secrete properly to predigest the food in the mouth, particularly the starches.

Thus the above mantra is a total body/mind rejuventation mantra, it helps develop control over mind with word 'M', N&T and to illuminate the mind with the divine Kundalini energy so kindled with the word 'S'.

2. Another 'OOMNI' mantra which helps us to imbibe in us the OOMNI knowledge of God is "OOMNI-Scient". Let us make it our breath.

Exhale with   =   OOMNI - SCIENT
Inhale with   =   ASHA - NAMMANT

3. And let us also imbibe in us the All-power-ful nature of God-by making the exhale mantra "OOMNI-POTENT" as our breath.

Exhale with   =   OOMNI-POOTENT
Inhale with   =   PANAMA - DANT

The word 'D' & 'T' are almost equivalent in their action.

This mantra particularly strengthens the teeth because it sets up to & fro resonant sonic vibrations in the teeth with the words - TENT & DANT.

Now all the 'OOMNI' breathing mantras given above are stress dissolving mantras, because God is the Greatest stress dissolver. And once we have faith in God and begin to feel HIS OOMNI PRESENCE everywhere, then we do no evil, think no evil and talk no evil and we also begin to surrender to God to cure us of all the stress and the stress automatically dissolves.

Now, we shall make many other suggestive and healing mantras with 'OOMNI' :-

4. Exhale with   =   OOMNI - PEACE
   Inhale with   =   SAPANAMMAÑ

5. And God helps those who help themselves, Here, we can help to heal ourselves by breathing with the following very suggestive breathing mantra.

   Exhale with   =   OOMNI - HELPING
   Inhale with   =   LAPAHANAMMANG

The above mantra includes 'H' the healing seed word of throat chakra, which strengthens the Thyroid gland which is called the watchman gland of our body/mind system and helps in fat/carbohydrate metabolism while also re-establishing the proper communication link in the cervical region of our spine.

6. Let us become as Diligent as God, and make it our breath;

   Exhale with   =   OOMNI-DILIGENT
   Inhale with   =   LAJADANAMMANT

Besides its many other benefits, it is also a heart friendly Mantra because of its seed word 'J'.

It also strengthens the teeth with the words T & D besides yoking us with infinity with Nammañ

7. Let us fill ourselves with the God's bliss and make it as our breath.

Exhale with   =   OOMNI-BLISS
Inhale with   =   LA-SBANA-MAÑ

8. Similarly let us fill ourselve with the Grace of God and make it our breath.

Exhale with   =   OOMNI-GRACIOUS
Inhale with   =   SHA-RA-GA-NAMMAÑ

9. Similarly we can feel as pleased as God.

Exhale with   =   OOMNI-PLEASED
Inhale with   =   LAZAPA-NAMMAND

10. Let us invoke the Healing Power of God and get healed in the process.

Exhale with   =   OOMNI HEALING
Inhale with   =   LAHA NAMMANG

11. Last but not the least let us link ourselves with God, so that God begins to reveal to us.

Exhale with   =   OOMNI-YEE-REVEALING
Inhale with   =   LAVARA-YA-NAMANG

The above mantra stimulates all the energy chakras of our body/mind system except the throat chakra, which the mantra no. 10 contains i.e. the seed word 'H'. Thus if we can inhale/exhale with mantra No. 10 for two minutes (20 times) and with mantra No. 11 for 4 minutes (40 times) every morning and evening daily in a pollution free environment we will soon get filled with the God's all pervading pranic life energy to heal us completely with no disease ever coming near us.

When we exhale with OOMNI-PLEASED, I am pleased within, I am inner pleased i.e. OOMNI-PLEASED because the Soul which resides in our body is thus pleased and as beautifully said by Jeremy Taylor.

"It is not the eye that sees the beauty of the heaven, nor the ear that hears the sweetness of music or the glad tidings of a prosperous occurence, but the soul, that perceives all the relishes of sensual and intellectual perfections and the more noble and excellent the soul is, the greater and more savoury are its perceptions."

Thus, it is the OOMNI-SOUL which feels blissful with the breathing mantra-OOMNI-bliss, which is our own soul, thus all the breathing mantras with 'OOMNI' uplift our soul and our total self, our total BEING, May we feel the OOMNI PRESENCE and OOMNI-EFFULGENCE of God always within us.

OM-TAT-SAT (AMEEN)

Chapter - 7

THE MANTRA
PRA

'PRA' is a mantra of PRAN (Life), PRANA (Life Motivating Energy), PRAYER, Improve, PRANAM (Salutation) and above all for Pramatman (God). The word PRA helps to breathe totally i.e. both from the abdomen with R and from the lungs with P. This mantra PRA is similar to the word BRA in its effect which is also the SEED MANTRA for total breathing.

There is a separate chapter devoted to - What is PRANA, but here we use it as an inhale mantra:

1. Inhale with   =   PRANNAÑ
      Exhale withe   =   INNI-PREEÑ

(i) The word 'R' in PRA helps to give FIRE to our body by properly digesting the food and its proper assimilation by secretion of Insulin by the pancreas and strengthening all the abdominal glands including liver and pancreas.

(ii) The word 'P' helps cardio-vascular system to breathe and circulate oxygen and the pranic energy.

(iii) The word 'N' is the seed word for brow chakra, it strengthens the left brain and eye sight and also the pituitary gland which is the master gland controlling the secretions of all other glands in our body. Thus, its strengthens our total immune system.

(iv) The word Ñ Yokes us with infinity - the superconsciousness to draw in as much pranic life energy as possible and even store it, in the solar plexus. Thus the mantra PRANA is the simplest life giving mantra true to its name.

(2) We can add NATH to PRAN (which means master of my life)

Inhale with	=	PRAN- NATH
Exhale with	=	INNI-PREET
		(which means Inner

Love)

3. We can add, M at the end of the word 'PRANA' to strengthen our right brain, mind and the pineal gland.

Inhale with	=	PRANAM
Exhale with	=	MUNI-PREE

The word PRANAM in Hindi means salutation.

4. Thw word PRAMATMAN in our Sanskrit/Hindi language means-God, the word PRAM means ultimate and ATMAÑ means Soul. And it is a unifying mantra with God.

Inhale with	=	PRAMATMAÑ
Exhale with	=	IMTI-PRAIM (This means
		I am the Love)

In this mantra, we have included the word T, which is the seed word for taste glands and also helps to improve our all tastes in life, to live life fully for the ATMA (Soul) to enjoy all tastes to its satisfaction while holidaying in our body temple.

5. The word "ASHA' in Hindi language means 'HOPE' and if we attach ASHA to PRAMATMA, it means, O, God help me to give me the Hope for life and Hope to survive my illness etc.. Also the word 'ASHA' helps us to breath right from

the bottom of our legs. Thus, it strengthens the legs, boosts the sex power and also kindles the divine kundalini to move it upto the crown chakra with M. Thus the following mantra is a mind illuminating one to give us that Great Hope.

Inhale with	=	ASHA-PRAMATMAN
Exhale with	=	OOMNI-PRIEST

6. We have also said above that the 'PRA' is also a mantra of 'PRAYER'

Inhale with	=	PRAYER
Exhale with	=	RAYA-PAÑ
		OR

7.
Inhale with	=	I AM IN PRAYER
Exhale with	=	ARRA-YA-PANAM or
		YA- PRANAM

(A separate chapter is devoted to this mantra)

However, I must stress that the word 'PRAYER' gives double stress on the word 'R' which is the seed word of navel chakra/solar plexus. It helps to improve liver action, the pancreas and all other secretions in our abdomen to digest and assimilate food to give 'FIRE' to our body. The word 'R' also stimulates our emergency life saving Adrenal gland. And the word Y is the seed word for Heart Chakra, so that Mantra prayer also strengthens our Heart, and gives our heart the compassion to love the whole humanity to say - we are all the children of this beautiful world and LET NO ONE SLEEP WITHOUT A SQUARE MEAL.

OM TAT SAT (AMEEN)

Chapter - 8

DEVELOP WISDOM TEETH
"I AM PRUDENT"

"You cannot turn back the clock;
but wind it up again"

— BONNIE PRUDDEN

The above quotation by Bonnie Prudden is indeed very prudent and with the following breathing mantras you can rewind your chronological clock by 10 to 20 years and these mantras will also help you to become prudent and grow wisdom teeth.

1. Exhale with = I AM PRUDENT
   Inhale with = PRAMA DANT

   OR

2. Inhale with = PRADHANNA- DANT
   Exhale with = INNI - PRUDENT

   OR

3. Exhale with = OOMNI - PRUDENT
   Inhale with = PRANAMA - DANT

i) The word 'PRA' helps us to breathe totally both from the abdomen with R and from the lungs with P to fulfill our BEING.

ii) The word 'N' is the seed word for Brow chakra. It stimulates the left brain, the eye sight and the Pituitary gland to boost our immune system.

iii) The word 'M' is the seed word for Crown Chakra. It strengthens the right brain, the pineal gland and the mind.

iv) The word D&T are the seed words for teeth. The word DANT & DENT help to send to & fro pranic life energy between the teeth to set up sonic resonant vibrations to strengthen teeth. Thus, this mantra will help to develop WISDOM TEETH & also rewind the clock of life.

Chapter - 9

RE-JUVENATE YOUR HEART

It is indeed a great MIRACLE of nature that our heart can circulate blood continously in our body for more than 100 years without even a second's rest. It is one of the most robust organs in our body, provided we do not damage it by overdrinking alcohol or overstressing the heart in so many other ways.

The seed word for strengthening heart is Y and its associated word is J. They say, you are as young as your heart. Thus, make 'young' as your breath to Juvenate the heart.

1. Inhale with   =   YOUNG-SPOKEN as YANG

    Exhale with   =   YOONG

2. Inhale with   =   SO YOUNG-Spoken as SAU-YAANG

    Exhale with   =   You SING

If your heart is strong and full of compassion, life becomes a song and most of the young persons are found singing in their bathroom. Thus, keep singing with the above breathing mantra and become young.

3. Another heart friendly mantra is

    Inhale with   =   SAYYAN

    Exhale with   =   NEEY - YEES or NEW YES

The exhale mantra is also suggestive, giving a

74

hypnotic suggestion to say Yes to life, say yes to every new day with new hope and new vigour. This mantra also strengthens the Brow Chakra with its seed word N to strengthen the left Brain and also the eye sight, besides the pituitary gland with the resonant sonic vibrations of N to boost our immune system. The word G in mantra no 1 is also an associate word for left Brain and the Brow Chakra.

4. Another similar heart friendly mantra is

Inhale with   =   SAYYAM
Exhale with   =   ME YOU SHE

Here we have replaced 'N' with 'M' which is the seed word for Crown chakra. It strengthens the right Brain and the pineal gland.

Before we proceed with other heart friendly mantras, let me say a word about emergency heart problem. Angina Pectoris is the first stage of heart disease, when the heart muscle cries for Oxygen and shows itself as pain in the heart region and left arm. This is an emergency situation which must be attended to by a competent heart Physician. There is a Micro Cylinder of Oxygen available in the form of Dinitrate (Sorbitrate)tablets which should be immediately procured from the nearest chemist and kept below the tongue before the heart physician reaches the patient or the patient is sent to a Heart Clinic. There is also a Homoeopathic medicine — Gloinine 3x, which also supplies Oxygen and should be kept in the home for emergency use or a pack of Dinitrate tablets.

For curing people of Angina, heart surgeons are also now resorting to Laser Beam Therapy in which the Laser Beam pierces Micro-holes in the diseased portion of the heart muscle. It results in creating new path ways of blood channels for supplying Oxygen directly from the arterial blood supply of the heart into these microholes created by the Laser Beam.

And if we make our thought move alongwith the breathing mantra, it pierces the Heart Muscle with the Thought Laser Beam, because the thought is the most refined form of Pranic Energy, more mono-directional and Coherent than even the Laser Beam, because powerfully beamed thought energy can even cure as well as harm another person even at a distance. Thus, the word Y by its resonant sonic energy can make micro-micro-holes, supplemented by the thought power, if we end the breathing mantra at Y and give a convenient PAUSE there of one or two seconds, concentrating and thinking good of the Heart. The word PRIYY ends at Y and is thus very suitable for the above practice. And the word YA will then fulfill the heart with Oxygen and Pranic Life Energy and Compassion.

5. Thus exhale with =   OMNI - PRIYYYY
    Inhale with   =   YA - PRANNAM

The word PRIYYA means LOVED ONE and it is the loving person who is capable of showing compassion and love for one and all. This is the seed mantra of heart rejuvenation.

The above breathing mantras will surely strengthen the Heart Muscle though the method is slow but steady and sure to cure heart disease, supplemented with heart friendly diet, provided we inhale/exhale with these mantras by speaking them silently and rhythmically by focusing our thought on the heart, when we inhale and exhale with the word Y or J. Do it for 5 to 10 minutes both morning and evening in a pollution free environment and soon you will begin to notice the beneficial effects on your heart functioning and thus you will not need a knife of a Heart Surgeon because they demand 10 bottles of blood to be donated by ten different persons. Is it ethical to live on with so many other peoples' blood flowing in our veins to survive?

6. Another very beneficial mantra for the heart is Hindi/Urdu word JWAN which means Young and the word J is also a word which strengthens the Heart as said above.

   Inhale with   =   JWAN

   Exhale with   =   JEEVUN or JUVEEN

7. The word JUVENATE is also a Juvenating mantra for the Heart.

   Thus exhale with =   JUVENATE

   Inhale with   =   VAJATAN

8. In order to give a Hypotic feeling of continuous process of rejuvenation:-

   Exhale with   =   JUVENATING

   Inhale with   =   VAJATANNANG

9. In order to metabolise fat and food properly so that the harmful fatty Cholesterol does not accumulate in our blood arteries, we strengthen the Liver/abdominal & Pancreas secretions with the seed word of Navel Chakra ' - R in breathing mantra No. 4. Also we include the word H in the breathing mantra to strengthen the Thyroid gland which also helps to properly metabolise fats as well as Carbo-hydrates in our body. It also establishes the communication between the heart and the Brain through the

cervical region of the spine.

Thus inhale with =   SARAYAHHAM
Exhale with   =   MIHHI-YOU-REESH

The above breathing matnra is a very very potent one to rejuvenate our body and heart. This is another seed mantra for Heart Rejuvenation.

10. We are all seeking glimpses of JOY and the day we lose track of that Joyous vision in our life, depression sets in, the heart as well as digestion slackens and life starts losing its meaning. This is the beginning of our heart problems. Thus, keep up the spirit of enjoyment, and make it your breath. And the word 'JOY' contains the words J & Y - both the seed words for heart.

Thus exhale with =   I AM JOYOUS
Inhale with   =   SAYAJAMMAÑ

11. Exhale with   =   I AM ENJOYING
                       OR
                       IMMI - ENJOYING

Inhale with   =   AYYA JANAMMONG

But, we must enjoy with-in our body limits. The motto-Eat, Drink & Be Merry is O.K. as long as it is with-in our body limits because over-eating, over-drinking and over-merriment can then become a torture for our body - to our Being & thus detrimental to our heart. So we have to live within the discipline for which the Hindi word is NIYYUM. This is also a heart friendly mantra,.

12. Exhale with   =   NIYYUM
Inhale with   =   YANAM

This mantra also stimulates the left brain,

pituitary gland with N- and the right brain & pineal gland with M.

13. Another great mantra for heart is to keep up the spirit of youth and warmth and our heart will never fail us for which I always say, "Twenty warm embraces a Day keeps the heart surgeon away."

First, because Embrace is so joyful & heart warming; ii) It gives physical warm Pulsations to the heart muscle besides mental pulsations of Joy. Its benefits are many many fold,just not two fold.

Thus inhale with = WARM
Exhale with = EMBRACE

14. The simplest heart friendly mantra is SANJEEV

Inhale with = SANJ
Exhale with = JEEV

The word SAÑ yokes us with the Infinity - the super-consciousness to draw in as much pranic life energy as possible and then ends at J - the seed word for Heart. Then we exhale with JEEV (which means a living Being in Hindi language). The word 'V' is the seed word for Ovary Chakra and lower intestines where the digested food is absorbed in the blood for circulation to all the cells of our body. In view of its importance, a separate chapter is devoted to it.

15. Last, but not the least, our modern day Managers need to possess a very strong heart to support them in their mad mad race for competition, efficiency & power.

For this exhale with = MANAGERIAL
Inhale with = LARA JANAM

It is indeed a total body and heart rejuvenating

mantra because it stimulates the divine Kundalini
energy with L, the liver, the Pancreas and emergency
adrenal glands with R, the heart with J, the left
brain and Pituitary gland with N and the right brain
and the Pineal gland with M.

Now, a few words about the heart friendly
exercises. Walking is the most natural aerobic
exercise very very good for the heart. Walk at your
convenient pace for 30 to 40 minutes in the
morning (See chapter on Walking). If due to some
disability, one is not able to walk, then sitting in
a chair or lying in bed on the back, alternate
movement of the hands up and down as in walking
tones up the heart. Do it for 10 to 20 times. Rest,
then repeat again as convenient. Similarly, you
can move your legs alternately up & down as in
walking, conveniently, for 8 to 10 times. Rest and
repeat as it suits you.

Regarding Heart friendly diet, volumes of books
have been written. The sum and substance of all
these books is to take ample supplements of fresh
seasonal fruits and vegetables in the form of
Salads, fibrous food i.e. Oatmeal, porridge, sprouted
grains and to avoid fried foods as far as possible
and also to limit the intake of non-vegetarian food
to prescribed limits. I usually advise taking one
clove of garlic everyday with milk at Breakfast to
take care of the naughty cholesterol. The Garlic
also discourages clotting of blood and also stimulates
the immune system by supplying some of the
required nutrients.

Whenever, I get a mild chest pain in the heart
region due to over-eating or otherwise, I rejuvenate
my heart/digestion with the breathing mantra No.
9 i.e. inhale with **SARAYAHAM** & exhale with

MIHIYOUREESH and the pain vanishes in a few minutes. If the pain continues, then immediately take one tablet of Dinitrate and consult the Doctor.

This chapter is dedicated to my sweet niece 'PRIYYA' for her well being. She is the darling of all hearts at RAJNEESH ASHRAM, PUNE.

Chapter - 10

THE MANTRA
IMPERIAL - LIVING

If you can become your own Emperor and develop an Imperial personality, you can rule over the hearts of all other persons. Thus, make imperial living as your way of life and BREATH.

1. Exhale with   =   IMPERIAL - LIVING
    Inhale with   =   LAVARA PAMMANG

The inhale mantra really helps us to develop the imperial personality because:

(i)   The word 'L' helps to kindle the divine Kundalini energy, gives power to the sex organ and the legs to make our style of walking imperial.

(ii) The word 'V' helps to strengthen the ovary, the lower intestines for better assimilation and elimination processes of body and keeps us EVER-GREEN, by the proper water action which is necessary constituent of all cells and life processes in our body.

(iii) The word "R' which is the seed word for Navel chakra, boosts our metabolism, by stimulating liver, Pancreas and all abdominal secretions.

(iv) The word 'P' helps the cardio-vascular system to circulate blood/oxygen in a more efficient manner and to develop the compassion to become IMPERIAL to look after all people with compassion.

(v)   The word 'M' is the seed word for crown chakra, which strengthens the right brain and crown chakra which is the top Imperial chakra.

(vi) The word MAÑ helps us to yoke with Infinity-
the super-consciousness to draw in all imperial
energy from Infinity.

(vii) The word 'G' stimulates the left brain.

Thus the above breathing Mantra rejuvenates
our total body/mind system, to continue to look
and feel IMPERIAL.

Chapter - 11

BECOME TALLER
MANTRA 'INCREASE - LENGTH'

Growing taller is the greatest obsession of children between the age of 13 to 18 years - the age when the children become taller every day to reach the full height potential which is mostly controlled by the inherited genes. However, some height can be added by taking good nutrition and the will-power to increase the height and some hormonal stimulation which we can achieve by strengthening growth-glands like pituitary gland with N, and Thyroid gland with H, and the sex glands - the Mulandara chakra to give strength and length to the legs with the word 'L'.

1. For this inhale with   =   LAHHAN
    Exhale with   •   =   NIHHIL

Also we can exhale with a very very suggestive mantra given below, which contains the word 'R' to help improve metabolism.

2. Exhale with   =   INCREASE LENGTH
    Inhale with   =   LAKRA ZAGANNATH

Similarly, another suggestive breathing mantra which also contains H, the seed word for Thyroid gland is :-

    Exhale with   =   INCREASE - HEIGHT
    Inhale with   =   SAKRAHA - GANANT

And the word NAÑ-yokes us with infinity-the superconsciousness to draw in as much pranic life energy as possible to fulfill our BEING with life force for fuller growth to our maximum potential. And above all, the above two breathing mantras will enable you to increase length and make you taller by their hypnotic suggestive power, as we know that thought is the most refined form of pranic life energy to motivate our MIND. Thus, you will surely be able to add one or two inches to your height, provided you support it with a well balanced nutritious diet of proteins, fats, carbohydrates, vitamins and minerals for growth and one or two inches of extra increase in height of a person matters quiet a a lot, which can thus be achieved, provided you are below 18 years of age.

Chapter - 12

A SALUTATION MANTRA
'NMEESTAI'

"Twenty Claps a Day Keeps the Heart Physician Away."

The English speaking people and Europeans greet each other with a warm handshake, partaking each other's warmth in their hand. The Muslims usually greet each other with a Hearty Hug, while we Hindus greet each other with salutation in the form of folded hands which we call Nmeestai. It literally means - I bow to Thee in Salutation with all my mind and heart.

Every form of greeting has its own merits and since this chapter is devoted to Nmeestai, I will highlight its merits. In this, we press the palms and fingers of both right and left hands, finger to finger and palm to palm, pressing against each other affectionately. As it is well known now that the reflex points of total body/mind system are located on our both hands, these, thus, get pressed against each other. We, thus, inadvertently, press the bio-energy switches of our body/mind system, and thereby, activate all of them in self love, each time we say - Nmeestai. And simultaneously we also join the bio-energy circuit of both hands, thus conserving the body/mind energy.

Similarly, clapping with both hands with a devotional song also achieves the same purpose, besides giving an added benefit of prayer with a Bhakti Song-Yoking us with God, through the medium of devotional song. This is why, I have highlighted the importance of clapping by saying - "Twenty claps a day, keeps the heart physician away".

I, myself, do these hand clappings while exhaling with the breathing Mantra - NMEESTAI and then pressing both hands firmly with each other without making a sound, so that other persons are not disturbed in the process. Then, I start inhaling, while out-stretching my hands to 180 degree angle, inhaling with the mantra "SDA-NMAÑ" which means - O God, I always (Sada) respectfully give my salutation to you. I do this clapping exercise as above by facing the early morning Sun while keeping my eyes closed. I do it as a prayer to the giver of Solar Energy, to make of me a warm hearted person.

An ex-Prime Minister of India - Indira Gandhi once quipped very aptly "You cannot shake hands with a clenched fist", that is very true but you can definitely humble (win) the other person with a warm Namaste because you need not shake hands. This mantra - Sda - Namañ/Namaste makes the person humble and can turn politicians into statesmen to serve the people. So doing, the humanity can be uplifted to be hunger free. Then alone, no one will sleep without a square meal in this world.

PRAYER TO GOD WITH MANTRAS

Inhale with		Exhale with
O, God	—	A good day
O, God	—	A good food
O, God	—	A good deed
O, God	—	A good sleep
O, Lord	—	I AM GRATEFUL TO THEE

Chapter - 13

A NOURISHING MANTRA
FOR THE MIND

It is the innate nature of Mind to engage itself in some pleasing activity or the other. Once the mind is free, it can become naughty and a devil's workshop and can make hell out of heaven and heaven out of hell. So, the best Way to nourish the mind, besides its craving for nutritious and tasty food is to keep it nourished with some useful activity and motivated with fruitful endeavours. All this is conveyed beautifully by the inhale mantra - "SDA-RAMANNA", which means always totally involved in pleasing pursuits.

Inhale with	=	SDA-RAMANNA
Exhale with	=	NOURISHMENT
		or
		NOOREESH-MIND
		or
		NOURISH-MIND

Thus, the mind requires both food and also nourishment with pranic life energy which the above exhale/inhale mantra helps to amply provide.

The word 'S' helps to take the breath from its seat of origin about mid way between the Navel and the bottom of the spine to the Solar Plexus/Navel Chakra-the seed word for which is R which ignites the Fire Energy in our body/abdomen and then the breath imparts strength to all the organs of the brain and mind with the words M,N,D. Thus, this inhale mantra very adequately nourishes the mind with the pranic life energy The exhale mantra Nourishment is self explanatory and it is similar to the Hindi/Urdu word-NOOREESH which means- the eyes full of bliss because the above inhale/ exhale mantra gives sparkle to the eyes with the word N. Inhale/Exhale with the above mantra silently for five minutes in the morning and evening and the bliss will begin to radiate from your eyes - an insignia of well nourished mind/ brain system. This happens because N&M stimulate the total brain, the pituitary gland & the pineal gland to boost our Immune system.

Chapter - 14

INVEST IN YOUR HEALTH
THE MANTRA
I AM INVESTING

Our investment in our health is our best investment and the yogis are able to store pranic life energy in their brow chakra (N), located between the two eyebrows, wherein is located the 3rd eye of Lord Shiva or the single eye of Christ. Its seed word is N and by it sonic resonant vibrations, it strengthens all the conscious organs of our brain. And the following mantra helps to move the dormant kundalini energy into the brow chakra (N) and crown chakra (M) with the power of the words S & V.

Thus exhale with = I AM INVESTING

Inhale with   = SHAVA-TANAMMANG.-

or

SHTA-VANA-MANG.

The words S/Sh. are the seed words for breath origin and also constitute the mouth of Kundiline Vessel, which is constituted of the word V, S and L. The seed word for Swadistana Chakra is V. It represents water principle and movement. The word V by its sonic resonant vibrations strengthens the lower intestines for absorption of digested food into the blood stream and also helps in eliminative process of stool etc.

And the word T stands for taste gland and helps to strengthen the salivary glands in the mouth. And M is the seed word for crown chakra and the right brain and the end of the inhale mantra-Mang, yokes us with infinity-the superconsciousness to draw in all the needed pranic life energy to store in the brow chakra and to activiate the sense endings of various conscious organs. Thus, with the inclusion of the words T, M, N and NG, the total mind, brain and super intelligence is invoked and is thus a very healing mantra for the mind and is capable of storing the extra pranic life energy into the brow chakra with the word N & the word N & M strengthen pituitary and pineal glands, which together control all glandular activity in our body/mind system, thus boosting our Immune system.

Inhale/exhale with the above mantra for five minutes in the morning and five minutes in the evening by speaking the mantra inwardly, smoothly and rhythmically and non-violently to simulate the natural breathing as nearly as possible. This will indeed prove a very good investment for your health.

"He who has health, has hope, And he who has hope, has every thing".

— *'Arabian Proverb'*

Chapter - 15

THE MANTRA
I KINDLE LIFE

The word Kindle has its root in the word Kundalini-which is the vessel of potential life energy, lying dormant, like a coiled coil serpent but it can be made kinetic by the sonic resonant power of the words L,S and V-the words constituting the VESSEL.

When the sex moves down, one can enjoy the ecstasy of sexual union for progeny or other-wise and when the sex power moves up, our personality starts kindling and shines like a jewel, first appearing as a bright blue diamond, in between the two eye brows, off and on, and soon we become a lamp to ourself and then to all others. For this,

1) Exhale with = KINDLE
   Inhale with = LAKKAND

After practicing to inhale/exhale with the above mantra- the mantra to be spoken inwardly, smoothly and rhythmically while giving stress on L, the sonic resonant vibrations of which will make the dormant Kundalini dynamic and make it move up with the breath upto the K, N&D-sense centres in the brain. Now, we add the word M to make the Kundilini power to touch the crown chakra, the seed word for which is M.

2) Exhale with = IMMI-KINDLE
   Inhale with = LA-KAMMAND

The word 'kammand' is like the English Word-

Command and in order to make the breath continuous, the inhale mantra should be spoken as LAK-KAMMOND.

And we can also use the hypnotic and very suggestive power of the line 'I KINDLE LIFE.'

3) Exhale with   =   I KINDLE LIFE
                         or
                         IMMIK KINDLE LIFE

   Inhale with   =   ALFA-KAMMAND
                         (COMMAND)

The word F is the seed word for lungs, and hence its strengthens the lungs with its resonant sonic energy to breathe to its full capacity., and this mantra particularly strengthens the mind to put it in a commanding position with the word Kammand which it deserves. The word 'kundalini' itself helps to kindle the divine kundalini with the power of the word - L provided we make it an exhale mantra - by spelling it 'KUNDILINI' which should be its proper spelling.

   Exhale with   =   KUNDILINI

   Inhale with   =   LAKA - ANAND

This mantra stimulates the brow chakra, left brain and pituitary gland with seed word N besides endowing us Bliss by the word 'ANAND'.

And, last but not the least, let us not forget that in order to kindle our life, we have to live a stress free life of Satyam (truth) Shivam (godliness) and Suderam (Beauty).

Chapter - 16

MANTRA
I AM FLOWERING

The word 'Flower' is indeed a very rejuvenating mantra for us to spread the aura/fragrance of our health around, just like a beautiful flower, and this can happen, if we can exhale with the mantra 'flower' pronounced as floower, as originally intended by the linguists.

1. Exhale with   =   FLOOVVERING
   Inhale with   =   LAVARAFONG.

   And

2. Exhale with   =   I AM FLOOVVERING
   or
                            IMMI-FLOOVERING.
   Inhale with   =   LAVARAFAMMONG.

(i) The word "L' is the seed word for the basic Muladhara chakra which strengthens the sex organ and the legs and helps us to illuminate by kindling the dormant kundiline to move up, with the breath.

(ii) And the word 'V' is the seed word for Swadhistana Chakra which represents the water principle and it helps to strengthen the ovaries which nurture life and also helps to strengthen the lower intestines, where the digested food alongwith nutrients gets absorbed in the blood stream for circulation to all cells in our body. It also helps to strengthen the kidneys for proper elimination of urine etc.

(iii) The word 'R' is the seed word of Manipur Chakra which represents the fire principle in our body, and the word 'R' gives resonant sonic vibration to the total digestive/assimilative process in the abdomen, to release the proper digestive juices, as and when required, and strengthens the liver and the pancreatic gland to release proper insulin for proper assimilation of glycogen in our body.

(iv) The word 'F' is the seed word for lungs, which it helps to breathe to its optimum capacity - the oxygen/pranic life energy to motivate life.

(v) The word 'M' is the seed word for crown chakra, it helps to strengthen the right brain and the pineal gland and the word Mañ yokes us with the superconsciousness to draw in as much pranic life energy as required by us and the mantra ends with the word 'G' and the total word 'MONG' gives sonic vibratory power to the conscious sense endings in our brain like eyes, nose, throat etc. and also activates the pituitary gland in the left brain which is the master gland to control the total glandular activity in our body. Thus, the inhale mantra 'lavarafammong gives resonant sonic power to the total body/ mind system and above all, it strengthens our sex organs with the power of the words L N & G to increase our retentivity and sex power of 'LING' (Sex organ in HINDI) and as long as a person is sexually active, he is flowering, he thinks I am still young. That is indeed a great rejuvenating feeling and then we can say things to others with flowers.

OM TAT SAT/AMIN

Chapter - 17

A MEANINGFUL HEALTH MANTRA

Life for every individual is the only meaningful entity, If we are there in this world, then alone, everything has meaning otherwise it has no value for us. For that let us make our life meaningful & healthy by making the word meaningful as our breath. Thus

Exhale with	=	MEANINGFUL
Inhale with	=	LAFANAMANG

The word 'LAFANA' in our Urdu language means-Infinite age and the word 'Mang' means-Ask for. Thus the inhale mantra-Asks for agelessness and the breathing mantra will indeed help us to score healthy hundred years if we so desire to live, but for that we also need to live a stressfree life of Satyam (truth), Shivam (godliness) and Sunderum (beautiful life) which should be satisfying to our soul, so that the soul likes to continue to embody us and is reluctant to leave it.

The above mantra helps to

(i) stimulate our divine kundalini energy with its seed word for muladhara/basic sex chakra - L, which gives strength to our legs and increases sex power and illuminates us when the kundalini moves up to the crown chakra (M).

(ii) The word F is the seed word for lungs to breathe in optimum oxygen/pranic life energy to rejuvenate us.

96

(iii) The word N is the seed word of Brow chakra and it stimulates the pituitary gland and strengthens the left brain.

(iv) The word M is the seed word for Crown chakra. It helps to strengthen the right brain and the mind control and also the pineal gland. And the pituitary and pineal glands help to boost our total body/brain Immune system.

(v) The word MAÑ helps us to yoke with Infinity-the super-consciousness to draw in as much pranic life energy as possible and also store it in the Brow chakra.

(vi) The inhale mantra ends with the word G which is the seed word for nasal sense endings. It strengthens the Immunoglobin A which is present in the nasal cavities to boost our immune system to fight outside germs.

Thus, the mantra 'Meaningful' is very suggestive to give meaning to our health restoration and its build up.

Chapter - 18

SKY IS THE LIMIT MANTRA
ASMAN

Sky is the limit for the man to scale any heights. It is man's ingenuity that he has reached the moon and returned home to the earth safely again and again. The Word 'Asman' means 'Sky' in Urdu/Hindi Language, and is a good inhale mantra to develop the left brain (N) and the right brain (M) of a person & together the words N&M resonate with their sonic energy with the pituitary & pineal glands respectively, which direct the total glandular orchestra in our body, thus keeping our body/mind healthy for any challenging task. And the word 'AS' helps us to breathe from the bottom of our legs and the total inhale mantra Asman helps to take the the breath to the top crown chakra(M) through the brow chakra (N).

1) Inhale with   =   ASMAN SPOKEN as
                       ASSMAN
   Exhale with   =   MUNEESH

Before we practice with the above mantra, there are two simpler mantras:

2) Inhale with   =   ASSAN
   Exhale with   =   NEESH

This very easy mantra will help cure eye defects like Myopia, Hypermetropia & Cataract by providing pranic life energy to the eye sight organs with the help of seed word N. Also

3) Inhale with   =   ASSAM
    Exhale with   =   MEESH

This mantra will strengthen the right brain
and the mind & helps to take the Kindled Kundalini
alongwith the breath to the crown chakra, thus
helping us to illuminate our personality. Give a
small pause after inhaling with the above mantras
as well as a small pause after exhaling with the
above mantras. So doing you will benefit greatly
because it brings about fusion of the inhale &
exhale currents bringing bliss in the mind. This
mantra wil thus help us to scale all heights — Sky
is the Limit, by building up our brain power.

Chapter - 19

A FLUORESCENT MANTRA

The persons who discover something new, I call them fluorescent people, just as in a fluorescent tube, the invisible radiation becomes visible. And use of this word 'Fluorescent' as mantra for exhaling the breath also brings shine on our face. How?

It can be seen below:-

1. Exhale with   =   FLUORESCENT
   Inhale with   =   LARA-SHFANT.

   or

2. Exhale with   =   I AM FLUORESCENT.
   or
                        IMMI-FLUORESCENT.

   Inhale with   =   LARA-SHFA-MANT

The word 'L' is the seed word for Muladhara Chakra, the basic sex chakra and its sonic resonant vibrations kindle the dormant kundalini; which the breath with the word S/Sh helps to take it to the crown chakra M. The word 'R' is the seed word for Manipur/Navel Chakra/Solar plexus and represents the fire principle and gives sonic resonant vibration to the total digestive organs/assimilation system to strengthen them to release properly the digestive juices as and when required, and the word Mant yokes us with the superconsciousness to draw in as much pranic life energy as required and ends with the word 'T' which improves our all tastes in life, strengthens the gums of our teeth and also helps to strengthen the salivary glands in the mouth for proper pre-digestion of starches. Thus the above mantra brings about a total rejuvenation in our body/mind system to shine and become fluorescent. And the word 'F' is the seed word for Lungs which it helps to breathe to its optimal capacity. And the word Shfa' in Urdu means — Heal-some. Thus, the above breathing. Mantra helps to restore our health completely.

Chapter - 20

"WANT TO BE WEALTHY"

"On Material gains, depends the Realization of Dharma and Pleasure".   — Arthasastra.

However much we may scoff at the very rich persons, all of us want to become rich, because money can provide us with all comforts and above all, it makes the mare go. But the trouble starts, when in the mad rush to acquire wealth, people begin to adopt dubious means to get rich-quick. Then, the total aim of such persons becomes-money, money, money. Let us stop this mad race for money, but we should acquire enough riches, with the Honest means, to provide us a good house, a car and a beautiful wife and something spare to help the poor to become self sufficient. I remember President Bush saying once "I do not believe in giving away a Fish to a poor person, I want to teach him how to catch fish.".

Thought is our Being and the mantra "Want to be wealthy" motivates us to become wealthy. And we are using this mantra also to breathe with. So to become wealthy in a natural way we make this desire our breath-our Being. And, this is a sure beginning to become rich.

Inhale with   =   WANT
Exhale with   . =   TO BE WEALTHY

i) The word 'L' in Wealthy is the seed word for basic Muladhara Sex Chakra. This represents

102

earth principle and gives power to the legs and kindles the kundalini to move up with breath.

ii) The word V is the seed word for Swadhishatana/ ovary chakra which represents water principle and strengthens the ovaries, and the lower intestines for better assimilation and elimination processes in our body.

iii) And the word Wañ yokes us with the Infinity - the Super-consciousness to draw in as much pranic life energy as possible and the inhale mantra ends with T, which is the seed word for taste glands. It helps to improve all our tastes in life, strengthens the salivary glands in the mouth for better pre-digestion of starches in the mouth and also boosts the immune system, by stimulating partially the pituitary gland.

Inhale/Exhale with the above mantra by speaking the mantra inwardly, smoothly and rhythmically, to simulate the natural breathing as nearly as possible. Do it for five minutes in the morning and for five minutes in the evening. This mantra besides helping us to enjoy a vibrant health, gives us that hypnotic impetus to become wealthy. So let us become rich both in health and wealth.

OM-TAT-SAT/(AMEEN)

The opulent man who is liberal towards strangers, while his family lives in distress, has counterfeit virtue which will first make him taste the sweets (of fame), but afterwards make him swallow the poison (of punishment in hell).   *Laws of Manu 11.9*

Chapter - 21

A BEAUTIFYING MANTRA

"A thing of beauty is a joy for ever." Keats.

Every child born in this world, is essentially beautiful, because he/she is born in the image of God. The child is God's own creation and every person is like an Actor on the stage of life, to fulfill his/her assigned role as said by Shakespeare. But some persons come in this world and excel in their roles and thus make this world a more beautiful place to live in.

There is no doubt that youth is beauty because this is like a fully blossomed flower, radiating the fragrance of youth and it is all a rejoicing period of one's life. But once the first signs of wrinkles appear in our mirror image, we begin to feel sad. So health is beauty and beauty is health and let us rejuvenate ourselves by breathing with the following mantra, and say goodbye to the wrinkles and old age.

(1) Exhale with   =   I AM BEAUTIFUL
                       or
                       IMMI-BEAUTIFUL

    Inhale with   =   LAFA-YA-BTAMMAÑ

In the above mantra, the world 'L' is the seed word for basic Muladhara sex Chakra. It helps to kindle the divine Kundalini with its resonant sonic energy to make it move up alongwith the breath and the breathing optimised with the seed word 'F' for lungs. Inhale as much as possible the oxygen and pranic life energy from the cosmos.

The word 'Y' - the seed word for heart chakra helps improve the circulation of blood/nutrients and makes us more compassionate. Thus, it is also a heart strengthening mantra. The word 'T' improves the taste for all things in life and also improves the digestion of starches by strengthening the salivary glands in the mouth and the word 'B' combined with 'T' helps to improve our speaking power to improve our total personality and ultimately the word 'M', the seed word for crown chakra improves our right brain and our control over our mind. for an impressive beautiful personality, because ultimately the Kundalini divine energy when it becomes kinetic, it reaches the crown chakra to illuminate us with its effulgence, to make us Beautiful.

(2) Similarly, the word - KHOOBSOORUT which also means 'beautiful' is a mantra which suggestively helps us to remain beautiful, particularly to give lustre to the eyes with its seed word 'KH' contained in it. Also it increases the fire in our body with the word 'R' and improves our taste with the word 'T'.

Exhale with   -   KHOOBSOORUT

Inhale with   -   SARA - BTANKH

Thus, so doing, you will continue to remain beautiful (Khoobsoorut).

Chapter - 22

A HEART WARMING MANTRA EMBRACING

"Twenty warm embraces a day will keep the
Heart Surgeon away".   — Author

A warm embrace is the best massage for the
Heart Muscle and there cannot be better exercise
done lovingly for the Heart than this. In fact, this
is the only feasible daily exercise for the Heart.
Even the Heart Surgeon, as a last resort, gives a
sudden jolt to the heart muscle to revive it when
a person's heart has stopped beating and many a
time the Heart revives. The word 'embracing' is
also a good exhale mantra.

1) Exhale with   =   EMBRACING
    Inhale with   =   SA-BRA-MANG

When we fall ill, our breath becomes shallow
and the word SA is the seed word for breath origin
in our body about 7 cms. below the Navel and the
word BRA helps the bronchial tubes to breathe to
their optimal capacity. This also helps to breathe
from the abdomen, because R is the seed word for
Manipur/Navel chakra in our body and it helps the
Liver, the abdomen, the Pancreas for proper digestion
and assimilation of food in our body. And the total
word 'BRA' helps us to breathe both from the
abdomen as well as from the lungs, very effective
word to help total breathing.

Word 'M' is the seed word for crown chakra. It

helps to strengthen the right brain and the pineal gland. And the word Mañ yokes us with Infinity-the Super-conscious-ness to draw in as much pranic life energy as possible. And the total word MANG helps to strengthen all the conscious sense endings in the brain. and the words, M,N,G, together activate the pituitary and pineal glands which are the master-glands directing the total glandular activity in our body/mind system. Thus, this breathing mantra helps to boost our immune system.

Inhale/Exhale with the above mantra by speaking it inwardly, smoothly and rhythmically, to simulate the natural breathing as nearly as possible. Do it for five minutes in the morning and for five minutes in the evening to boost your total health to make of you a warm hearted person.

Chapter - 23

THE MANTRA
'MINGLE'

The mantra 'Mingle' is apt, practical and suggestive mantra to yoke ourself with God and ultimately, one is so much part of the God almighty just as the water mingles up with milk to become in-separable from it.

Exhale with   =   MINGLE
Inhale with   =   LAGGANM

Inhale/exhale with the above mantra by speaking the mantra inwardly, smoothly, and softly so as to simulate the natural breathing as nearly as possible.

The word 'L' is the seed word for the basic Muladhara Chakra and by the sonic resonant vibrations of the word L, the dormant kundaline becomes kinetic and this energy can move up alongwith the breath, with the word 'Lag' up to the left brain and the word gañ yokes us with the superconsciousness to draw in the pranic life energy from the Infinitum source, and the breath ends at the crown chakra for which the seed word is M. This word M strengthens the pineal gland, as well as the right brain.

Thus, this mantra helps to take the breath from the bottom of the spine upto the crown chakra and thus one can illuminate oneself with the power of kundalini provided one lives a stress free life of Satyam (truth), Shivam (godliness) and Sundram (beauty). And one will start radiating bliss all around if one constantly practices to breathe in with this mantra for about half an hour in the morning and half an hour in the evening and also constantly thinks of mingling with God to become one with God's superconsciousness. You flow into the God with your thoughts and God starts flowing unto you, to become One with God's Super-Conciousness.

OM-TAT-SAT/AMEEN

Chapter - 24

A GREAT HEALTH IMPROVING MANTRA

'IMPROVING'

Out of all the living beings, only human beings have been endowed with the will-power to improve their health or improve their fate, if they so desire to do.

The word 'Improving' is really wonderful, it can prove a great mantra in health management and help in eradicating the disease with the power of its healing words, as seen below:-

1) Exhale with   =   IMPROVING
     Inhale with   =   VAPRAMMONG

(i) The word V is the seed word for ovary/ Swadhishtana Chakra and represents the Water principle, and it helps the absorption of digested food & nutrients in the blood stream in the lower intestines., it also helps the elimination of waste matter like Urine and stool, improves the action of the Womb which nurtures life.

(ii) The word 'R' is the seed word for Navel/ Manipura/Solar plexus Chakra, which represents the fire principle and hence, helps to digest the food and improves the action of Liver, proper release of digestive juices in the abdomen and the action of pancreatic gland for proper absorption of glycogen in the blood.

(iii) The word 'P' helps the lungs to breathe in to its

optimum capacity and the combined word 'PR' fortifies the total breathing by helping to breathe from the lungs with 'P' and from the abdomen with 'R'

iv) The word 'M' is the seed word for crown chakra, located in the head and it helps to stimulate the right-brain, our mind control and the word 'M' gives resonant sonic energy to the pineal gland, which releases the pacifying hormone - Melatonin

(v) The word G gives resonant sonic energy to our left brain to strengthen the eyes and the pituitary gland to boost our Immune system.

An allotropic modification of the above breathing mantra, which is complementary in its action to Mantra No. I is given below :

2) Exhale with   =   IMPROVEEMENT
   Inhale with   =   VAPRAMMANT

Here, the word 'T' has been substituted for 'G'. This improves all our tastes in life plus helps to strengthen the salivary glands to release proper juices in the mouth for pre-digestion of food. The word T also strengthens the gums holding the teeth, and the pituitary gland.

Thus, inhale/exhale with the above two mantras for three minutes each, both in the morning and evening by speaking these mantras only inwardly, smoothly, deeply, and rhythmically and non-violently so as to simulate the smooth natural breathing as nearly as possible.

In order to improve Will-power

3) Exhale with   =   IMPROVE-WILL
                        OR   IMPROVILL

Inhale with　　=　　LAVA PRAMMAÑ

The words L, V kindle the Kundalini and thus strengthen our will power as well as impart blissful shine in the eyes.

MANTRAS FOR ALL ROUND HEALTH IMPROVEMENT ARE GIVEN BELOW :-

4. IMPROVE - LIVER
5. IMPROVE - STRENGTH
6. IMPROVE - BRAIN
7. IMPROVE LEG COMMUNION
8. IMPROVE HEAD COMMUNION
9. IMPROVE ILLIAC COMMUNION

The above Mantras will bring about an all round improvement in our health i.e., by improving Liver, legs, brain and inter-communion in the brain.

These are all exhale mantras. Then inhale deeply from the bottom of the spine upto the Crown Chakra.

Chapter - 25

THE SELF SEARCHING MANTRA
MYSELF/SWATMAÑ

Our body is a temple of God who has animated our BEING — our temple with the soul (Atmañ), part of that infinitum soul, which we in Hindi language call Pramatman which means the Greatest Soul-the soul of souls, encampassing the whole universe, the super-soul, being Omni-Scient, Omni-present and Omnipotent through the power of which this whole universe is in purposeful vibration and radiance.

Each person has its own individual soul, rich with its past experience in its onward journey of evolution through ages, as per our Hindu religion. Our life is like a flowing river becoming bigger and evolving, with merger of new streams and ultimately this individual river becomes one with the sea, at the end of its journey. But as long as it is flowing on land, it has its own identity, its own origin, its own name, its own path to follow, but with the difference that the human kind has been endowed with the wish and will power of its own, to change its own destined course, if it desires to do so.

And human beings are more like the river which is about to merge into the sea, the waves of sea also incoming into the river to upgrade it, uplift it, to rejuvenate it and this in the breathing mantra therapy is denoted by the word AÑ, when through the current of breath, one gets united with the infinitum source. the super-consciousness.

113

And the Kundalini - a potential life energy source, which according to the sages, is normally lying dormant like a coiled serpent, but can be made dynamic with the sonic resonant vibrations of the power of the words L, S, V- the words constituting the VESSEL. Thus, Kundalini is the Vessel full of potential energy. I am comparing Kundalini to the SNOW in the mountains, which when melts gives the current of flow of water to the river at its source, which continuously gets melted with heat and solar energy and is thus the primary source, feeding to the river, it is also like a Bank Balance of Energy- if it has rained more, the snow is more, if the sun is more hot, the flow of water current is more. Thus, we have also to continuously feed ourself with food energy, which gives us the heat, and flow of life.

Thus Inhale with =	SWATMAÑ or
	SHAVA-ATMAÑ
Exhale with =	IMTEESH-SHIV
	or
	IMTEEV-WISH

The inhale mantra SWA-ATMAÑ is a good mantra to inhale with, first it reminds me about myself (SWA) as part of that super consciousness, secondly, as said above, the word SWA can Kindle the Kundalini and move it up alongwith the breath to join our self with the super consciousness, with the power of the word ATMAÑ. The word AÑ stands for superconsciousness as said earlier and the word M is the seed word for crown chakra in the Head and strengthens the right brain, mind and the pacifying pineal gland and the word T strengthens the muscles of the teeth and improves our tastes for all things in life and also strengthens the salivary glands in the mouth, and pituitary gland to boost our immune system.

Inhale/Exhale with the above mantra by speaking the mantra inwardly, smoothly, rhythmically and deeply and as non-violently as possible to simulate the natural breathing. Let us give a pause of a second or more, at the end of each inhalation and exhalation. The larger the pause, better it would be but convenience is the watch-word, never exceed your limits and that is the key to stress free existence in this world. You will start experiencing bliss during these pauses, after practice, with these mantras for sometimes, because of the fusion of inhale (male) and exhale (female) breathing currents during pause period.

Thus, this mantra helps to melt the snow in the Kundilini and yokes it with the super soul; thus establishing our link with God for our continuous upliftment and thus we can enter the Kingdom of bliss, which is our ultimate aim.

2) Last, but not the least we can also inhale/ exhale with the slight modification of the above mantra. to make Swatmañ into Swatman (myself)

The word 'N' the seed word of brow chakra stimulates the left brain & the master pituitary gland.

Indhale with   =   SWA-ATMAN
Exhale with   =   OOMNI-SWEET

Thus, inhale deeply the God's Sweetness and spread it all around saying things to one and all with flowers.

OM TAT SAT (AMEEN)

Chapter - 26

A FRAGRANT MANTRA

Every person in this world has an Aura of fragrance about him or her. This is how we feel attracted instantly. And more healthy & more cheerful our personality, the greater aura we have, to win friends and influence people. The following breathing mantra will help your whole personality to be filled with the fragrance of youth.

The word fragrance is both male & female i.e. it can be used both as an inhale as well as exhale breathing mantra depending upon how you pronounce it.

1) Exhale with = FRAIGGRAINT
   Inhale with = FRAAGGRAANT

Inhale/Exhale with the above mantra which should be spoken inwardly, smoothly and rhythmically, without any violence to our body/mind system so as to simulate the natural noiseless breathing. Do it for the five minutes in the morning and five minutes in the evening every day.

This is a rejuvenating mantra and uses the word R twice and it is the word R which activates the Solar Plexus/Navel Chakra and gives our body the FIRE to remain vigorous and young. And I recall my youthful days when we husband & wife, though sweating, would swear fragrance, in each other's body, when we are well locked in embraces and in ecstatic sex but now say, after thirty years of married life, my wife may externally apply the

116

choicest perfume to attract but still she goes unnoticed. This is what the following rhyme coined by me says:

"Aik Zamana Tha
Keh Unkai Psinai Maiñ Bhee
Ati Thee Khusboo
Ab Kya Zamana Aya
Keh Voh Itter (perfume) Lagati Haiñ
Aur Hmaiñ Khaber Tak Nheeñ Hoti"

This all happens because our senses get dull with age and even loving partners slowly, slowly start losing interest in each other, though this is not universally true- I would love my first wife Indu Rai any time, any age and perceive her fragrance at all ages because she is my first youthful love, and remained so for 30 years of our married life.

After you have got practice with breathing mantra given at (I), we can slightly extend the mantra for better benefits.

2) Exhale with   =   I AM FRAIGGRRAINT
                         or
                         IMMI-FRAIGGRRAINT
   Inhale with   =   FRAAGGRAANT-MAÑ

Thus, let us live a life like a fully blossomed flower, with all its fragrance. Once we are healthy and fragrant, we can say things to people with flowers.

OM TAT SAT (AMEEN)

This chapter is dedicated to my first wife 'Indu Rai' for Her Well Being who as said above, I would love any time, any age and feel her fragrance at all ages because she is my first youthful love and remained so for 30 years of our married life (1955 to 1985).

Chapter - 27

DEVELOP IMPRESSIVE PERSONALITY

Every one of us wants to possess a healthy impressive personality. This is quite possible if we make the Mantra 'IMPRESSIVE' as our breath.

(1) Exhale with   =   IMPRESSIVE
    Inhale with   =   SHAVA-PRAMMA

(i) The word 'SHA in the inhale mantra helps to kindle the divine Kundalini power and takes it alongwith breath to the crown chakra (M).

(ii) Thw word 'V' is the seed word for Swadhishtana Chakra, it represents water princ!ple and helps to keep us ever green, because it strengthens the lower intestines to absorb digested food alongwith water in the blood to reach all the cells of our body. It also helps in the elimination processes in the lower intestines.

(iii) The word 'R' is the seed word for Solar plexus. It strengthens all the abdominal secretions to help in digestion and assimilation of food and to give FIRE to our body.

(iv) The word 'P' helps the Cardio-vascular system for proper circulation of oxygen/nutrients through blood circulation. And the word 'PR' helps to breath both from the abdomen (R) and from the lungs (P).

(v) The word 'M' is the seed word for crown chakra which by its resonant sonic vibrations helps to strengthen the right brain, the mind and the pineal gland. And the mind illuminates when the divine kindled Kundalini reaches the crown chakra to give us an IMPRESSIVE personality.

Chapter - 28

LIVE EMINENTLY

All of us want to achieve Eminence in one field of activity or the other. And the word EMINENT as exhale mantra definitely helps us to stimulate our total BRAIN/MIND to help us to reach an eminent position in our life. Thus :-

1. Exhale with   =   EMINENTLY-LIVING
    Inhale with   =   LAVATA - NAMANG

2. Exhale with   =   EMINENT JEEVVUN
                           (JEEVUN MEANS LIFE)
    Inhale with   =   VAJATAN-NAMMAÑ

(i) The word L- the seed word for BASIC Chakra kindles the divine Kundalini and helps to illuminate us.

(ii) The word V - the seed word for ovary Chakra preserves us by stimulating the assimilative and eliminative processes in the lower intestines.

(iii) The word 'J' helps our cardio vascular system for better circulation of blood.

(iv) The word T is the seed word for taste glands and it also strengthens the salivary glands.

(v) The word 'N' - the seed word for Brow Chakra strengthens the left brain, the eye sight and the pituitary gland to boost our Immune system.

(vi) The word 'M' the seed word for crown chakra strengthens the right brain and the mind. It illuminates us when the divine kundalini energy reaches the crown chakra. It also strengthens the pineal gland which releases the Melatonin hormone to calm our stressed mind.

(vii) The word MAÑ yokes us with Infinity - the super consciousness to draw in as much pranic life energy as possible to fulfill us.

(viii) The word 'G' also stimulates the left brain. It also stimulates the immunoglobin A in the nasal cavities to boost our immunity.

Thus, inhale/exhale with the above mantras speaking them inwardly for a period of five minutes in the morning and in the evening and you wil begin to enjoy a very good healthy body/mind system to achieve EMINENCE in life.

Chapter - 29

BECOME A LAMP
THE MANTRA
'YOU RE-ILLUMINATE'

"What in me is dark - Illumine,
What is low-raise and support" John Milton

Become a Lamp first, to yourself and then to all others. The mantra, "You-Re Illuminate" helps us to achieve this speedily, provided we also simultaneously lead a life of Satyam (Truth), Shivam (godliness) and Sunderam (Beauty). Once we attain this self illumination, we can radiate the effulgence of beauty and bliss all around, and "A Thing of Beauty is a Joy for Ever," as said by the poet Keats.

In our youth, our youthfulness radiates and a poet has gone so far as to say that-O, Youthful, lady, inspite of the fact that you are blind as well as deaf, but still you look so beautiful, because of your radiating youth. This is what a punjabi poet sings thus:-

"Vah Jwani, Vah Jwani;
Tere Jaiñ Nhieñ Dekhi
Akhooñ Anhee, Kannooñ Bohli
Phir Sohni, Di, Sohni".

But, with advancing age, this youthful radiance slowly loses its lustre, but we can regain it, if we re-establish our link with the God Almighty, by

122

drawing in the pranic life force abundantly and thus get rejuvenated. For this.

1. Exhale with   =   YOU-RE-ILLUMINATE
   Inhale with   =   ALLARAYA - NAMMANT.

This breathing Mantra gives resonant sonic energy to Muladhara Chakra and the legs by (L), to Manipura Chakra (Solar Plexus/Navel chakra) with its seed word 'R', to Heart chakra with 'Y', and all the brain psychic centres with the words N,M,T and ultimately yokes us with the Super consciousness with Ñ in the inhale mantra, to draw in all the pranic energy which we can possibly absorb, thus helping us to kindle the divine Kundalini life force with the resonant sonic power of word 'L' to radiate the sparkle of bliss, combined with neutral mantra MAÑ.

This breathing mantra is a six stage inhale/exhale mantra to rejuvenate the total body/mind system by imparting it the pranic life energy. If we continue to inhale/exhale with the above mantra, slowly, smoothly, rhythmically and inwardly to simulate the natural breathing as nearly as possible for a few months, both morning and evening for about ten minutes each, then one begins to see first a blue diamond glow in between the two eyebrows, before we see the full splendour of superconsciousness. Thus, we can illuminate ourself and then all others.

And now I shall give the seed mantra of this book: .

2. Exhale with   =   HEY! YOU RE-ILLUMINATE
   Inhale with   =   ALLARA-YAHA-NAMMANT

This mantra in addition stimulates the Vishudha

chakra with its seed word 'H' to strengthen thyroid gland and to help re-establish communication between the body and the brain. This is a seven stage breathing mantra which can bring about Enlightenment and make us an Esteemed Self.

Chapter - 30

STAR-DAWN / INDUSTRY

The 'INDUSTRY' as its name implies, is to first dump your money 'IN-Dust- and then TRY'. This is true to a great extent, because Industry means a very risky investment, unless one has planned very-well in advance by studying the Demand/ Supply of the product in the market and its excellent production capability.

Plus, it also means - Try and Try again and again, inspite of initial failures during the teething period of the Industry, till one achieves the required success in one's venture.

Plus, as the name of the Industry suggests that one should be very very industrious, to put in all the hard-work necessary for the success of the Industry, since during the starting period of the Industry, the industrialist may have to work from 8 A.M. in the morning to 8 P.M. in the evening:- about 12 hours each day and even at night, one has to dream about one's industry - the work left still unfinished at the end of the day and as to how to solve those problems. And many a time, an idea will flash across one's mind at night which will solve the problem. And this comes only, when one is intensely devoted to one's industry. Then and then alone, one can leap forward to take one's industry to the crowned success.

And, this flashing of solutions comes to us from our subconscious which is collecting all the data and because our sub-conscious is yoked with the super consciousness - The God.

And the following breathing Mantra helps us to accomplish all this. The breathing mantra is :-

Exhale with   =   'INDUSTRYÑM'
Inhale with   =   'SARADATAÑM'

We have to inhale/exhale with the above mantra, while chanting silently, and smoothly. Thus, our breathing with the mantra should be as rhythmic, as deep and continous and as non-violent as possible to simulate the natural breathing as nearly as possible.

While, we are exhaling with the help of the mantra - 'INDUSTRYNM' we should be simultaneously feeling within ourselves, to be industrious and determined in establishing our industry. The word 'NM' has been added at the end of the mantra - Industry, to yoke us with the super consciousness - God, which will provide us with the sixth sense to avoid all the pit-falls in the industry. See, the beauty of the exhale mantra - Industrynm - the mantra 'Industry' has now become our breath - our life breath, because our industry is also our bread & butter By adding 'NM' (The silent 'N' with 'M'), it has become prayerful to unite us with the 'OMNI' - God's blessings.

Similarly, while inhaling with the mantra 'SARADATANM' you should be simultaneously feeling that it is all happening because of the Omni - God, because the word 'SARA' means "all" and the word 'Datanm' means, the Omni - Giver, and the inhale mantra also includes 'NM' to link us with the Omni' God.

Also, both the inhale/exhale mantras include 'R' - the seed word for Navel - Solar plexus to increase our metabolic rate and digestion of the nourishing food, to be able to put in all the hard work necessary to successfully implement the industry.

The above breathing mantra, also contains the word T/D which are the seed words for taste glands. It helps to improve our all tastes for life as well as strengthens the salivary glands in the mouth to release properly the digestive juices in the mouth for the predigestion of starches etc. in the mouth.

And the word 'S' is the seed word for breath-origin in our body-in between Muladhara Chakra and Swadhistana Chakra about 7 cms below Navel. The word 'S' helps to take the breath from its start point to the word 'M' which is the seed word for Crown Chakra in the head. The word 'S' also helps to kindle the Divine Kundalini to illuminate us.

And the word NM together strengthen with their resonant sonic energy the pituitary and pineal glands, which control all the glandular activity in our body/mind system, thus boosting our immune system to meet the challenge of setting up the Industry, because it requires a vibrant healthy condition of both body and mind system to successfully accomplish this task.

Another easy inhale/exhale mantra, to boost our health and indirectly our Industry is

2) Inhale with   =   STAR-DAWN
    Exhale with   =   INDUSTRY

This mantra is also very suggestive in nature

and the hypnotic influence of the word 'STAR-DAWN' as if a Star has dawned on the horizon of Industry to start a new chapter. This is indeed very helpful to give that great motive power to reach high and higher in the realm of Industry.

Thus, if we inhale/exhale with the above mantras for 10 minutes each morning in a pleasing and contamination free environment, it will not only augment the intake of oxygen/pranic energy in our body to keep us healthy, fit and disease free, but also it will provide us the necessary will-power and sixth sense to make our industry a roaring success.

OM-TAT-SAT/AMEEN

This chapter is dedicated to my youngest son - Vikas Chowdhry on his 37th birthday for his future WELL-BEING. He is a successful Industrialist and Managing Director of Logwell Forge Ltd. New Delhi.

Chapter - 31

BECOME AN IRON MAN

Nature manifests its Supermacy through Duality and it is through the Duality of the double valency of IRON that haemoglobin (an oxygen carrying substance in the blood) provides oxygen to the cells of the body, because iron can exist as Ferrous Iron in double valency and as Ferric Iron in triple valency and the ferrous iron has the property to trap oxygen to become ferric iron and ferric iron can part with oxygen to become ferrous again. But the total quantity of iron present in our body is only 1 to 5 gms depending upon the weight of the person, equal to the tip of an iron nail and our daily requirement of iron is only a few milligrams per day, though the requirement of pregnant ladies/ growing children and anaemic persons is slightly more. I am highlighting this, because we should not un-necessarily gulp iron supplements which usually contain more than 20 mgs. of iron and such iron capsules containing more than the daily need of our body are harmful for the body, because the extra iron can also drain away along with it other useful nutrients in our body. Experiments with radioactive iron have revealed that iron is stored in the body as an iron compound only upto a particular limit and no more. The extra iron has to be excreted from our body.

And if you want to develop the dual personality of a Politician to rule this world; then exhale/

inhale, with the following mantras:

1. Exhale with   =   I AM FERROUS or
                              IMMI FERROUS

   Inhale with   =   SARA FAMMAÑ

2. Exhale with   =   I AM FERRIC

   Inhale with   =   ARRA FAKAMMAÑ

So doing and thinking, we can become an iron man to rule this world.

Chapter - 32

WATER THE MAJOR CONSTITUENT OF BODY

We cannot live without water for more than 2 days as it is most essential for life processes in our body. Therefore, we must consume about 1.5 litres of water daily, taking a glass of water measuring about 250 cc, every 2 to 3 hours during our waking period, because water essentially acts as the medium for life processes in our body cells. Water is a major constitutent of our blood and gets absorbed alongwith the digested food in the lower intestines. It also helps in the elimination of body wastes by cleansing the bowels regularly with the help of proper intake of water. Water also helps to maintain the body temperature stable at 98.6°F in so many ways, and in summer, also by the process of sweating and evaporation which cools the body in hot summer environment.

About 70% of our body composition consists of water and incidently, it may not be out of place to mention that about 70% of our earth's crust is also constituted of sea water, but alas! the sea water is not directly fit for drinking because of its abnormal salt content. That is why, the poet Coleridge writes about his sea journey, thus :-

> "Alone Alone, All All alone,
> Alone on this wide wide sea.
> Water, Water Every where,
> But not a drop to drink".

But God is great, The sea water is purified by evaporation and then it is transported over the land in the form of rain clouds to provide water fit

131

for drinking through rains, which fill the rivers, lakes, ground water supply, snow which melts to fill the rivers for our drinking and irrigation of plants and vegetables and fruits and most of the vegetables and fresh seasonal fruits contains 70% to 90% water. Thus, fresh fruits and vegetables in the form of salads provide us water and nutrients directly in the most natural composition to our body, and these are the products to be consumed for living naturally a long healthy life.

And blood, through which all the cells in the body get their nutrition also consists mostly of water, sugar, fat, albuminous substances and salts of sodium, potassium, calcium and magnesium etc. and it also contains iron in its haemoglobin. And water is the medium for all cellular life reactions. Water is contained both inside the cell and also surrounds the cell, separated by cell membrance. The electrolytes of sodium, potassium, calcium and magnesium diffuse across the cell membrane because of the concentration gradient of the above electrolytes to provide electrical currents inside the human cell, such as transmission of information in the nerves, cell growth, cell division etc.

Also, the active transport of sugars and aminoacids into the human cell is linked to the electrochemical gradient of $Na+ - K+$ pump in the water electrolyte of each cell structure, while sodium sulphate ions help to regulate the excretion of superfluous water, while sodium chloride can attract water for furthering the division of cells for life processes etc., thus all the processes of life and cellular activity are carried out in the medium of water.

And, whenever any part of our body aches, it is crying for oxygen or glucose or water and the nutrients unless there is a direct cut or an obstruction of blood flow in the body. And thus many of our chronic ailments are cured by water therapy, and like all good things, too much intake of water is also not good, because it can drain away the essential nutrients.

In order to maintain proper health, let us start our day with a glass of water, preferably mixed with the juice of one lemon and one spoonful of honey and make the word - WATER as our breathing mantra for one minute only, every two hours after taking a glass of water.

Inhale with	=	WAT
Exhale with	=	TER

This mantra will help us to stimulate our lower intestines to absorb water properly for all life processes as mentioned above. The word/mantra WATER also stimulates the taste glands with the word T so to digest the food properly and it also helps the abdominal glands, by the resonant sonic vibration of its seed word R' to help digest and assimilate food properly in the abdomen by proper secretions to give FIRE to our body and we know that nutritive food and its digestion is the key to our health maintenance and to keep vigorous and kicking. And this book devoted to Self Healing would not have been complete without highlighting the importance of water in our body. And remember, only a dry leaf falls from the tree. Thus, consume enough water to keep green and waving with the sweet morning breeze.

And notice the miraculous action of water to make the water soaked grains of wheat, Bengal gram, Moong etc. sprout to become ALIVE and richer with nutritious vitamins and enzymes.

Chapter - 33

BLOOM & BLOSSOM AT ALL AGES
'MANTRA'
"I AM JUVENATING"

Who does not want to bloom and blossom at all ages! In fact, it is the innate desire of all human beings to remain ever young and delay as far as possible, the inevitable process of ageing. Because, youth is a period of peak enjoyment, when we do not know what is death, since we are passing through the saga of joy and merriment.

Mark Twain once said, "Life would be infinitely happier, if we could only be born at the age of eighty and gradually approach eighteen", a really tremendous idea; In this chapter, we want to achieve half of that dreamed target i.e. make people about twenty years younger than their chronological age, in the environment they are living-indeed, a great challenge to fulfill.

It is well known, that any ordered system of energy flow, when left to itself, will get ultimately into disordered state slowly, this is what the 2nd law of thermodynamics states and this happens to human beings also, what we call ageing. This can easily be illustrated from a fully charged 12 Volt car battery which when left to itself, will slowly get discharged, it needs to be recharged again to bring it back to its original charge-its original voltage of 12 volts. And the car battery can get damaged, if we overdraw the current heavily for a long period, more than its rated capacity, the battery will be damaged permanently though it can withstand much higher current discharge for a short time. The same is true of human beings also. If we over-work and stress our body/mind system for a short period and provide ample rest in between, our body can recuperate, but if we continue to stress it beyond its biological limits and that too, without giving it proper rest in between, the body, like the battery will get damaged permanently.

Thus, the first and most important criterion to remain healthy and fully charged is not to over work beyond our rated capacity and for that we have to respond in time to hear the feed back signal of tiredness of that particular sense organ being used, for example: we must hear the feeling of fullness of our stomach when we are on the dining table, otherwise, we become prone to an attack of indigestion.

And, we must continuously recharge our life's battery with proper breathing, and this chapter is devoted as to how to re-connect or connect ourselves properly with that infinite-reserviour of Pranic Energy to rejuvenate ourselves, by flushing our blood arteries with oxygen and Pranic energy to oxygenate and declog the semi-clogged blood arteries, to make them full blooded again, as in youth. this is what is called rejuvenation and it is possible to achieve all this in a slow but steady manner without even a shadow of harmful effect, which looms large, if we take rejuvenating drugs and herbs which though initially show quick results, but end up with greater damage to our body/mind system.

And the age of 50 years is a turning point in our

life, when there is a menopause period for Ladies and also the period when the sex power of men, begins to wane and dwindle, giving to men also a warning signal-'Men-O-Pause'. Too much sex indulgence at this age will drain us out. This is the stage when one starts reading books on Health & Rejuvenation and looks for rejuvenating drugs to regain that lost youth. Some persons wisely turn their mind to seek union with God to get the bliss, which they are now missing in sex. Now, they realise that their existence in this world is the greatest truth, time is now running short and we must get as much out of life as we can, and they come to realize that, to do so, our health is our greatest possession- because if health is lost, every charm in life is lost.

So, let us not lose hope and turn to our breath to rejuvenate ourselves. For that, the easiest breathing Mantra is

1) Exhale with   =   BLOOMMMM
   Inhale with   =   BLAAMMMM

The Exhale, Inhale Mantra - Bloom/Blaam, being single stage breathing mantra, is the easiest to use, but, with three fold benefits i.e. (i) it helps us to breathe more efficiently with the help of word 'BL' (ii) It also helps us to bloom again to youth because it helps the Sex energy to move up to the crown Chakra (M) with the help of Seed Word L of the Muldhara Chakra, thus imparting a sparkle of youth to us again. (iii) It also gives a boost to our sex power, by opening up the clogged channels of blood with the word 'L' to fully enjoy the ecstasy of sex at all ages.

Of course, there are many people who after the age of 50 years will feel that we have fulfilled the purpose of life by indulging in sex for the sake of procreation, as ordained by God and now, enough is enough, but even such persons even if they have no desire to enjoy the ecstasy of sex beyond the age of 50, will still relish that great feeling of youth, if they get erection in the morning hours of sleep just before waking up "Abhi Tau Main Jwan Hoon". (That I am still young)

Another breathing Mantra with exactly similar but fortified effect is :-

2) Inhale with   =   "BLOOSSOM" to be pronounced as
    =   BLAASSAAM"

Exhale with   =   "BLOOSSOOM"
or   =   I AM BLISS

The word 'S' is the seed word for the origin of breath about seven cms., below the navel and it also activates the divine Kundalini - the bank of divine life energy, to make the life energy to move up, with the help of breath to the crown in our head, thus giving us a look of a re-blossomed personality.

3) Exhale with   =   "BLOOMING" or
I AM BLOOMING.
Inhale with   =   "BLAMMANG"

This Mantra besides the advantages of 1st mantra, also helps to strengthen the pineal gland to produce Melatonin to pacify our nerves & give us good sleep, and the word 'G' stimulates the Master Pituitary gland. Also the word 'ING' gives us a great feeling of continuous tense of living in the present. The greatest aim of Yoga is to live in the present moment and not to brood over the past mistakes or build castles in the future.

What is Life- It is nothing but the ceaseless flow of pranic life energy in our body to impart it life movement and of course, kept in harmony, by soul - the Atma, and the words Y(J) and V, help this flow of pranic energy, as in the following mantra.

4) Inhale with   =   "JWAN"
    Exhale with   =   "JEEVUN"
                     and

5) Inhale with   =   SDA-JWAN
    Exhale with   =   JUVENATE

The word Sda-Jwan" is a Hindi language word which means — ALWAYS YOUNG

This Mantra imparts pranic energy to the lower intestines with V and improves the function of heart with the seed word J

6) Exhale with   =   "I AM JUVENATING"
                          or I AM REJUVENATING

    Then Inhale with =   " V A R A - J A T A - NAMMONG"

After the age of 50 years, the functioning of various vital parts of our body, i.e. Heart, Liver/ Stomach System, Pancreas, Kidneys start showing a sort of deterioration-resulting in poor assimilation as well as elimination resulting in piling up of toxic matter in our body, and because of poor digestion, the poor supply of nutrients to our already stressed and exhausted body organs further deteriorates their functioning. Thus, the process of ageing becomes a cumulative effect, and the above mantra arrests this process of ageing by giving a boost to our power of digestion by stimulateing Liver, Pancreas, adrenal gland & spleen action with the help of seed word 'R' and improves the pre-digestion of food in the mouth, particularly

Carbohydrates by activating the Salivary Glands in our mouth with the help of seed word 'T' in the above mantra. This mantra also gives Pranic Energy to our eyes-the most harrassed and over worked organ in these modern times, with the help of seed word-N. Thus, the Exhale Mantra - "I am re-juvenating"is a very powerful breathing mantra to rejuvenate us completely. But it does not strictly conform to the sequence of exhale breath for which 'R' should follow J. The inhale mantra is OK. The exhale mantra will also do no harm.

Another simple but effective and meaningful mantra is :-

7) Inhale with   =   "ALLA-YOUNG'
   Exhale with   =   "YOUL-LING"

The translation of "ALL' in our Urdu language is "SARA'. It is more effective, because, it includes the word 'R' the seed word for Navel Chakra (Solar Plexus)

8) Inhale with   =   "SARA-YOUNG"
   Exhale with   =   "YOU-RE-SING"

This Mantra rejuvenates us to again sing a song of radiating youth and joyful existence.

And last, but not the least I have coined a very powerful Inhale/Exhale Mantra with which we can dance, while standing at one place like Jogging on the tune of Cha, Cha, Chacha, Cha, --- A separate Chapter is devoted to it.

9) Inhale with   =   SA,RA, YAHAM-MAÑ
   Exhale with   =   ME YOU, RISHI, HOOÑ

Just a few minutes of dancing Me with Me, with the above Cha Cha Music, will regenerate bio-currents of youth reflowing in our nerves. It we can dance with the above mantra for five minutes both morning and evening, we-will continue to Bloom & Blossom at all ages, provided, we also nourish our body with balanced & nourishing food. Thus, so filled with new vitality and energy, we sing the following song, exhaling with the left side rhyme and inhaling with the right side rhyme.

The word 'O, BLOSSOM' should be spoken as — AU, BLASSAM as inhale mantra.

Exhale with	Inhale with
Say Yes to the new day	O, Blossom
The New Zest	O, Blossom
The New Vision	O, Blossom
The New Inspiration	O, Blossom
The New Search	O, Blossom
The New Wealth	O, Blossom
The New Ego	O, Blossom
The New Power	O, Blossom
The New Empire	O, Blossom
The New Challenges	O, Blossom
The New Worries	O, Blossom
The New Fights	O, Blossom
The New Introspection	O, Blossom
The New Surrender (to God)	O, Blossom
The New Peace	O, Blossom
The New Bliss	O, Blossom

O, Bloom & Blossom.

Thus, we have absorbed the whole fragrance of this universe which gives us New vigour & vision to say Yes to the New Day.

OM TAT SAT/ AMEEN

SECTION - III

IMPROVE EYESIGHT
AND
BRAIN POWER

Chapter - 34

IMPROVEMENT IN EYESIGHT
MANTRA
IMPROVE-VISION

Our eye sight is the most prized possession to enjoy this most beautiful world in all its hues and colours. Without this eye sight, the whole world is a total darkness - a living death for us. So we must take all the precautions to keep our eye-sight in perfect health.

But our modern technology is over-straining our eyes beyond its biological limits, particularly, with the on-set of printing media, books and books to read and television and flashing of strong lights for Cine Photography for long hours etc. which tires us at the end of the day. And, as a general rule, most of the eye defects (except congenital and those caused by physical injury or exposure to high dose of radiations) arise due to the over-use of the eyes and also, most importantly, due to under-nourishment of the body, of which the eyes are part and parcel. This is also asserted by W.H. Bates-the author of the famous book 'Better Eye Sight Without Glasses" in which he recommends various relaxation techniques i.e. palming of the eyes in which we cover the right eye with cupped right palm and the left eye covered with left cupped palm and we look into the darkness between the two eyes, with closed eyes. This is a sort of Meditation technique and quietens and rests the eyes and the mind to restore proper vision in case of Myopia and

Hypermetropia.

ANATOMY OF VISION

As we see an outside object, its image is refracted through the eye lens to get focussed on the retina of the eye in case of normal vision. Then, the optic nerves from both the right and the left eye carry the image neural signal at the visual cortex in the brain, the complete image mixed from both eyes 50:50 at the rear of cerebral hemisphere on visual cortex carrying information about the form, movement and colour of the object. Simultaneously, the optical neural signal carries the information to the Hypothalamus/left brain/pituitary gland conglomerate. While our eyes are the beholder, the left brain/pituitary gland/AJNA Chakra are the Charioteer of our body and we use the seed word of Ajna Chakra - N and its associated words K, Kh, G to stimulate the eyes. However, the optical image neural signal from both eyes also reaches the right brain for further processing in the memory cortex for which we stimulate the right brain, and the crown chakra with its seed word M., but it is the left brain which is mostly used by our present day education system and printing media, therefore, we usually correct eye defects by stimulating the left brain and pituitary gland with its seed word 'N' in the breathing mantra. As I stimulate the Crown Chakra with breath mantra SAHAM," it first stimulates the right brain, then the right eye, then the 3rd eye and then the left eye. Similarly as I stimulate, the Brow Chakra with mantra SAHAN, it first stimulates the left brain, the left eye and then the right eye.

Various Eye Defects : Stress, ageing and overuse of the eyes and malnutrition are the main causes of an early appearance of various eye defects given below: However, it needs to be stressed that it is the inter-play of sodium/potassium ions across the cell membrane which generates the varyng response to light, in the light sensitive cones and rods at the cornea and hence the necessity to nourish the eyes with bio-chemic salts besides vitamins of which we shall speak later.

1. **Hypermetropia** called Far-sightedness is due to the eye refractive index becoming less convex which results in the light rays getting focussed behind the retina. Convex corrective lenses are needed for close reading work. This eye defect can be corrected with the breathing mantra, by providing pranic life energy to the eyes alongwith nutritive food.

2. **Myopia** called near-sightedness is due to refractive power of the eye becoming too convex (thick) or the eyeball becoming too long. In both cases, the light rays are focussed in front of the retina, giving a blurred image. Concave corrective lenses are needed to focus on distant objects.

3. **Presbyopia** : a form of hypermetropia which develops naturally as the age advances because the accomodative power of the eye gradually declines with age.

4. **Cataract** in which the eye lense becomes transluscent and ultimately opaque with advancing age and gets speeded up with strong exposure to bright sun-light/flash lights/ exposure to X-ray radiations etc.

5. **Glaucoma** - where abnormal pressure is exerted on the eye ball called occular pressure, which, if left untreated, may lead to eye blindness.

And it also needs to be high-lighted that our emotions of love, anger and other moods as well as state of well being is noticeably reflected from the eyes and the face of a person - that shows the great interconnection of our body, mind, eyes and the soul with our BEING. And this connection, we use to heal the eyes by strengthening the brow chakra with N, the crown chakra with M and the unifying chakra with supersoul with its seed word AÑ. These eye defects, thus, get corrected with pranic laser beam.

Correcting Eye Defects with Breathing Mantras

The seed breathing mantra for correcting various eye defects cited above is the very suggestive breathing exhale mantra - 'Improve Vision', but we shall start first with the simplest beathing mantras for improving the eye sight :-

1. Inhale with   =   ASSAN or ASSANKH
    Exhale with   =   NEESH or KHUSHI

The Mantra 'ASSAN' means Easy and it is also the easiest Mantra, as its name implies, but a very efficacious mantra for improving the eyesight.

2. In order to make the breathing more efficient to supply pranic energy to the eyes, we introduce the seed word for lungs PH (f) in the above mantra.

    Inhale with   =   SHAFFANKH
    Exhale with   =   NOOFFEES or
                          INKHIFEESH

The word 'shaffankh' in Urdu means the healthy eyes and Nooffes means a fine gentleman & gentle lady. The word 'ANKH' in Hindi/Urdu language means Eyes

3. In order to give psychic sonic resonance energy

to the Solar Plexus - the Navel Chakra, to enable
it to manufacture proper glycogen and other nutrients
from food with the release of proper digestive
juices and release of Insulin-the hormone from
Pancreas, and the healthy Liver action, we use the
seed word 'R' for this purpose in the breathing
mantra.

| Inhale with | = | SARRAN |
| Exhale with | = | NOORREESH |

The word Noorreesh means full of sparkle and
this Healing Mantra really fills our eyes with all
the blissful radiance, because it helps to illuminate
the eyes with the divine Kundalini energy, so
kindled by the word S/SH.

4. Now, we also stimulate the heart chakra with
its seed word Y or J

Inhale with	=	SAYYAN or SAJJAN
Exhale with	=	NEEYYEES or NIJJISH
or		NEW-YES

5. Now, we stimulate the Thyroid gland with its
seed word H

| Inhale with | = | SAHHAN |
| Exhale with | = | NIHHISH |

6. Now, we yoke ourself with infinity - the super
consciousness to draw in as much pranic life
energy as possible with its seed word AÑ and end
at T, the seed word for strengthening taste and
salivary glands.

| Inhale with | = | SAHANT |
| Exhale with | = | TIHHISH |

Similarly, we stimulate the left brain/eyes
with the words K, KH and G.

7. Inhale with   =   SAHANK
   Exhale with   =   KIHHISH

8. Inhale with   =   SAHANG
   Exhale with   =   GIHHISH

9. Inhale with   =   SAHANKH
   Exhale with   =   KHIHISH

10. Use the King of Eye-sight mantra

   Inhale with   =   RAKA-GANNAÑ
   Exhale with   =   INNER KING

11. Now, we stimulate the ultimate chakra - the crown chakra, with its seed word M, to strengthen the right brain, the eyes and the pineal gland.

   Inhale with   =   SAHAM
   Exhale with   =   MIHHISH

12. The following is the simplest breathing mantra to stimulate the left brain the eyes and pituitary gland with N and the right brain, the eyes and the pineal gland with M.

   Inhale with   =   SMAN OR SMANKH
   Exhale with   =   MNEESH / MUKHEESH

13. Make nourishment your breath

   Inhale with   =   NOURISHMENT
   Exhale with   =   SARANAMMANT

It is indeed a great benefitting mantra for the eyes and the total brain.

14. And another very potent healing mantra for the eyes is

Inhale with	=	SARAYAHAN or
		SARAJAHAN
Exhale with	=	NIHI-YOUREESH

15. A very magnificient mantra to stimulate both the eyes and total brain is

Inhale with	=	MAGNIFICIENT
Exhale with	=	SFA-GANA-MANT

A separate chapter is devoted to it.

Now, I shall return to the seed breathing mantra for improving vision.

16.
Exhale with	=	IMPROVE-VISION
Inhale with	=	VARA-ZAPAN-NAMMAÑ

While exhaling with the above mantra, let us give a convenient pause at 'N' and let N reverberate in the brain to stimulate the left brain and the pituitary gland. The word V kindles the divine kundalini, the word 'R' improves our digestion and assimilation of food, the words Z and P help cardio-vascular system to circulate blood and breathe to its optimum capacity, the word 'N' stimulates the left brain and the word 'M' stimulates the right brain, thus it is a complete body/mind/eyes rejuvenating breathing mantra and also very very suggetive breathing mantra to improve vision, by its hypnotic influence. The world MAÑ yokes us with Superconscious Energy Field.

17. Another similar mantra using the Hindi language word 'NAIN' for EYES

Exhale with	=	IMPROVING - NAIN
Inhale with	=	VARA-PA-NAMMANG

18. Urdu speaking people can use the following mantra and mantra no 3 given earlier.

Exhale with	=	NZIR
Inhale with	=	RAZAN

19. For Hindi speaking persons, a very suggestive mantra is given below:-

Inhale with	=	SACHA-ANAND
Exhale with	=	NEESHCHINT

This is a great stress relieving mantra for the eyes/mind because inhale mantra - Sacha Anand means-A pure bliss and the exhale mantra Neeshchint means 'worry free" and this is possible only if we lead a stress free life of Satyam (Truth), Shivam (godliness) and Sundaram (a beautiful existence).

And let me suggest some breathing mantras which are emotionally related with our national boundaries. I have chosen countries with N contained in their country's name.

20.
Exhale with	=	INDIAN
Inhale with	=	ANAND
		(This means bliss)

And now many Westerners are looking to India to achieve bliss by their Yogic Meditation techniques.

21. Similarly for English speaking people:

Exhale with	=	ENGLISH
Inhale with	=	GLOW ON

This is a Tribute to English people.

22. Similarly for Americans :

Exhale with	=	AMERICAIN
Inhale with	=	RAKA- NAMA or
		RAKA-NAMMAÑ

23. Similarly for Japanese people :

Exhale with   =   JAPAN
Inhale with   =   NEE POOJOOÑ

24. Similarly for German people :

Exhale with   =   GERMANY
Inhale with   =   RAJA-NAM

and so on.

For correction of eye defects, Bates also recommends blinking of the eyes which gives exercise to the eye muscles for the blood to reach the eyes. While blinking, the water is released by the lachrymal glands in the eyes to moisturise and clean the eyes. These breathing mantras with healing words combined with the power of thought act like the micro-laser beam to cure all our eye defects, slowly but steadily without any harmful side effects.

Out of the twenty four breathing mantras given above to help us improve eye sight, we should use the first twelve breathing mantras, in the first week, repeating them five times each. This will take about 6 minutes or so. Repeat it both morning and evening, chanting them silently, smoothly, deeply and rhythmically alongwith respective inhale/ exhale breathing mantra and then slowly and steadily move upto the 16th breathing mantra which is the seed mantra for improving vision and in a month's period, you will start experiencing the on-rush of bio-energy currents into your both eyes and at the location of 3rd eye, and in the left brain with the mantras containing the word N at the end, and in the right brain with the mantra containing the word M at the end and above all, the sparkle in both eyes, with improvement of eye sight and removal of all its defects, achieving a very steady progress with time. Besides, these breathing mantras also give tranquillity/relaxation to our mind because we are expected to make our thought move alongwith the breath just as in Vipasna meditation, very powerful tranquillizing Yogic technique advocated by Lord Budha, where one's thought moves alongwith the breath. Now, we know which word arises from where in our body/brain, so we can also make our thought move alongwith the breath, as it traverses various associated chakras in our body.

Some Neck Exercises with Breathing Mantra :-
Our Neck is the junction passage between our brain and the body. Any blockage in the blood vessels of our neck will diminish the much needed blood supply and healing breathing mantras constituted with the seed word 'H' for Visudha/ Neck chakra, help to declog the neck arteries as well as fortify the thyroid gland which helps to burn fat in the body and regulate the carbohydrate metabolism in our body.

Move your neck towards the right slowly without a jerk while inhaling with the mantra "AHHAÑ" and then return to the front neck position with the exhale mantra "OHHOOÑ". Similarly, repeat it with the neck moving towards the extreme left position with this mantra. Do it 10 to 20 times as convenient without giving it any discomfort. Then, rest for a minute or so, by just a little stroll in the lawn.

Now move up slowly your neck from its lowest position to all up in the sky, inhaling with the mantra "AHHAÑ" and bring the neck down exhaling with the mantra "OHHOOÑ". Repeat it 10 to 20 times as convenient. Then, relax for a minute or so. Then walk a distance of bout 20 to 50 Meters, with interlocked fingers of both hands pressing softly the neck from behind. This will also help to strengthen the neck.

Now, first move up your left hand up, then right hand up, alternately, as if you are walking in the air with your hands alternately moving up and down. This is the best exercise to enliven the heart and neck muscles in an aerobic atmosphere, thus restoring the normal blood supply to the eyes and brain; and you will also notice, that if you start this alternate hand raising exercise with left hand first, then your left nostril will open up for breathing and vice versa. Thus, this exercise opens up both the nostrils, alternately by starting with right & left hand respectively to remove any blocking due to sinus problem and also brings about equilibrium in breathing from both the nostrils, thus, helping to reach the breath unto both the eyes, with equal fervour. This also helps to rectify the problem of cervical spondylitis while stengthening the eyes.

Now & then, Enjoy appreciating a green leaf on a twig of a plant,about 20 cms. from your eyes and then look far unto the distance at a green tree and then enjoy seeing unto the green lawn below your feet and then again at the green plants and trees around you and Lo! your eyes are feeling refreshed. How? because our eyes like the green colour the most and that is why nature is so green, but do not forget to enjoy the flowers in all their beautiful colours of a rainbow.This will relax your eyes and brighten you up, by giving your eyes and Mind the energy of full spectrum of sunlight.

And, last but not the least, stand in prayer to God in your lawn. Be thankful to God who has given you these beautiful eyes. Inhale deeply with the mantra "Pran-Nath" while raising your both hands slowly as you inhale deeply as if you are drawing in all the pranic energy from the cosmos into your BEING and your eyes.

Then, Exhale slowly while bringing the hands down slowly with the exhale mantra "Inni-Preet". The inhale mantra Pran-Nath means "O,God, the giver of life to me, and the Exhale Mantra "Inni-Preet means-the inward love for one and all, which the God Almighty has endowed us to love the whole humanity. It is when we transcend hatred and begin to love all, without any discrimination, then our eyes start sparkling with the God's bliss.

Food For Eyes : A balanced nutritious diet consisting of Proteins, Carbohydrates, Vitamins, Nutrient Salts, and Fats is essential for the proper upkeep of our body/eyes/brain system, and will go a long way in preventing the eye defects i.e. Vitamin 'A', prevents Night Blindness and is one of the main components, they say, in Retina-the light sensitive screen in our eyes. This Vitamin 'A' also helps to prevent cataract and also in the absence of Vitamin 'A' the eyes cannot withstand the glaze of sun light or bright lights. Also Vitamin 'A' helps the lacrymal glands to make the eyes sparkingly clean by secreting the tears while blinking. This Vitamin is present varyingly in whole milk, butter, cheese, carrots, tomato, lettuce, cabbage, greenpeas, SPINACH, wheat germ, papaya, oranges and dates, and for best results, eye doctors also re-commend the use of high potency vitamin 'A' Cod Liver Oil Capsules to make up for any acute deficiency. and above all we must protect our eyes against Bright sunlight with sun glasses.

Also vitamin B-2, vitamin 'C' & Vitamin 'E' are other vitamins which are essential for the proper health of the eyes. Also, vitamin 'D' is very essential for the eyes to see the distant objects. If vitamin 'D' is provided to children adequately, their myopia eye defects will improve. Also, lecithin is very good for the brain/eye system because it forms 30 percent of the dry weight of the human brain. Egg Yolk is a rich source of lecithin and also a rich source of cholesterol, now thought to be not so good for heart patients. Vegetarians & heart patients, can use Soybeans supplement or sprouted grains because two spoonfuls of sprouted grains provide most of the daily requirement of vitamins cited above and for breakfast I take for myself a small bowl of mixed fruit consisting of papaya, one banana and one apple or any other seasonal fruit, sprinkled with small lemon juice & I take one bread piece along with one egg on 3 days a week & on the remaining four days, instead, I take. 2 spoonfuls of sprouted grain at break-fast, instead of egg.

And I top it up with 250 grams of whole milk taking two cloves of garlic to keep the dirty cholesterol away.

Also, when the eyes get tired and stressed, in order to provide immediate succour to them, take slowly a large spoonful of honey or Glucose bit by bit on the tongue, followed by a glass of water, or enjoy the luscious taste and nutrition provided by taking about 20 gms of raisins (dried grapes), taken in 10 lots of 2 gms each; and musticated and enjoyed thoroughly in the mouth. This will provide immediate relief and evaporate stress from the mind/eye system by giving the much needed glycogen. This is particularly needed because brain/eye system does not have a storehouse of built-in energy resreviour like the muscles of the body. Besides, the requirement of blood, supplying Glucose/Nutrients is about nine fold more, in the brain compared to any other organ of the body because of a large network of nerves and neurons working to first register the various sense signals, interpret them, store them in memory; besides co-ordinating & directing all other life processes throughout the body-indeed a very great responsibility thrust on our brain system. Thus, we have to ensure a steady supply of Glucose and nutrients to our brain/eye system, which is the most harrassed organ of our body these days. Besides, we have also to provide more than adequate supply of oxygen and pranic life energy to enliven our eyes/brain with the help of breathing with the above healing mantras.

Since, we have to move with the times and cannot shut our eyes from the modern technology, I am sure this Chapter will help us to meet adequately the challenge of our modern times. For that, I give below an equally challenging breathing mantra for benefiting the eyes:-

Exhale with   =   HI, YOU RE-ILLUMINATE
Inhale with   =   ALLARA-YAHA-NAMANT

This is a total body/brain/eyes Rejuvenating breathing mantra unsurpassed in its excellent benefits.

OM-TAT-SAT/AMEEN

Chapter - 35

STRENGTHEN BRAIN AND MEMORY
THE MANTRA — I AM BRAINY

Our Brain/MIND is the beholder and Charioteer of our Body. All the time, it is busy collecting the data from what we see with our eyes; what we hear with our ears; feed the taste from our mouth and smell from our nose and touch sensations from our hands and the total body, alongwith emotional stimuli. Then, the brain processes this data and compares it with data already stored and responds accordingly and also stores all this in the memory to be recalled later when ever required.

Thus, the brain needs almost ten times more oxygenated blood than any other organ of the body, because, all the sense ending in the brain need oxygen for their action. The magnetic Imaging Technique has shown that whenever brain cells are called upon to carry out tasks like the recognising a face or seeing a picture etc., the brain cells release a chemical that summons oxygenated blood from tiny arteries in the brain. Thus, for proper brain function, we need to nourish it with oxygenated blood carrying also the glucose and other nutrients for the brain cells.And according to brain specialists, it is the left side of the brain which systematically collects this informatin from various senses of our body and responds to act accordingly. The pituitary gland which is called the Director of all glandular orchestra of our body is actuated by the left brain and total left brain alongwith pituitary gland is stimulated by the word N-the seed word of BROW Chakra. Also the subsidiary words K,Kh, G also stimulate the left brain and it is the left brain which is mostly used by our present day education system of collecting data and reading and memorizing it, while the right half of the human brain is used for more creative mental and intuitive functions and has the capacity to expand spatially because much of our brain's capacity remains unutilised. The right part of the brain is stimulated by the word M-the seed word for Crown Chakra. It comes to the help of over-strained left brain when ever necessary.

And the word AÑ yokes us with Infinity-the super- consciousness to draw in as much pranic life energy as possible. Thus, the word AÑ is the Transducer of super-consciousness and acts as a bridge between the left and right brain to expand the total brain's action and strengthen the inter-communion between the left brain and right brain. It also helps to give intuition and clairvoyance to our Mind.

Develop Left Side of the Brain

The simplest suggestive breathing mantra for stimulating the left brain is:-

(1) Exhale with   =   BRAINY
    Inhale with   =   BRANNAÑ

The word 'N' as said above stimulates the left brain and the word BR contained in the word brain also helps to improve our cardio - vascular system to breathe and circulate blood to its optimum capacity. The word BR helps to breathe from the abdomen with R and from the lungs with B to supply the much needed oxygen. The inhale mantra

BRANAÑ is like prana in its effects and is able to supply oxygen/pranic energy-life giver to the brain actions as said above.

Another very suggestive breathing mantra to develop the left brain is:-

(2) Exhale with   =   INTELLIGENT
    Inhale with   =   LAJATANANT

This Mantra stimulates the Muladhara basic Chakra with its seed word 'L' and kindles the divine Kundalini energy to illuminate the left brain with its seed word 'N'. The word J helps the heart to circulate blood to its optimum capacity to improve brain's action, while the word "T" helps to stimualte the taste sense endings in the brain.

Develop Right Side of the Brain

As said above, the seed word for strengthening the upper right side brain is "M' and the word Premium can provide Pranic life energy to it because the word 'PR' like 'BR' helps to breathe to our optimum capacity from the lungs with 'P' and from the abdomen with 'R' thus augmenting inhalation of oxygen and Pranic Life Energy. Also the words 'MIUM' set up resonant sonic vibrations in the right brain to stimulate the neurons, because of double'M' present as MAM/'MIUM' in the Mantra.

(3) Thus exhale with =   PREMIUM
    Inhale with   =   PRAMMAM

Another breathing mantra for the right side of the brain is ;-

(4) Exhale with   =   MEMORY-RE-ZOOM
    Inhale with   =   ARRA-ZAMAMMMM

The word 'R' gives fire to our body by helping in proper digestion of food we take, and the word 'Z' helps the heart and the lungs to breathe to its optimum capacity to augment the supply of pranic life energy to the right side of the brain with 'M'. It really helps to rezoom the action of right brain.

Develop Both Left And Right Brain

If we add the word 'M' to the breathing mantra No. 1, given above, we stimulate the left brain with 'N' and the right brain with 'M'.

(5) Exhale with = I AM BRAINY/
IMMI-BRAINY

Inhale with = BRANAM-MAÑ

(6) Similarly Exhale with = I AM INTELLIGENT
OR
IMMI-INTELLIGENT

Inhale with = LAJATANAMMANT

As we age, our upper body sags which can create kinks in the spine that squeeze the two arteries passing through the cervical region of the spinal column to the brain. This results in inadequate supply of blood to the brain and according to Dr. Schemerl "This diminished blood supply to the brain can cause fuzzy thinking and forgetfulness." Hunched over posture can contribute to stroke like symptoms known as transient ischemic attacks which are brief black out periods. To overcome this, try always to sit up straight. Besides sitting straight, we also use the word H in the breathing mantra to strengthen the thyriod gland as well as to re-establish the communication links in the cervical region of the spine around the neck :

(7) Inhale with = ALLA-BRAHAN-NAMAND

Exhale with = MINHI-BRILLIANT

This is indeed a rejuvenating mantra for both sides of the brain to make it brilliant. This is the ultimate breathing mantra to bring about SYMPHONY of BODY, MIND AND SOUL.

i) The word L kindles the divine kundalini energy to illuminate our mind.

ii) The word R improves our digestion to feed the proper nutrition to our brain from the nourishing food we take to provide heat/fire to our body also.

iii) The word B helps us to breathe better. The word breathe itself contains the word BR because it helps us to breathe totally i.e. from the lungs with B and from the abdomen with R.

iv) The word H as said earlier is the seed word for throat chakra. This strengthens the thyriod gland for better carbohydrates/fat metabolism in our body and improve the communication link between the heart and the brain through the cervical region of the spine.

v) The word N is the seed word for brow chakra. It strengthens the left brain and pituitary gland.

vi) The word M is the seed word for crown chakra. It strengthens the right brain and the pineal galnd.

vii) The word MAND yokes us with Infinity – the super consciousness to draw in as much pranic life energy as possible and settle at the word D which helps to improve our all tastes in life. The word MAND helps to improve our Mind.

Thus, if we inhale/exhale with the above breathing mantras silently for five minutes in the morning and evening in a pollution free atmosphere, slowly and steadily, we will completely rejuvenate our brain/memory system.

Last but not the least, a very suggestive breathing mantra to impart brilliance to our modern day Managers who have to use a lot of brain/memory power is:-

(8) Exhale with = MANAGERIAL
    Inhale with = ALLA-RAJA-NAM

This mantra stimulates both the left brain with N and the right brain with M. Thus, this very suggetive mantra goads us to become good managers as well as fulfill our total brain with pranic life energy and with God's Effulgence with L.

A Wisdom Gaining Mantra

As we age, we may loose some brain power and recent memory but we gain wisdom becuase of our interaction with the world. But it is in the very nature of human beings to continue to ERR. Thus, many times we behave foolishly. As beautifully described by someone :-

As a rule, a man's a fool;
When it's hot, he wants it cool;
When it's cool, he wants it hot.
Always wanting what is not.

Only a person who has the capacity to laugh over oneself and atone for one's own mistakes and foolish behaviour has the capacity to become wise. On such occasions :-

(9) Exhale with = I AM FOOLISH
    Inhale with = LA-SHFAMMAÑ

When we exhale with 'I am Foolish' but actually we turn a wise man, fulfilling our mind with oxygen and pranic life energy with F, illuminating our mind with the kindled kundalini energy with L and SH which reaches with this mantra to the Crown Chakra with M to make us wise by making us aware of our right place in this universe.

Another Mantra to help us gain wisdom is by a very suggestive breathing mantra given below:-

| (10) Exhale with | = | IMPROVE-WISDOM |
| Inhale with | = | VAZAPRADAMMAÑ |

Thus with the above breathing mantra we have stimulated the right brain with M and inter communion with total BRAIN with AÑ

Thus we can improve our brain power, memory capacity and gain wisdom using the above very potent and at the same time suggestive breathing mantras. However, I shall now go into the mechanism as to how to enhance memory capacity.

Enhancing Memory Capacity :

It is the use that determines the health of any organ, while its over use, inadequate rest and non-supply of nutrients for its proper functioning can damage it. Within the small volume of human brain, there are about 100 billion or so nerve cells, fantastically intricate in the growth of neuronal branches called dendritic channels or tree like branches which receive the incoming sense signals from areas of various sense Cortex which are stored in the pattern of molecular transformation in the dendritic trees, where all the recollections of sight, sound, smell, taste and associated emotions are stored in these linked beautiful dendritic impressions. However, according to brain experts, only a small percentage of total brain capacity is actually utilised, thus intellectuals with active brain have unlimited scope to grow new neuronal branches to utilise the brain's full potentiality.

Now, recollection is achieved by re-activating the same sensory events that formed it. But, in older people with ageing, the chemicals in the brain which help neuro-transmission get depleted, thus the inter-communication to retrieve the memory gets slowly blurred. But let us not despair, the memory capacity can be enhanced as well as their inter-communication re-established by breathing with healing mantras; which help to regenerate these Neuro-trans-mitter chemicals in the brain.

i) First stimulate each sensory section of the brain and then (ii) re-establish the communication by setting up to and fro pranic life energy re-vitalisation by resonant sonic vibrations between the various sense endings in the brain cortex, with the words T, D, K, Kh, G, N, M, & Ñ. Simple two stage breathing mantras for activating these are given below:

With words T & D (Taste & Salivary Glands Centre):

11. Inhale with = SHRAFFANT
    Exhale with = FREESH-SHIENT

12. Inhale with = SHRAF-FAND
    Exhale with = FREESH-SHIEND

The words T,D, Th stimulate various areas of the top soft Palate in the mouth to give strength to salivary glands. Many Yogis advise a breathing practice by asking to touch the Soft Palate at the top of the mouth, which is located just on the other side of pituitary gland to strengthen this pituitary gland. This is a difficult yogic practice. The same advantage with greater potency can be achieved with the above breathing mantras which also stimulate the divine kundalini energy with Sh, strengthens the liver and digestion with R, re-inforce optimum breathing with lungs with 'F', yokes us with Infinity - the super consciousness with AÑ to draw in as much pranic life energy as possible to fulfill our Being and then ends at T or D or Th to stimulate pituitary gland and the salivary glands.

And the word MIND is beautifully designed, because our total brain/mind is stimulated by the words M, N & D.

Stimulate Left Brain With K, KH, G & N

13. Inhale with   =   SHRAF - FANK
     Exhale with   =   FREESH - SHEENK

14. Inhale with   =   SHRAF - FANKH
     Exhale with   =   FREESH - SHIENKH

This breathing mantra particularly stimulates the eyes including the third eye.

15. Inhale with   =   SHRAF - FANG
     Exhale with   =   FREESH - SING

16. Inhale with   =   SHRAF - FAN
     Exhale with   =   FREESH - SHEEN
                       (FRESH - SHEEN)

This mantra truly gives a fresh shine on our face and in the eyes.

Stimulate the Right Brain with M :

17. Inhale with   =   SHRAF - FAM
     Exhale with   =   FREESH - SHEM.

18. We can also yoke our breath with superconscious-

ness to stimulate the ultimate crown chakra to get
the spiritual enlightenment for that

Inhale with = SHRAF - FAÑM
Exhale with = FREESH - SHEEÑM

Stimulate Total Brain with Neutral Breathing Mantra

19. Neutral Breathing mantra :

Inhale with = SHRAFAÑ
Exhale with = FREESH - SHEEÑ

This breathing mantra being neutral does not
prefer any side of the brain but communicates with
the total brain and the super-conscious energy
field.

And the great advantage of the above breathing
mantras is that they end with the same specific
seed word K, Kh, G, T, D, N, M & Ñ both in
Inhalation mantra as well as in exhalation mantra,
for which we give a convenient pause both at the
end of inhalation as well as exhalation, to enhance
the Quality & Quantity of stimulation. These nine
breathing mantras given above are the ultimate
breathing mantras in stimulating the brain/Memory/
Mind system. Inhale/Exhale, with each of the
above breathing mantras for 10 times which will
take one minute each mantra, thus all the above
nine mantras will take nine minutes or so. Do it
both morning and evening and soon you will be
bubbling with sparkling brain/memory and mind
system. These also rejuvenate the total body/mind
system and bring about HARMONY in the BODY/
MIND/SPIRIT to dissolve any stress and no disease
can ever touch us, so powerful are these healing
mantras. These breathing mantras will also halt
the progess of Alzheimer's disease to which a

separate chapter is devoted. However I shall give below a breathing mantra which will reverse the progress of Alzheimer's disease.

HALTING THE PROGRESS OF ALZHEIMER's DISEASE.

Since memory retrieval is activated by the combined action of the same sensory route which forms it and all the brain senses become dull and less sensitive with age including the eye - sight, hence the need to stimulate all the sense organs by the healing breathing mantras given above. Also I also must stress that some of the old persons who suffer from Alzheimer's disease shut their MIND to out-side world which becomes the greatest impediment in memory retrieval. Thus, this negative emotional response of older people is the most difficult to correct. For that, their interest in life and the outside world has to be re-generated by very congenial and friendly company. They must regenerate HOPE to LIVE on independently, which the above breathing healing mantras will reinvoke by showing progress in the rejuvenation of all sense organs. i.e. eye sight, taste sense and above all the hunger and lust for good-food - thus proper nutrition will provide the necessary fillup to regain taste for life.

However, a breathing mantra is given below which not only helps to inter-communicate between all senses in the brain, but generates the desire (Kamana) to interact with people and society at large.

20. Inhale with   =   SHRAFA - KAMANA KANT
     Exhale with   =   FREELY - COMMUNICATE

(The word SH & L are equivalent)

The mantra COMMUNICATE/KAMANA KANT is indeed wonderful.

The word **KAMANA KANT** means - I am full with the splendour of DESIRE to live and the word communicate is very suggestive to give us the hypnotic power to really communicate with all sections of the brain with the words - K, M, N, K, & T - all the seed words of brain, where-in, it sets up to & fro resonant sonic vibrations to stimulate all the sense endings simultaneously. This stimulative & CELEBRATIVE DANCE of various sense endings re-unites them to become WHOLE and it brings about the much needed HARMONY in Body, Mind and Soul.

Balanced Nutrition for Brain/Memory

However, a balanced nutritious diet of carbohydrates/proteins, fats/minerals/vitamins is a must for healthy development of body/brain. I must stress that pituitary gland and all other glands have protein structure plus the receptivity of neuron sites is greatly enhanced by the migration of a protein called protein kinase. The protein moves from the cytoplasm of a cell to the membrane altering a neuron property so that the particular input signal triggers impulses more readily. They say, one third of the dry weight of our brain is composed of Lecithin which is present in the eggs and Soybeans etc. Besides proteins, sodium, potassium and calcium salts play a great part in life processes in cells. Arrival of a nerve impulse brings about a change in the permeability across a cell membrane causing sodium ions to enter the cell and the potassium ions to leave the cell, thus creating a potential difference to allow an electrical activity to propagate. Also calcium ions serve as ionic messenger. The calcium ion is also involved in such diverse processes as the regulation of muscle contraction, the secretions of hormones to develop immunity against inflammation of the brain as well as in the production of neuro-transmitters in the brain which get depleted in older people. These calcium ions are polarised to act as a switch turning on and off the cellular processes. But in fact, calcium ions can carry out this role/information role only at very low concentrations, because higher concentration of calcium is detrimental to normal cell function. That is why I usually recommend using Five Phos 3X or 6X (in older people) as tonic for brain/memory function. In five phos 3x and 6x, calcium, sodium, potassium, Ferrum (Iron) and Magnesium phosphates are present in milligram and microgram quantities respectively and also potenciazed, to be directly absorbed on the tongue to strengthen the brain/body system to carry out vital cellular reactions.

And for protien and Lecithin requirement, I recommend - one or two eggs a day for students, and younger group and 3 eggs a week for older people alongwith one clove of garlic to look after the naughty cholesterol accompanying the yellow of an egg. The garlic also supplies sulphur and other minerals for proper functioning of the glands/hormones. But we must not forget to take an ample quantity of fresh seasonal fruits alongwith vegetables salads to supply antioxidants like vitamin C, A & E alongwith other vitamins, minerals, fructose in their natural form. Ten almonds with 10 gms of Raisins is a good tonic food for the brain.

Also, there is a well known Indian herb called BRAHMI (Centella Asiatica) which has been used since ages to boost memory power. This herb is

---

170

found to increase protein synthesis in the brain cells, resulting in the increase in the efficiency of brain's function. It also soothes the brain to remove stress by also inducing good sleep.

The Herb "SHANKHA PUSHPI (CONVOLVULUS Pluricaulis) is also a brain tonic par excellence.

Chapter - 36

ENJOY MAGNIFICENT MEMORY

MANTRA
MAGNIFICENT

The exhale Mantra 'Magnificent' can bring about excellence in total brain/mind health, as it contains the total spectrum of brain/memory words like M, N, G, & T and thus helps us to improve memory, brain, eye-sight and sense endings of taste, smell and hearing etc. and then also establish inter-connections in the brain so as to ward off the onset of Alzheimer's and Parkinson's diseases.

(1) Thus exhale with =   MAGNIFICENT
    Inhale with   =   SHFA-GANA-MANT

And the inhale Mantra also conveys it to be a magnificent song of health, because the word 'Shafa' in Urdu/Hindi language means - Health, the word 'GANA' means - song and this Mantra really helps to endow us health because

(i) The word 'SH' helps to kindle the divine Kundalini energy and moves it alongwith the breath upward to

(ii) The Heart Chakra with the word 'F' which also helps to augment the breathing with the lungs to provide optimum oxygen/pranic life energy intake for circulation in the body.

(iii) The word 'N' is the seed word for BROW

171

Chakra, strengthens the left brain and the eye-sight and stimulates the pituitary gland to improve the immune system of our body. The word 'G' is also the seed word for smell sense endings in the brain, which it strengthens.

(iv) The word 'M' is the seed word for the Crown Chakra and it also stimulates the pineal gland in the brain. It helps to improve the right brain and the mind control.

(v) The word MAÑ helps to yoke us with the Infinite - the super-consciousness to draw in as much pranic life energy as possible, which one can also store in the Brow Chakra.

(vi) The inhale Mantra ends at 'T', the seed word for the Taste endings in the brain to improve our all tastes in life including pre-digestion of food in the mouth.

Thus, the breathing mantra Magnificent is indeed a very great health impartng Mantra for the body and for the brain/memory system, endowing Magnificence to our personality.

SECTION - IV

SLOW DOWN AGEING PROCESS

Chapter - 37

SLOW DOWN AGEING PROCESS

Slowing Down Ageing and making old age the most enjoyable period of one's life is the aim of this book, in order to enable us to age gracefully, so that we can continue to act on the stage of life with fervour and vitality till the last moment of our life.

Our birth and death are both quantum phenomenon. In our birth, soul energy animates life when the negatively charged male sperm fertilises the female ovum in the vagina or otherwise. Then, it gets nurtured with food and pranic life energy till death, when the life sustaining factor becomes less than one and the reactor of our body is not able to sustain life due to many poisons accumulated in our body, then the soul energy departs, leaving the body cold and motionless.

The aim of this book is to help keep the life factor in our body reactor greater than one, so that we can go on loving and living. Thus, both our birth and death are Quantum Events-one shot process; while life is a beautiful integration of life sustaining processes. And the stress causing factors like disease etc. act like poisons to make the life factor less than one, while our immune system and other life asserting processes try to make the life factor greater than one - thus there is a constant battle going on between life assertive processes against the disease causing agents. Now, with mantric breathing, a new hope, a New Door has opened to heal ourself and to continue to keep the life factor greater than one for as long as we desire, so that we can conquer old age as well as death and thus become ageless. Death will become a tool in our own hands to say "Enough is Enough", we have enjoyed life fully and leave this world at our sweet will. Thus, we can become the master of our own life.

All of us attain our youth around the age of 20 years, when all our faculties reach their peak performance and this plateau in peak performance continues till the age of 25 years when the process of ageing starts and the metabolic rate of our body begins to decline at the rate of 5% every 10 years on the average and similarly all our body/mind faculties start declining. No one escapes this decline in various faculties, though there is a great variation in its degree and effect on persons of the same age depending upon the inherited genes, the food we take, the environment we live and our mental make up to keep our life battery charged up.

Ageing is usually brought about due to the diminished supply of blood and nourishment with age to the brain's neurons and the cells of our body. This happens because the blood arteries and veins become slowly narrower due to the deposits of calcium and other salts, uric acid and fatty cholesterol deposits in the blood arteries. As a result of this diminished blood supply, body repair mechanism becomes slower, causing loss of elasticity in all organs in our body. Muscles start losing strength, shape, size. Leg joints become stiff and painful. Brain, liver, heart and kidneys become reduced in size and their functional ability decreases with ageing. Also, as a result of the diminished blood supply/nutrition to brain neurons, age old defects in eyes of Presbyopia, Cataract and glaucoma begin to develop which we can correct by making use of the word N in the breathing mantra - the seed word for brow chakra. Also, the other senses of touch, taste, smell and hearing also deteriorate with ageing. Their onset can be considerably slowed down by incorporating the words T, K, G, H, N, & M in the breathing mantras.

As long as we can run, we are young and fit, the day we lose the capacity to walk fast or the pace of our walking becomes slow and not so firm - this is the first sign of old age infirmity which affects all other faculties i.e. Heart function, digestion, liver action, process of assimilation and elimination also start declining because of non-movement due to this disability in walking, then there is a geomertic progression in the ageing process, each declining body organ's performance affecting the other. Thus, once walking disability appears, then the body starts rusting, loosely speaking, because all body parts become further stiff and inflexible due to their limited movement, thus, accelerating the on-set of old age diseases, because in walking, we move both the legs and the hands, which keep the spinal chord functioning to keep its communication links with the mind/body functioning and once walking disability appears, then the incurable diseases of old age like Parkinson's disease and Alzheimer's diseases start appearing and by the age of 90 years, about 50 per cent of the persons begin to suffer form Alzheimer's disease which renders the person in-capable of taking care of himself and may proceed to a point at which the person forgets his relations and even his/her own name. This is the most horrendous degenerative disease of old age, when a person becomes totally dependent upon others for day to day survival and thus a total **BURDEN ON SOCIETY.**

Thus, to ward off old age, keep moving & walking. This is the mantra of healthful existence. Mantras to become Ageless and Conquer Old Age are given in the following chapters.

Chapter - 38

EXPERIENCE THE TIMELESSNESS
MANTRA
SMAÑ

The word 'SMA' in Hindi language means 'to get submerged', to become one. That is what happens in the ecstastic sexual union, when the time stops and we experience timelessness. The word 'S' also stands for breath centre (SANS) and sex centre and the word 'M' denotes mind. Thus when we yoke our breath with our thought, we also experience timelessness. Similarly we can experience timelessness when we yoke ourself with super consciousness by breathing with the following Mantra:-

Inhale with   S M A Ñ
Exhale With   M S I E Ñ

And at the end of inhalation and exhalation, if we give a pause in breathing, then we experience the fusion of inhale breath (male) and exhale breath (female) and we experience bliss - the ecstastic bliss - the timelessness, similar to the bliss as in sexual union. During the pause period, we experience the real timelessness.

This Mantra also stimulates the crown chakra and the pineal gland with its seed word 'M' And the pineal gland releases the tranquillity endowing hormone - Melatonin to destress our mind and it also helps in inducing deep sleep and it is during our deep sleep period when we experience deep relaxation and the state of TIMELESSNESS.

Chapter - 39

BECOME AGELESS
THE MANTRA
LAPHAN-NI

Men may come, Men may go, but some men continue to live in our hearts for ever, because of the noble work they have done during their life time and I remember a poem by H.W. Longfellow

> *"Lives of Great Men*
> *All Remind us*
> *We can make our lives sublime*
> *And Departing*
> *Leave Behind us*
> *Footprints on the sands of Time".*

And all of us have to depart one day or the other, however much we may extend our health span. But, if we can score a healthy 100 years - that is one of the greatest achievements, particularly in this world with polluted environment and life full of so much stress and strain now. However, we can cope with all this, provided we use the following mantras as help in breathing by speaking the mantra inwardly, smoothly, rhythmically, without causing any violence to our body, so as to simulate the natural breathing as nearly as possible.

1. Exhale with   =   I AM AGE-LESS
                              or
                              IMMI-AGELESS
   Inhale with   =   LA-SA-JAMMAÑ

180

And there are people like an Oil-Magnet and a famous Geologist named Mr. Miller Quarles who wants to become ageless and live for ever and thinks 'Never Say Die' and he is funding research on Rejuvenation. The above mantra will go a long way in achieving this (i) firstly, by the hypnotic power of thought because Thought is our Being and as beautifuly said by Swami Vivekanand "Matter is Mighty but Thought is Almighty" and if we think young, we remain young (ii) secondly, by inhaling deeply and fully by the power of breathing with the above mantra which makes the breath to start deeply from the bottom of the spine with the word 'L' which is the seed word for Muladhara Basic Chakra, which strengthens our sex power as well as gives power to our legs and this word 'L' also helps by its resonant sonic energy, to kindle the kundalini - the dormant potential energy in our body. The word 'L' thus makes this life battery energy to move up to the Crown chakra, the seed word for which is 'M' and this word also strengthens the right Brain and the pineal gland which is called the Transducer of super-conscious field. And the word S, which is the seed word for breath-start helps to take this awakened kundalini energy, made mobile by the power of word 'L,' to take it alongwith the breath to the Heart Chakra for which the seed word is Y or J. This word J strengthens the heart for better circulation as well as to fill our heart with God's compassion to embrace this whole humanity, when we can say that 'We, all, are the children of this Beautiful World'. And the inhale mantra ends with Mañ which means mother in our Hindi language, it helps to Yoke us with Infinity - the superconsciousness to draw in as much pranic life energy as needed.

And the secret of longevity is to keep our life battery fully re-charged with the help of these breathing mantras.

Another modification of the above breathing mantra is

2. Exhale with = AGELESS — BECOME
   Inhale With = LA-SAJJA — BAKKAM

This mantra gives us a commandment to become ageless and you can live infinitely, if you fill your total being with the desire to live on and on and that Mr. Miller Quarles, you possess in abundance.

3. In order to really become ageless, we have to make our inner life processes ageless. For that :-

Exhale with = INNI - AGELESS
Inhale with = LA - SAJNAÑ

This mantra stimulates the left brain and the pituitary master gland with N and Yokes us with super consciousness with AÑ to continue to boost our life factor to be always greater than 1.0.

4. The word - LAPHAN-NI in Urdu language means immortal. It is indeed a life prolonging mantra to make us live a healthy 100 years, because (i) it helps us to breathe long from the bottom of the spine with 'L' (ii) it helps to fill the lungs with its seed word 'PH' to its optimum capacity to impart splendid health to us, and it stimulates the Brow chakra, left brain / Pituitary gland with N.

Inhale with = LAPHAN

Exhale with = NEE/NEW - FEEL

So, cheer up, you can **now** become ageless with this new feeling every **moment**/every day.

Chapter - 40

CONQUER OLD AGE

Conquering old age is the greatest challenge posed to human kind and his most fertile mind. We have to embark on a new reverse journey, against the Natural ageing currents of life, but this reverse journey of generating ordered life currents is the most enjoyable journey - the journey of rejuvenation for our total body/mind system. How happy and victorious we feel, when we swim a noticeable distance against the water current in a canal or river.

All of us want to become immortal but mortality is written within our genes. God has made our body in-mortal, not immortal and now, we have to convert N to M to become immortal. How? Through the thought of MYSELF — 'I Am', then this in-mortal will become immortal because thought is our BEING. If we think and act young, we become young.

We have come in this world through sex, and they say you are as young as your sex glands. If you can keep your sex activity alive, your will live on & on. And 'L' is the seed word for basic sex Muladhara Chakra, located between the bottom of the spine and the genital organ. It strengthens the sex glands and gives power to the legs. Dwindling sex and dwindling gait are the first signs of old age. The word 'L' gives power to the legs as well as to the sex glands, through its resonant sonic energy. The word 'L' also helps to kindle the Kundalini-the dormant life energy battery currents to move up as effulgence in the crown of the Head for which the seed word is 'M'.

When we fall ill, our breath becomes shallow, so we are as young as the depth of our breath. Make your life breath deeper and longer and you live as long as you wish. That is why the word for living long, long life in English is LONGEVITY.

2. Thus Inhale with = LONG
    Exhale with = GEVITY
                  or
                  GIJEVITY

The total Inhale mantra becoming LONG-GIJEVITY. Make longevity your breath, Inhale long and deep. With the Inhale word 'LONG' you can inhale as deep as you want, and it yokes us with infinity - the super-consciousness to draw in as much pranic life energy to rejuvenate our total BEING, to live as long as you wish. According to Hindu thought, we come into this world with certain fixed number of breaths. If we can make our breath slow and long, then we can live longer. So make life breath as long as you can, as deep as you can and you can live longer and longer. The Urdu/ Hindi language word for agelessness is 'LAFFANI', again starting with the word 'L'.

(2) Thus Inhale with = LAFFAN
     Exhale with = NI/ NEWFILL

As if, we are filling our being - our life battery with new charge. Thus we are rejuvenating by recharging our life battery with pranic life energy, with the word 'F', seed word for lungs; to help to fulfill the lungs with pranic Energy.

(3) In order to conquer old age, we have to re-

kindle the FIRE of our Body engine i.e. increase our metabolic rate to digest food properly. Our metabolic rate decreases by about five percent every ten years, after we cross the peak youth age of 25 years. In order to increase the FIRE of our body engine, we use the resonant sonic power of the word 'R' the seed word for Manipur/ Navel Chakra/ Solar plexus. A simple English word 'MIRROR' gives double stress on R and can activate the total abdominal glandular system for reactivating our metabolism.

Thus Exhale with = MIRROR
Inhale with   = ARRAM

If we Inhale/ Exhale with the above mantra for one minute every morning and one minute in the evening, the glass mirror will start showing that wrinkles from our face have started slowly disappearing. So you are as young as your Engine Fire Power. Re-establish it with the above breathing mantra.

(4) But fire needs fuel to burn. So, we have to feed ourself with the balanced natural diet of proteins, carbohydrates, fats, vitamins and minerals to our body engine in their required proportion to supply glycogen and nutrients to all the cells of our body through the circulation of blood by the Heart/ Lungs system. Thus make nutrition your breath.

Exhale with   = NUTRITION

Spoken as NOOTTREESHUN

Inhale with   = ASHA — TRANN

This breathing mantra strengthens the left brain (N) and all the conscious sense endings in our brain with words N & T. As we age, the eye sight becomes dim. This mantra will strengthen the eyes and will cure eye defects like Myopia, Hypermetropia and cataract, and even glaucoma defect.

(5) And they say, we are as young as our brain, make the suggestive mantra "I AM BRAINY" as your breath.

Thus Exhale with =   I AM BRAINY
Inhale with   =   BRANNAM

This mantra helps us to breathe to our optimal lungs/abdomen capacity with the help of the seed word 'BR', and this mantra also strengthens the left brain (N) as well as the right brain (M) and the words N & M together strengthen both the pituitary and pineal glands, which together direct the total glandular activity in our body/mind system, thus boosting our total immune system. Though, we have activated the pituitary and pineal glands with the above mantra, but so far we have forgotten to activate the thyroid gland individually which helps to control both carbohydrate and fat metabolism in our body and also boosts the communication link between the body and the brain, through the cervical region of the spine. The seed word for Throat/Vishudha chakra is 'H'. For this :

(6) Inhale with   =   SAHHAM
    Exhale with   =   MIHHISH

This mantra helps to cure cervical spondylitis.

(7) And in order to conquer old age, we must also concur with nature. Let us not exceed the biological limits of our body/mind system and load it with unnecessary stress. Make concurring with nature as your breath:-

Exhale with   =   I AM CONCURRING

Inhale with	=	ARRA-KAN-NAMMANG

This mantra also helps to re-establish the communication links within brain with the help of words - K,N, M&G and also increases the fire in our body with the help of the word 'R'.

(8) And in order to conquer old age, we also have to have that great spirit of conquering - that great will - power - that committment - that great purposeful actions to conquer old age. Make the spirit of conquering your breath.

Exhale with	=	I AM CONQUERING
Inhale with	=	ARRA-YAKA-NAMMANG

As compared to mantra No.7, this mantra includes the word Y (U), which strengthens the heart for proper circulation of blood.

(9) And as we grow old, our liver becomes sluggish, and our assimilation processes become slow. In order to improve this :-

Exhale with	=	IMPROVE LIVER - JEE
Inhale with	=	LAVARA - JAPAMMA

This will completely rejuvenate our body.

(10) And last, but not the least, let me stress that that when we grow old, the communication links between the brain, the memory and the body get slowly partially blocked, resulting in causing old age diseases like Parkinson's disease and Alzheimer's disease. For that we have to rejuvenate the total body/mind/memory system:-

Exhale with	=	HI - YOU WILL RECOMMUNICATE
Inhale with	=	ALLA - VARA - YAHA - KAMANAKANT

This Exhale/ Inhale mantra, besides being very suggestive, is the fountain of longevity and has the power to cure people of the dreaded diseases like Parkinson's disease as well as Alzheimer's disease to which a separate chapter has been devoted in this book.

This breathing mantra encompasses all the conglomerates of energy centres called wheels or chakras in our body, which control the total glandular activity in our body. They say, we are as EFFICIENT as our glands.

Let us breathe ten times with each of the above breathng mantras, both in the morning and evening, by speaking the mantra silently, smoothly, rhythmically and as non-violently as possible, so as to simulate the natural breathing as nearly as possible. It will take about ten minutes or so. SO DOING, we have conquered the old age.

OM - TAT - SAT (AMEEN)

"If wrinkles must be written upon our brows, let them not be written upon the heart. The spirit should not grow old."

— *James A Garfield*

Chapter - 41

A SONG CAPSULE TO CURE ALL DISEASES

DANCE MANTRA
"SA, RA, YAHHAN, NAM"
MUNI, JEE, RISHIH, HOOÑ

Dance with a good music can enchant us, elevate us, transform us and even cure us of stress is known by all of us. Now, a dance with a healing mantra can cure us almost of all the diseases of our body/mind system in a slow but steady manner., has been coined by the author, and is given a little later in this chapter.

According the Hindu scriptures, God-The Creator is like a Dancer and this whole Universe-His creation is his Dance, because it is known that all creation including atoms and the planets and the stars are all revolving and dancing i.e. the electron in the hydrogen atom is dancing around the proton of the hydrogen nucleus; the earth is revolving around the sun and is also itself revolving on its own axis to create the days/nights, and the beautiful changing seasons with all the different fruits, and vegetables all the year round. Thus, all creation is His Harmonic vibration like a dance. The creator is continuously dancing to create. Do we not feel 'RE-CREATED' after dancing or even watching the beautiful dance. They say, "Bank moves the money, but the Dance moves the Soul".

And I have coined this dance breathing Mantra after song on a brilliant cha cha music :- *"Cha, Cha, Chacha, Cha"*. This is also a SIDHA MANTRA.

The Inhale Mantra is
"Sa, Ra, Yahhan, Nam"
And the Exhale Mantra is:-
"Muni, Jee, Rishih, Hooñ"

We can, dance alone- Me with Me, like jogging at one place or dancing around, singing inwardly and rhythmically with "Sa, Ra, Yahhan, Nam, while vibrating the body as in a dance and also taking hands up in a dance waveform, our hands slowly going up into the sky, and also stretching up the spine to become lofty and united with the superconciousness, the hands out-stretched upwards in prayer as if united with God. Similarly, then, exhale rhythmically with the mantra, singing inwardly - "Muni, Jee, Rishih, Hooñ" while destretching the spine, as well as vibrating our body sonorously and the hands coming down, in a dance form.

This dancing breathing mantra resonates with all the seven known chakras - the conglomerates of energy centres of our body/mind system known by the Hindu sages, fills them with pranic life energy, and imparts resonant sonic energy to them. This dancing mantra is able to make each cell and each neuron of our body/mind system dance and bring it into lively vibration to rejuvenate and if we can provide our body with the required quantity of balnced nutritious food, then no disease can ever dare to come near us. And slowly and steadily, it can help us also to eradicate all diseases from our body/mind system, provided we are determined to do so and develop the necessary will-power to do so and inhale/exhale or dance with the above mantra for 10 minutes or as convenient; both morning and evening.

Now, how this dance breathing mantra is so potent? because, as said before, it resonates as well as provides pranic life energy to all the seven known wheels of energy-the conglomerates of nerve centres of our body emanating and distributing various hormones by their secretions in the blood stream.

(i) "The word 'S' stands for breath centre and is able to awaken the kundalini-the potential life energy in our body, which can be activated to become kinetic energy-an energy which can move up the spine along the so called sushumna opening alongwith the breath upto the crown of our head.

(ii) The word 'S' besides activating the kundalini and the breath, also stands for both (a) Muladhara chakra (seed word L) denoted as basic sex boosting chakra as well as for (b) Swadhistana chakra (seed word V) which denotes the movement of water/elimination process like urine and stool and absorption of nutrients in the blood in the lower intestines besides giving strength to the ovaries, which nurture life.

(iii) The word 'R' activates the navel/solar plexus chakra, which boosts digestion and gives heat to our body and it improves liver and pancreas action also.

(iv) The word 'Y' activates the heart chakra, which boosts circulation of blood/breath and imparts compassion to our heart.

(v) The word 'H' is the seed word for throat chakra, which activates thyroid gland. This controls fat and carbohydrate metabolism in our body and also establishes the communication link between the brain and the body.

(vi) Similarly, we give pranic life energy to the left brain and conscious senses like eyesight etc with 'N'. This also stimulates the pituitary gland - the director of total glandular activity in our body.

(vii) The word 'M' is the seed word for crown chakra, which energises the right brain and strengthens the action of pineal gland which releases the hormone - Melatonin to quieten and pacify the mind.

In the above dance mantra, we have provided pranic life energy and sonic energy to (i) muladhara (L/S) and swadhistana (V/S) chakras only indirectly through their common representative word 'S' which only partially resonates with these two chakras. In order to give full resonating sonic energy to these two chakras, we modify the above song mantra as follows to dance similarly on the cha-cha music.

(2) Inhale with   =   LA, VA, YAHHAM, MAÑ
    Exhale with   =   ME, YOU, VOULAI, VOUH

The Exhale words Voulai Vouh sound like the famous French phrase for "I Love You" (Voulez Vous). This is really a very invigorating mantra and gives sparkle to our body/mind system.

These two mantras, thus, boost our total immune system. Thus, we can dance with the above two mantras for five minutes each, as convenient but before changing over to next dance mantra, rest for a minute or so in-between. In this pause period, you can watch beautifully the on-rush of boi-energy currents rushing in your hands/ brain system. Thus, the above dance mantras encompass the whole spectrum of bio-energy centres, in our body/mind system and are thus the most rejuvenating capsule full of pranic life energy. The whole science of the power of healing words has been laid bare and compressed in this chapter/ article and any committed person, who happens to use this breathing system consistently with the power of healing words as above will benefit very greatly.

Joseph Conrad, while speaking of the words said, "Donot talk to me of your Archimedes lever-give me the right-word and the right accent and I will move the world." And those right healing words are right here, to rid people of various ailments.

And, the above dance mantra can also be used while standing stationary or sitting comfortably in an arm-chair or sofa, but with the spine fairly straight, for equally good benefits without dancing. This is for people suffering from arthritis or Parkinson's disease or persons with some walking disability or for a person who is not so inclined to dance. These can be used as inhale/exhale mantras, speaking the mantras silently.

The above breathing mantras are indeed very beneficial so much so that these mantras can even kindle the kundalini, and make the person sidha (Enlightened Person) but for that a great dedication is required to practice this mantra sitting silently for many many hours during the day, plus it becomes necessary to lead a pure, non-violent,

stress free life of Satyam (Truth), Shivam (godliness),
& Sunderam (Beauty). All the same, it will endow
sparkling health to all those who use this breathing
mantra even for ten minutes morning and evening
each day. This will, thus, help to make life a
blissful experience.

Chapter - 42

INCREASE HEALTH – SPAN

THE MANTRAS

1.	INCREASE	—	SPAN
2.	INCREASE	—	STRENGTH
3.	INCREASE	—	LIFE
4.	INCREASE	—	LING
5.	INCREASE	—	COMMUNION
6.	INCREASE	—	ILLIAC COMMUNION.

All the above exhale mantras are very suggestive and indeed very very useful. Then inhale deeply or

(i) Exhale with   =   INCREASE — SPAN
     Inhale with   =   SPAZA KRANNA

In this inhale mantra, the word 'S' kindles the divine Kundalini and moves it up alongwith the breath. (ii) The word 'R' gives 'FIRE" to our digestion by proper digestion and assimilation of food (iii) The word 'P & Z' help the lungs and the Cardio - vascular system to improve blood circulation, the word 'N' is the seed word for Brow Chakra, it strengthens the left brain, the eye - sight and the Pituitary gland to improve our total immune system and the word 'K' also helps to strengthen the sense endings in left brain; thus the above Mantra 'INCREASES' the sensitivity of our senses and boosts our immune system to increase our life span.

(ii) Similarly, we can exhale with INCREASE STRENGTH and then inhale deeply from the bottom of spine unto the brow chakra. It will really increase our body strength.

(iii) Similarly exhale with   = INCREASE LIFE
and inhale with   =   LAZAFAKRANNA

The word 'L' is similar to 'S' and kindles the Kundalini and gives strength to the legs and the word 'F' helps the lungs to breath to its optimum capacity to increase our life span.

(iv) Also exhale with   =   INCREASE — LING
Inhale with   =   LAZAKRANANG

This Mantra helps to increase the length of the male organ and boost sex power with the resonant sonic vibrations of words 'N & G' (See Chapter on Sex Power). The word 'G' also strengthens the sense endings in the brain and also stimulates the immunoglobin 'A' in the nasal cavities.

In breathing Mantras Nos. 5, 6 the word COMMUNION helps to restore the sagging communion between the brain and the memory with age. This is re-established with the resonant sonic vibrations of the words 'K, M, N.', thus helping to cure old age diseases like Parkinson's, and Alzheimer's slowly and steadily supplemented with proper nutrition.

Chapter - 43

RE-IGNITE YOUR BODY FIRE
THE MANTRA — 'MIRROR'

Mirror is a beautiful word describing its own action of mirror-to reflect R as R as in the word 'ROR' exactly, while omitting the word MI - the Myself- the Soul motivating the body .The actual glass mirror also reflects only our outer personality and not the ATMAÑ (Soul) animating our Being.

And the Atmañ (Soul) also resides in our body, as long as Fire is burning in our Body Temple and the fire can continue to burn with the resonance power of the word R, the Seed word for Navel/ Manipura chakra/the Solar Plexus; when supplied with nourishing food.

Our metabolic rate is the mirror of our youth and after we cross the youthful age of 25 Years, the metabolic rate of our body starts declining by about 5% every 10 Years and we can almost forestall the natural death of a person because the metabolic rate makes a sharp nose dive about a few months prior to one's impending death and the person starts losing one's hunger with consequent sharp decline in one's weight before one's natural death, not as a rule, but as generally observed in sufficiently old persons.

However, it is quite possible to Regain our metabolism to a considerable extent by activating the Navel Chakra by its resonant word RA, which represents the fire principle in our body as said earlier. This word RA helps to strengthen the Liver and also the stomach linings to secrete proper digestive juices for proper digestion, and activates the pancreas, the gland which manufactures the hormone Insulin, responsible for assimilating glyogen/sugar in the blood. The pancreas also help to inject necessary enzymes into the upper intestines for digesting proteins, fats and carbohydrates.

The following mantra 'Mirror' gives double stress on the word R and is hence a very apt word for RE-igniting the fire in our body.

Thus Exhale with=   MIRROR
Inhale with   =   ARRAM

The above mantra also contains the word M which is the seed word for crown chakra, which by its resonant sonic power strengthens the right brain and the pineal gland. In order to stimulale the left brain & the master pituitary gland, we replace M with N

2) Inhale with   =   ARRAN
    Exhale with   =   NIRROR

Inhale/ Exhale with the above two mantras by speaking the mantra inwardly, rhythmically and as non-violently as possible so as to simulate the natural breathing as nearly as possible. Do it for ten minutes early morning before break-fast and also for ten minutes in the evening half an hour after evening tea and just with a few weeks' practice, you will start feeling a great improvement in Your digestive power with proper assimilation of food with resultant shine on your face and you will start feeling pleasure in seeing your smart healthy personality reflected in the Mirror, provided you are feeding yourself with the necessary balanced nutritious food-the fuel to burn in your stomach engine. This is indeed a very simple but very effective mantra to regain our metabolism slowly but steadily in the most natural fashion. This mantra will also help to cure the diabetic patients of excess sugar present in the blood-stream.

OM - TAT - SAT (AMEEN)

Chapter - 44

MANTRA FOR LIVER IMPROVEMENT
IMPROVE — LIVER

Give me a healthy liver and I shall live for ever; because liver manufactures/stores glycogen to supply us the energy and is thus preserver of all organs of our body by feeding them with proper nutrition. As we age, our liver also ages, because we damage it with intoxicants like alcohol, tea, coffee and over eating etc. The seed word for stimulating LIVER is R and it appears in the above exhale mantra twice. Thus it is eminently suited for strengthening liver.

1. Exhale with = IMPROVE LIVER
    Inhale with = LAVARA — PRAMMAÑ

(i)   The word L the seed word for basic chakra kindles the divine kundalini, boosts sex power and gives strength to our legs to walk on & on.

(ii) The word V the seed word for ovary chakra which irrigates all the cells of our body by stimulating the lower intestines for proper absorption of digested food in the blood.

(iii) The word R the seed word for Navel Chakra helps to stimulate the LIVER, the pancreas and all the other abdominal secretions to properly digest our food to give our body the required FIRE.

(iv) The word 'P' stimulates the cardio - vascular system for better circulation of blood & nutrients to our body/mind system.

(v) The word 'M' the seed word for crown chakra stimulates our right brain, the pineal gland and the mind with its resonant sonic vibrations.

(vi) The word MAÑ Yokes us with Infinity-the superconsciousness to draw in as much pranic life energy as possible to fulfill our BEING.

Thus, the above mantra not only stimulates our liver; but rejuvenates our total BEING.

Chapter - 45

PREVENT TOOTH DECAY

Our teeth are the presiding diety of our food digestion system and the decaying teeth are the greatest problem in old- age, accelerating old age by spreading infection from the teeth, which goes to the abdomen, mixes with the blood in the lower intestines alongwith digested food and water and thereby reaches all the cells of our body to enhance congestions and pains existing in various parts of old persons.

It is very interesting to note that the Hindi/ Urdu language word for teeth is DANT which is quite similar to TEETH i.e. constituted of T, D & Th - all these words are the seed words for taste/tooth endings in the brain. They say that prevention is better than cure. Thus make 'prevent tooth decay' as your breath :

1. Exhale with   PREVENT — TOOTH — DECAY
   Inhale with   VAPRA — KA — DANT

2. Exhale with   IMPROVEE — TEETH
   Inhale with   VAPRAMA DANT

3. Exhale with   OOMNI — PRUDENT
   Inhale with   PRANAMA — DANT

4. Exhale with   OOMNI — POOTENT
   Inhale with   PANAMA — DANT

5. Exhale with   PRESIDENT
   Inhale with   PRAZA — DANT

6. Exhale with   PRECEDENT

Inhale with   SAPRA DANT

All the above breathing mantras are very very potent indeed to strengthen our teeth and gums. Since the words DANT/ DENT/ TEETH form the last part of the inhale/exhale breathing Mantras given above, the word DANT/ DENT/ TEETH sets up resonant sonic vibrations in the teeth to strengthen them. Inhale/exhale with the above Mantras silently for five minutes in the morning in a pollution free environnment, these will not only strengthen the teeth but also rejuvenate the total body. Give a small pause and focus attention on the teeth with the word DANT/TEETH. This will amplify the above benefits.

Last but not the least, gargling with a dilute solution of ALUM ($K_2 SO_4 Al_2 SO_4$ 24 H_2O) called potash alum twice in a week will go a long way in preventing any serious infection in our teeth, because ALUM is a disinfectant as well as possesses tissue building property and hence very effective in controlling tooth decay. This is in addition to brushing teeth daily with proper tooth paste.

Also, I advise taking 4 tablets of Calc. Phos 3X and Calc. Fluor 12X twice daily only for two days in a week. This will help to prevent tooth decay by supplying the proper nutrients for the teeth.

Chapter - 46

BOOST SEX POWER

MANTRA 'INCREASE — LING'
INCREASE — PHALLUS

"Desire never rests by enjoyment of lusts as Fire Surely increases, the more butter is added to it". Laws of Manu 2.94.

We are the Embodiment of Sex- we have come into this world through the ecstatic Union of a male and female body. In fact satisfying sex act is the most unifying experience of two bodies into common love bondage- the most blissful union of two better halves made for each other. And each person has an aura of sex around him or her, the more the aura, the more we get attracted to each other. Mind is the door to sex arousal, the same mind also becomes a barrier, when the sex senses get dulled. The aim of this chapter is to boost sex control in young people., and help sex arousal in aged persons if they so desire.

Sex is the release valve, for the over-flowing life energy in our body. In peak youth, this energy is full to its brim and the sex enjoyment, both its quality and quantity is also at its peak. But, soon the Bank Balance of Life Energy starts getting depleted; unless we continuously fill it up by the interaction of Pranic Life energy with the intake of highly nutritious food. This is the secret of enduring sex power in most of the people showing greater sexual vigour.

Since life is Breath which charges our Life

battery with Pranic Life Energy, we make use of this breath, both to control and arouse sex, with the resonant sonic vibration of certain words which strengthen our sex glands, i.e. L, S, V and increase the fire in our body with word R and boost fat metabolism with the word 'H' and develop mind control with the words MANT, MIND, MENT etc.

Lord Krishna in Hindu Religion, besides his other great qualities, is also known as the apostle of sex. His own name Krishnañ gives power to the sex glands and includes both the inhale (Male breath) and exhale breath (Female breath)

1) Exhale with   =   KRISH
   Inhale with   =   SHNAÑ

The words K&N dictate sex in the brain. These are the seed words for Brow Chakra and pituitary gland in the brain. It is the pituitary gland which sends the signal of arousal to the sex glands, after the mind is aroused by the sexual aura of the opposite sex and the sex glands as said earlier are strengthened by the words S/ SH/ L/ V. The words LOVE, voules vous, SEX, LING (sex organ) are all constituted of the words L, V, S, K, G, N etc. while 'R' is the seed word for Navel/ Manipur Chakra which strengthens the Fire principle and provides us the Fuel to our sex power. Thus, the word Krish- Shnañ is indeed a very potent single stage mantra complete in itself to strengthen the sex vigour.

But proper fuel & balanced nutritious diet is a must for continued sex virility. In fact, once, competing in a prize winning entry for Glaxo Advertisement, I wrote, "I like Glucose-D because it keeps me Healthy, Vigorous and Naughty, though long back, I crossed forty".

2) Another single stage breathing mantra for boosting sex power is to use the power of the word L - the seed word for basic Muladhara Chakra, located between the bottom of the spine and the genital organ. It strengthens sex glands, stands for earth principle, gives power to the legs and boosts sex power.

Exhale with   =   KLIEÑ
Inhale with   =   LAKKAÑ

3) The word for sex organ in our Hindi Language is LING. This is good exhale mantra for boosting sex power.

Inhale with   =   INCREASE LING
Exhale with   =   LARA - ZKANNANG

This is indeed a powerful mantra to boost sex power, because it contains words K, N, G, L, all sex boosting words.

Another very powerful sex boosting mantra and also very suggestive in nature is

4) Exhale with   =   INCREASE - PHALLUS
   Inhale with   =   ALLA - SARA - FZAK -
KAN

Another very very potent sex power boosting mantra as well as giving the mind control for Retentivity is :

5) Inhale with   =   LAVA - BRAHAMAND
   Exhale with   =   HOO - BROO -
                       VOULIEMENT

The word Brahamand in Hindi language means- the whole Universe The Inhale mantra connotes as if semen is the creative "Lava of Universe". This is a five stage breathing mantra which rejuvenates the complete body/mind system and strengthens the total glandular activity of our body.

Now, let me speak how the above words actuate various glands in our body/mind system is given below :-

i) The word L/S, as said earlier, are the seed words for basic sex chakra and hence by its resonant sonic vibrations strengthens the sex gland.

ii) The word V is the seed word for Swadhishtana Chakra, it strengthens ovaries which nuture life, It stands for water prinicipls, it also helps in both assimilation as well as elimination processes of life, in the lower intestines.

iii) 'R' is the seed word for Manipur Chakra which represents FIRE principle, it helps to give fuel to our body/sex by providing better digestion of food by strengthening liver, pancreas and all abdominal secretions.

iv) The word H is the seed word for Throat/Vishudha Chakra. It strengthens the Thyroid gland, which helps in the metabolism of fats and carbohydrates. It also helps to open up the clogged arteries (with age) in the upper cervical spine region for better communication between the brain and the body. They say, You are as young as your Thyroid Gland because it helps to make us look attractive for proper sex appeal.

v) The word 'BR' helps the bronchial tubes in the lungs to breathe to their optimum capacity and it also helps to breathe from the abdomen with the help of seed word 'R' for better digestion and assimilation of food.

vi) The word 'PH' helps to fulfill the lungs to provide pranic energy to all the cells of the body including sex organ.

vii) The word 'M' is the seed word for the crown chakra, which helps to strengthen the right brain, the word 'N' is the seed word for brow chakra which strengthens the left brain and the words M & N together strengthen both the pineal and pituitary glands which control the total glandular activity in our body/mind system and the words M, N & D help to control the total mind and the intelligence which is the charioteer of our body. Thus, the breathing mantra No. (6) provides pranic life energy to the total body/ mind system - rejuvenating it completely by charging the life battery and also strengthening the total body immune system to make us, healthy and vigorous which is essential for vigorous sex, as they go together. The word MAND/ MIND helps to improve sexual retention and this rententivity in sex will improve further, if we give a convenient pause at the end of the breath, both at the end of inhalation and exhalation. And we should try to extend this pause period and more the pause period, more the power of semen retention is achieved.

Inhale/exhale 10 times each with all the six breathing mantras by speaking the mantra inwardly, smoothly, deeply and as non-violently as possible to simulate the noiseless natural breathig. This will take about 7 minutes. Do it both morning and evening; or if you can practice with the all potent mantra No. 6 alone for seven minutes, it will have a superlative effect to rejuvenate our body/mind/ sex power completely.

Conjugal relationship : No male person is impotent, except through injury. Impotency in men is mostly psychological, because men are expected to prove their erectile and staying power. That becomes the cause of fear - psychosis for newly married men, particularly in India where premarital sex is a taboo. And this first night experience has a lasting impression on conjugal happiness. However, there is wide variation in sexual power as in any other human activity. I remember some-one reciting that three girl friends got married on the same date and decided to go for honeymoon also to the same destination/hotel and decided to relate their first night experience to each other by their coded language as to how they speak the morning salutation "Good morning" on the breakast table when they meet in the hotel restaurant next morning.

Next morning, one girl meekly pronounced 'Good morning' indicating that sex union was not very satisfactory, the other girl said very happily, "Very Good Morning" and the third girl said "Good morning, Good morning, till morning".

And all persons can enjoy a very satisfying sex relationship provided they use the above breathing mantras to boost their sex power. Since all glandular activity and the hormones secreted are essentially protein in composition, a balanced nutritious diet of protiens, carbohydrates, vitamins and minerals is required to provide fuel to the body and the sex activity. Honey, raisins (dried grapes), eggs, fish, meat, milk, grains, nuts, raw sugar (Gur), mangoes, all boost sex power. Onion / Garlic help to clean the arteries of fatty deposit to give greater erectile power. A mixture of a spoonful juice each of Ginger, Onion and honey is a very good aphrodiasic.

There are also other powerful aphrodiasics available in the market, particularly the most recently advertised potent aphrodiasic called DHEA - the short name of medicine "dehydroepian drosterone" which is converted in our body to "testo-sterone" and ostrogen. As we age, levels of DHEA slowly drop in our body which can be supplemented now by taking this newly manufactured drug orally, but many scientists are suspicious about its long term side harmful effects like any other drug, taken for a long time.

There is also a very potent drug called Nux Vomica, used both in Indian Ayurvedic system of medicine as well as in Homoeopathic system of Medicine. This is a polychrest medicine, extracted out of the seeds of the fruit of tree- strychnos Nux Vomica, grown in Cormandal coast in India and Cochin China. This medicine is also a potent aphrodiasic and potent polychrest medicine to cure many many human diseases including drunkeness and many stress related diseases.

Similarly, there is also a herb-called Ashwagandha (Asgandh) long known in Ayurvedic system of medicine. This again is a very good aphrodiasic and is known to give the power of a stud, as its name suggests. and a nerve tonic and a polychrest medicine.

Similarly, another Indian Herb — SHATAVARI (Asparagus racemosus) is an all round rejuvenating and sex boosting tonic specially for women.

And also there is another potent aphrodiasic called Yohimbinum ($C_{22} H_{30} N_2 O_4$). It is a powerful stimulant of the genital function in males and is good medicine in the congestive stage of old men, but it should be taken diluted, otherwise it can harm the system.

But, all aphrodiasic medicines are harmful and violent like Alcohol which when taken gives us a feeling of being on the top of the world for some time but next morning, it gives us the dirty look of a hangover, with headache etc.

However, the above breathing mantras help us to develop sex power slowly and steadily in the most natural manner by recharging our life battery by filling our 'BEING' with pranic life energy and by supplementing it with good nutritious diet. And thus we can continue to enjoy sex - as long as we want, and at any age. Age is no barrier to sex activity, though the age of 50 years is a turning point in sexual activity as "ordained by nature". For men, it is "Men- O- Pause", while for women it is the menopause period, when the mensturation cycle ceases. And at this juncture, some men will give a full stop to their sex activity thinking that sex is for procreation purpose and now enough is enough. But there are other men, who want to carry on and on, even beyond 80 years. As long as there is breath, there is sex, and it also depends to a great extent on the genes we inherit, the environment we live in and ultimately the key to sex is held by the conjugal partners and our mind.

And the ultimate aim of all sex tantrics is also - An Erect Phallus, to be kept in Erect position for as long as possible preferably for more than an hour which is also achievable through the medium of above breathing mantras.

But , it is this stage of life beyond 50 years when we need the help of these sex boosting breathing mantras to help us to continue to enjoy stimulating sex throughout life, though the frequency of sex relationship dwindles with advancing age but sex is there till our last breath. There is no better rejuvenating feeling than when we get an erection in old age in the morning hours because this is a sign of youth. So let us keep up this youthifying invigorating sex activity with the help of these sex boosting breathing mantras for as long as we wish. Last but not the least there is no better aphrodiasic than the sweet kiss of a lovely heart - throb; while an erect phallus can stimulate any willing woman partner.

"Power is the ultimate Aphrodiasic"

— Henry Kissinger

Chapter - 47

A LIFE REVIVAL MANTRA
SANJEEV / SANJEVINI

Life is another name for breathing and circulation of pranic life energy in our body, while it is the lungs which help us to breathe, but it is the heart which circulates the blood loaded with oxygen, glucose and other nutrients to reach each and every cell in our body. When we fall prey to some disease, then our breathing is the first casuality i.e. our breath becomes shallow and erratic and thus heart is not able to give the full supply of oxygen and pranic life energy to all parts of the body, thus further compounding the disease. In order to restore our natural healthy breathing, we can take tha help of the word - 'SANJEEV'.

1) Inhale with the word =   SANJ
    Exhale with the word =   JEEV

It is the simplest single stage breathing mantra which simulates the natural healthy breathing as nearly as possibe. Inhale with the help of the word 'SANJ' spoken inwardly to breathe in softly, rhythmically and as deeply as possible without causing any violence to our body and similarly exhale with the help of the word - 'JEEV'. This breathing mantra restores the breathing to its normal pattern, thus helping to restore our health. How it achieves this?

i) First by helping to start the breath from its seat of origin in our body about 7 cms below the navel. Now, the word S also originates from the same place in our body, as the breath. Thus, I call 'S' the seed word for the start point of the inhale breath. Both the breath and the word 'S' originate midway between Navel and the bottom of the spine.

ii) Secondly, the word 'SAÑ' helps to inhale the breath upto the other extremity of breath- the Infinity - the seed word for which is AÑ. This Infinity constitutes the Super consciousness, the Infinitum pranic life energy source from which we draw in our life energy. We are united with God through the breath, At one end is our BEING and at the other end the super consciousness and this breath is the connection between the two, because with the last exhalation, we are no more.

iii) Thirdly, the word 'SA' helps to awaken the divine Kundalini Energy stored as Bank Balance of the potential life energy, and it is through breath, that this kundalini becomes kinetic and finds a passage through the so called 'SUSHUMNA" Channel located in the spine to flow upwards to the crown chakra in the head, when the kundalini power illuminates us with the 'GOD's Effulgence of Glory & Bliss.

iv) Inhale mantra 'SAÑJ' ends with the word J which alongwith 'Y' are the seed words for 'Heart Chakra' and this is how, this mantra helps to strengthen the heart, by drawing in through breath all the pranic life energy with the help of the word 'SAÑ' and deposting it at the station-Heart, with the sonic resonant power of the word 'J'.

v) Then we exhale with the help of the mantra

"JEEV" which in Hindi language literally means - "A LIVING BEING" and life also means the flow of soul energy, which is further enhanced with the power of the words J & V. As already said above, the word J stands for heart / lung system., circulating blood oxygen/pranic energy throughout the body, and the word 'V' which is seed word for Swadhistana Chakra which stands for water principles, and as we know, our body is constituted of 70% water, and each cell of our body contains water both inside the cell as well as outside the cell to help carry out life processes. The word 'V' also strengthens the WOMB, and the lower intestines where the digested food and nutrients alongwith water are absorbed by the blood for circulation and supply to all the cells/neurons in our body. The word 'V' also strengthens elimination process of Stool.

Thus, the inhale / exhale breathing mantra complete in the word SANJ — JEEV, helps us to draw in all the needed pranic energy from the Infinitum source, and then helps to circulate it throughout the body. Thus, it is indeed a great health imparting mantra, particularly good for Heart.

Once, in a social function, held to celebrate the marriage anniversary of a friend named 'SANJEEV', I was asked to speak a few words, at the end of party. After thanking and congratulating the couple, I advised Madam Sanjeev that in order to impart further shine to her personality, she should daily breathe for a few minutes, with her husband's name- SANJEEV, as it will impart three fold benefits.

"Saihhit Kee Saihhit Hai
Mohabbat Kee Mohabbat Hai
Aur Ibadat Kee Ibadat Hai"

At this, the whole gala gathering burst into hearty laughter and clapped joyously. The above couplet means:- With this, you will become

(i)   An Embodiment of Health

(ii) An Effulgence of Love

(iii) And an offering of prayer to your husband.

And this poetic utterance becomes particularly relevant, because in India, husband has so far been the sole bread earner and is thus given the elevated status of a Semi - God in the household.

The Mantra Sanjeevini

The word SANJEEV derives its name from a Life Saving Herb called 'SANJEEVINI' grown in the the Himalayan Mountain region, as mentioned in the Ramayana Epic, when during the fight in the Lankan War, - the brother of Lord RAM — Lakshman was injured seriously, and the physician attending on Lakshman told that his life could be saved only if the herb- Sanjeevini is immediately brought from the Himalayan Region, thousands of miles away. Lord Hanuman a great devotee of Lord Ram through his Yogic Powers, flew immediately to the Himalayas, but was not able to distingiush and recognise the herb — Sanjeevini, from other herbs grown in that region. Then, with his sheer might and power, he lifted that portion of th HImalayan rock alongwith the herbs and brought it well in time to save the life of Lakshman.

And recently on 9th April 1995, I was invited by a Homoeopathic Doctors Society called Hahnemann

Dhanwantri Medical Society group, Gurgaon to give a small talk on the birthday of Dr. Hahnemann, the founder of Homoeopathic system of medicine. And it was a strange coincidence that it also happened to be the "Ram Naumi" — Lord Ram's Birthday, which is celebrated as a holiday by Government of India. Realizing this happy coincidence, there and then, I coined a small poem, thus :-

"Bhagwan Ram Kai Bhagtauñ Maiñ
Hanuman Jee Sai Nheen Hai Kowee Baihter
Aur Duniya Kai Doctoroon Maiñ
Doctor Hahnemann Sai Nheen Hai Kowee Baihter
Aur Doctor Hahnemann Aur Hanuman Jee Kai
Yaksan Nam Sai
Yakeen Hau Jata Hai Mujhai
Kaih Zroor Yeh Bhagwan Ram Kai Vardan Ka Ntija
Hai
Keh Hanuman Jee Nai Janam Liya Hai
Doctor Hahnemann Bankar.
Bhaija Hai Bhagwan Ram Nai
Daikar Yeh Vardan Aur Puraskar
Dikha Dow Duniya Kau
Zara See Dawa ka Chamatkar
Kar Dow Duniya Kai Her Mreez Kau Baihter
Zara See Chutke Bher Methhee Dawa Dekar

This poetic rendering in Urdu is translated thus :

"In this whole world:
There is no one better than Hanuman
Amongst the Devotees of Lord Ram
And there is No One better than Doctor Hahnemann
Amongst the Doctors of Medicine
To Cure Millions of People

With the magic of
Millionth part of the Medicine
This is Surely
The Blessings of Lord Ram
Granted to Novice but devoted Hanuman
To take Birth as Lofty Dr. Hahnemann
Seeing from the wonderful Similarity
In the names of Hanuman
And Dr. Hahnemann :"

The word "Sanjeevini" can also be used as Inhale / Exhale breathing mantra.

2) Inhale with   =   SANJ
    Exhale with   =   JEEVVINI

The Exhale mantra Jeevvinni is a two stage exhale mantra and thus doubly potent, because it helps to exhale from the conscious organs like eye sight/ brain, (N) thus creating vacuum, to be filled in with pranic life energy during inhalation with SANJ.

And I am sure, millions of persons can get rid of their ailments simply by inhaling/exhaling properly with the simplest breathing mantras 'Sanjjeev (ii) Sanjeevvinni, the cure also speeded up by the hypnotic influence of the magical name of the life saving herb - Sanjeevvinni. A person lying on the death - bed will surely revive if he/she recites sincerely the life saving mantra - SANJEEVINI.

This chapter is dedicated to my eldest son named Sanjeev Chowdhry, for his further well being. He is an Engineering Graduate, now settled in Los Angeles (U.S.A.).

Chapter - 48

A MANTRA TO LIVE
HUNDRED YEARS
MEDITATION

Meditation is the art of concentrating on an outer or inner body object to still and quieten the turbulent mind, by making the thought concentrate on a single point when it ultimately becomes monodirectional and coherent like the laser beam. Our sages in India claim to live many many hundred years by the technique of meditation and while also living stress free life of Satyam (Truth) Shivam (Godliness) and Sunderam (Beautiful Existence). The ultimate stage of meditation is the totally relaxed silence of our being. A poem written on meditation earlier by me is also reproduced here.

Mantric breathing is also a form of meditation, because we make our thought move alongwith the breath as it traverses various Astral/ body chakras. Also make the word Meditation as your breath

Exhale with   =   MEDITATION SPOKEN
                        AS MEDITAISHUN

Inhale with   =   SHTA — NAMMAND

The inhale mantra is a mirror image of the exhale mantra. The inhale mantra 'Shta — Nammand' means I salute the person who lives hundred years. The aim of this book is to make us live a healthy and vigorous 100 years, this breathing

219

mantra is potent enough to helps us achieve this as follows :

(i) When we inhale with the very very suggestive word - Shta Nammand - the mind moves alongwith the breath from the bottom of the spine with SH to the brow chakra with N and then to the crown Chakra with M, and then our thought yokes us with the infinity - the super consciousness with the word MAÑ to draw in as much pranic life energy as possible and then the breath ends at the soft dome palate of the mouth with the word D — We give a small convenient pause, by concentrating on the dome of our mouth. This is called VIPASANA MEDITATION advocated by Lord Budha.

(ii) The word SH helps to resonate with the Divine Kundalini Power to kindle it, and move it to brow chakra with N and the crown chakra with M to illuminate our total being. The word 'Sh' helps to strengthen the sex glands and also the assimilation and Elimination processes of our body occuring in the lower intestines.

(iii) The word 'N' strengthens the left brain, the eye sight and the pituitary gland to boost our Immune system to live healthy hundred years.

(iv) The word 'M' illuminates the mind, the right brain as well as strengthens the pineal gland to produce the pacifying hormone melatonin which helps remove depression from the mind.

(v) The words T & D besides helping to stimulate the taste sense endings in the brain, also strengthen the salivary glands for proper digestion of food in our mouth and also help our MIND, which is stimulated by the combined words M, N & D.

Thus, breathing with the mantra 'meditation' and its inhale counter-part, fulfills our total BEING with pranic life energy as well as stimulates the Endocrine glands of our body to boost our immune system while in conventional meditation we may even be starving the legs (of the pranic energy) which may become weak. Thus, make the breathing mantra MEDITATION/ SHTA NAMMAND as Vipasana Meditation and live a healthy hundred years.

VIRTUES OF MODERATION

"Verily, yoga is not possible for him who eats too much, nor for him who does not eat at all, nor for him who sleeps too much nor for him who is always awake, O Arjuna. Yoga becomes the destroyer of pain for him who is moderate in eating and recreation, who is moderate in exertion, in actions, who is moderate in sleep and wakefulness."

— Bhagavad Gita VI 16-17

'MEDITATION'

— Dr. L.R. CHOWDHRY

Do not Muse
Do not Moan
Over the Past
Which is gone
Into the By-gone
Why dream to be born again?
To re-live
Without Blemish
Without the past mistakes
It is not possible
Because
We will commit other mistakes
If not the same
We are a tool
In the Hands of Destiny
One can be born 'Poor'
One can be born 'Lame'
Mend it
If you can
As I have done
Otherwise
Be wise
Accept it
Surrender!
Unto the God's Will
You can see the light of Lights
The Inner Light
Every enlightened person
Sees that 'Illumination'
And Sings of it
Make life 'a song'
Inhale the 'Life' Breath
Rhythmically
Deeply
Smoothly
Joyously
With Fresh Air
With Fresh Thoughts
For Pleasant Today
And Pleasant Everyday.

SECTION - V

MANAGEMENT OF CHRONIC AILMENTS

Chapter - 49

MANAGEMENT OF ALCOHOLISM

"Say- Yes to Life and - No to Alcohol & Drugs."

What is Alcoholism : — A few pegs of alcoholic drinks when consumed bring cheers and festivity, but it creates its opposite effect of depression of the mind and consequent hangover next morning. But inspite of this, human beings of all races, and through all ages, have resorted to taking alcoholic drinks to drown their immediate worries and to enjoy the euphoria of being at the top of the world for some time.

But, the liver in our body is not able to metabolise more than about one peg of whisky per hour. Any excess alcohol which is not able to be metabolised by liver enters the blood stream through the lower intestines and thus reaches each and every cell of our body and in the process, each cell of our body gets dehydrated and functionally disturbed, Many cells of our body & neurons of the brain thus die, as a result, but in youth times there is enough replenishment of the new cells. And also a drink or two initially removes the inhibition in sex and makes the sex act intoxicatingly more enjoyable and playful. Thus, in youth times, an alcoholic drink acts like adding fuel to the fire, but soon this so called fire of whisky starts extinguishing the person and starts impairing the supply of blood and sex hormones to the male sex organ and as Shakespeare has aptly said, "Drink provides the desire, but it takes away the performance." Almost everyone, who drinks in excess goes through this experience and if not, he is an extra- ordinary person made of much better genetic stuff.

This alcohol which is a slow poison, can be life saver too, particularly in too cold weather when the mercury drops to freezing water temperature and below, because alcohol can provide quick Calories to heat up the shivering body, but alcohol provides only the empty calories without any vitamins or minerals and alcohol in larger quantity damages the liver, irritates the heart and damages the neurons of the brain, by starving them of oxygen, causing memory loss/damage, with prolonged use. And above all, it gives a dirty look of 'Hangover' on our face next morning. And this damage to the body/mind system is cumulative. If a person continues to consume more than 4 pegs of whisky for more than 5 years or so, then, his **drinking of alcohol becomes compulsive which we call "Alcoholism".**

And according to W.H.O., Alcoholism is one of the three major killer diseases in the world. It not only breaks up health but also shatters the family life of alcoholic addicts, and it may involve many other persons due to rash senseless driving accidents, by overdrunk persons. This happens all the year round but is particularly evident during festive seasons like Christmas and New Year.

TREATMENT OF ALCOHOLISM USING MANTRIC BREATHING:

As we know by now that mantric breathing helps us to acquire quickly and effectively the pranic energy from the cosmos. This can thus be of help to cure a person both in the acute and chronic stages of alcoholism, as seen below.

When overdrunk and face to face with stupor stage , I have saved myself by inhaling deeply and rapidly, with inhale Mantra "WANT" and exhaled the breath with Mantra "TO LIVE".

This Mantra first of all, creates the desire to "LIVE ON" in the face of imminent danger. And as Swami Vivekanand has aptly said, "Matter is Mighty but THOUGHT is Almighty"; because God has endowed only human beings with the will power, which is the greatest of all powers; as said above. Thus, Thought is our Being.

Besides, rapid exhaling with the above exhale mantra- TO LIVE" detoxifies the intestines of alcohol, as if, we are flushing out the alcohol through the exhale breath. And inhaling rapidly with the inhale breath mantra "WANT" fills our abdomen with much needed oxygen/ pranic energy to metabolise alcohol rapidly. Besides the sound word W (V) in "WANT" is the seed word for Swadhishantna Chakra in Kundalini Yoga, located about 5 cms below navel. This is almost the seat of breath and also represents water principle and the lower intestines. And it is in the lower intestines where most of the unmetabolised alcohol gets accumulated before being absorbed into the blood stream.

Thus, the inhale mantra "WANT" not only makes the breathing more effective in the intestines, abdomen, brain, supplying at a much faster rate the much needed oxygen to these vital parts affected by alcohol, but this mantric breathing also imparts vibratory sound resonance energy to them, so as to release their respective psychic energy to fight this depraved state of the body/ mind system due to excess of alcohol. And above all, the word

WAÑ yokes us with Infinity- the Super consciousness to draw in as much pranic life energy as possible to fulfill our body/conscious brain to detoxify it.

Another breathing mantra which can be of great help in detoxifying the stomach from alcohol is :-

2.   Exhale deeply with half mouth open with = FROOÑ
     Inhale deeply with   =   FRAAÑ

The word 'FR' is the combined seed word for abdomen and lungs system to breathe to their full optimal capacity; It is also useful in the nausea/ vomiting sensation which one feels after drinking.

Since liver is the most affected organ due to taking excess alcohol, we can heal it by giving it the pranic life energy by exhaling with

3.   Exhale with   =   HEAL LIVER — JEENM
     Inhale with   =   LAVARA — JAHAÑM

It is really a very very effective and rejuvenating mantra for the liver as well as for the whole body/ mind system affected by over- drinking. And this great mantra helps the alcoholists to get over the habit of alcoholism by developing their WILL Power by giving vibratory sound energy to the Swadhishtana (V) as well as Muladhara Chakra (L). Our will power thus gets strengthened with these words. And it is the will power which the alcoholists lack the most, which is very much augmented by this healing breathing mantra.

Also, the words L & V kindle the divine kundalini energy to illuminate our mind to develop control over alcoholism. The word 'R' is the seed word of Navel Chakra which stimulates the much harassed liver, the pancreas and it re-establishes all the abdominal secretions to digest food. The word 'R' also strengthens the adrenal glands - the emergency life saving gland which comes to our help when over-drunk.

The word 'H' strengthens the thyroid gland and helps to re-establish, the communication link between the body and the brain. The word HAÑ yokes us with Infinity - the superconsciousness to draw in as much pranic life energy as possible to fulfill our being to detoxify us.

The word 'M' strengthen the crown chakra, the right brain and the pineal gland to pacify the nervous system from the stress of alcoholic drinks. It comes to the rescue of over-worked left brain/ pituitary gland due to alcohol.

And a separate breathing mantra is given below to stimulate the left brain and pituitary gland, which is the master gland to boost our Immune system against the damaging effect of alcohol. For this

Inhale with	=	VARAYAHAN
Exhale with	=	NIHI — YOUREEV

This mantra stimulates the lower intestines with V, which helps to irrigate the dehydrated cells of our body/brain through blood circulation and the word R strengthen the liver and the abdomen, the word Y rejuvenates the heart, and 'H' stimulates the Thyroid gland and most important of all, the word N strengthens the left brain and the pituitary gland and the brow chakra to re-establish the shattered immune system of alcoholics. And this breathing mantra will completely rejuvenate the total body. To support it, I am suggesting the following homoeopathic medicines to help in quicker recovery from the acute effects of alcoholism.

Homoeopathic Treatment

Homoeopathic Medicines are being used increasingly to over-come not only the acute effects of alcoholism, but also its long term chronic effects. besides being of help to decrease the craving of the individual for alcohol, thus helping to get rid of the habit of alcoholism.

The most effective homoeopathic medicines for acute effects of alcoholism are (1) Nux Vomica (2) Glonoinum $(C_3 H_5 (NO_3) O_3)$ Both of these medicines in low potency provide the much needed oxygen for the starved neurons of the brain which are affected the most because of their much higher demands on oxygen. Thus for curing the acute effects of alcoholic drinks like Nausea and stupor- the initial stage of delirium of brain, give.

Nux Vomica 3x every one hour
or
Glonoinum 3x every one hour

After the patient has crossed the acutest stage, then give

Nux Vomica-3 four hourly
or
Glonoinum -3 four hourly.

And after two days, give Nux Vomica 6-Six hourly or Glonoinum 6-Six hourly.

On the first morning, after the acute stage of alcoholism has subsided by giving Nux Vomica 3x or Glonoinum 3x, give only liquid food to the patient, consisting of the following:

(1) A glass of fresh orange juice or sugar cane juice which will help the liver to recuperate by providing fructose directly plus minerals plus

vitamins, a great boon to the over-worked liver.

(2) And/or Lemon juice in water with a large spoon-ful of honey or Glucose D.

(3) A glass of butter milk made from, churning Yogurt/Curd with water and brown sugar and a pinch of common salt.

These liquid foods can be repeated as required till full recovery is achieved alongwith the above medicine, and mantric breathing.

The acute symptoms of alcoholism are taken care by Nux Vomica or Glonoinum in low potencies, when the drugs administered are in their milligram quantities to provide First Aid and immediate succour to the deranged/oxygen starved body/ mind system, followed by Nux Vomica 6, otherise the reactive effect of Nux Vomica 3x will start appearing. It is here where homoeopathy scores a greatly marked advantage over its allopathic system of medicine because in homoeopathic treatment, we can administer the more potenciazed but much smaller quantity of the same medicine only in picro-gram quantity of the original homoeopathic medicine, which completes the cure, thus, obviating the bad side effects, as in allopathic drugs, after their long use.

In chronic alcoholism, all the body/brain functions get deranged, body excretory system will also be impaired causing bleeding or blind piles. Simultaneously, all the mental faculties get impaired and even the will power to recover is lost. In this stage the patient should be advised to take homoeopathic tonics like 'Avena Sativa' or Alfa Alfa' Tonic, atleast twice daily to recuperate.

(2) Use of homoeopathic medicine 'Quercus' taken

10 drops in water three times a day takes away the abnormal craving for alcohol and it also removes some of the bad effects of chronic alcoholism later followed by Quercus 3x- four hourly.

And also, you can follow it up with Sulpur-3- three times a days. This also helps to control the craving for Alcohol.

Then, follow it up with Sulphur 30 in the morning and Nux Vomica 30 in the evening for one week, to complete the cure on pure homoeopathic principles of treating with the resonance power of the homoeopathic medicine in its 30th potency of "Like cures Like" when the drug has been highly diluted, but potenciazed to develop its Sublime power of Cure, in its infinitesimal quantity, which I call the Blessed phenomenon of "Hahnemannization".

Also, there are many more Homoeopathic medicines for treating alcoholism as given in various Homoeopathic books which I will not delve into for want of space.

And with this combined treatment -Homoeopathic as well as healing affected by the Mantric breathing, particularly by the last mantra which heals the liver in a slow and steady manner and also helps to develop the will - power, will go a long way to get over this dreaded habit of Alcoholism, provided the person desires to do so.

And before I close this chapter on ALCOHOLISM, let me say a few words how alcohol affects us in the old age. As a general rule, all the ill effects of over-intake of alcohol become much more pronounced in old age. Therefore, we must decrease the in-take of alcohol in old age. And using mantric breathing, I have got over my habit of over-drinking by developing control over my mind. Now, I have almost stopped drinking except once in a week, when I take only two pegs of whisky on a dance evening, when I let myself go in a dance party; thus getting completely intoxicated in the dance music, so much so that I become the dance and my dance becomes meditative. I continue to dance and dance, but next day the pain in my knee joints is very much enhanced. First because of too much stress of dancing on the legs; and secondly alcohol also increases the uric acid content in the body and also because the fragile bones in the old age are more brittle. However, with the help of mantric breathing and taking recourse to nutritous diet as above, I am able to recover in 24 hours which other wise would take more than 48 hours. But this is not possible without providing the nutrients to form the new cells in the body to repair the damage done to the body due to alcohol. And again when the mercury falls below 5°C in Delhi, I fall a prey to an alcoholic drink. Those days, I relish to take only one peg of brandy or cognac if I happen to get hold of it, which indeed provides warmth to the heart on a very cold night in Delhi and one large drink can indeed be life saving during severe winter nights any where. But we must always remember that too much of all good things turns into sadness, because every joy has hidden within itself a tinge of sorrow.

Chapter - 50

CURE OBESITY

Fat in our muscles is the reservior of energy, it is also the body's cushion, it is like a Bank Balance of Energy, but like all good things, too much of every thing is bad. And obesity means a 'FATSO/COUCH -- POTATO PERSONALITY', which is a complex combination of un-wise over-eating and heredity programmed into our genes.

Obesity also developes with age, because the metabolic rate of our body starts slowing down by about five percent every ten years, after the peak youth age of about 20 years. Since, mostly our food intake remains the same as a habit, our body weight starts increasing as we advance in age, for some years, and the extra calories getting stored as fat in our body. Then, accumulation of too much fat becomes a curse, as it entails an extra work for the Heart, thus, starting a chain reaction of various associated diseases in our body, particularly awkward appearance of abdominal bulge, which makes us less mobile, and leads to further accumulation of fat. Then, a time comes, when a person wants to put a stop to all this over accumulation of fat on the body. About 30% of population in an affluent country like USA is obese and almost the same percentage of affluent people in India also suffer from obesity, which thus can be called an off-shoot of affluence, except those cases, in which it may be due to some hormonal dis-order in the body.

Naturopaths advise food restriction, fasting for a few days or fasting on juices or on fruits and salads to fight the obesity as well as all other diseases. They also advise to reduce the intake of common salt, which can become the cause for retention of water in the body, causing increase in weight.

But, living on fruits and juices is something which is not easily acceptable and very difficult to adhere to for long periods, though diet restriction with balanced nutritious diet is more easily accepted, except an occasional freedom to go gay gay; otherwise, what is this life worth living for?

And one of the most natural and the best of all methods to fight obesity is to regain the depleted metabolic rate in a slow and steady manner by rejuvenating ourself, by recharging our body's life battery with pranic life energy and boost body's glandular activity by the resonant sonic power of certain healing words, in the form of breathing Mantras as follows :-

1) Inhale with   =   SARA — JAHAN

   Exhale with   =   NIHI — JEE — RISHI

The inhale mantra means - the whole universe - the total creation of God and in this, the word 'S' is the seed word for the origin of the breath located about mid-way between the Navel and the bottom of the spine. It also represents the basic sex chakra i.e. Muladhara Chakra which stands for earth principle and gives power to the legs. The word 'S' also represents Swadhishtana Chakra which represents water principle, strengthens the ovaries, and the lower instestines. It also kindles the divine kundalini to take it alongwith breath to the next chakra (ii) called Navel/ Manipur Chakra/ Solar plexus for which the seed word is 'R' which helps to give fire power to digest the food, by helping to activate the abdominal glands including pancreatic glands for proper assimilation of glycogen.

(iii) The words F/J/Ya are the seed words for lungs/heart chakra, these help the heart for proper blood circulation and the lungs to do optimum breathing.

(iv) The word H is the seed word for Vishudha/ throat chakra, this activites the Thyroid gland which regulates Carbohydrate and fat metabolism in the body, by helping to secrete proper quantity of its hormone 'Thyroxine'. The word H also helps to re-establish the communication link between the lower body and the brain which begins to sap with old age with consequent accumulation of fat and salt deposits in the blood arteries.

v) The word 'N' is the seed word for brow chakra and it strenghtns the left brain, and the pituitary master gland, to boost our immunity.

It is this mind which revels in enjoying all the sense pleasures and to fight obesity, we must develop control over our taste sense, to control eating too much of tasty and delicious snacks. And once we get determined to control our obesity, over - eating etc gets subordinated to it, because thought is our being. And it is common knowledge that no method of obesity control will succeed if we continue to gulp food indiscriminately beyond our biological needs. But, above all, it is the Aroma of good food which prompts the mind to enjoy to its brim, to its full satisfaction. But it is the intelligence which is the charioteer of our mind which will help us to control this uncontrolled craving which is the root cause of all our troubles in this world including over-eating and the resultant obesity.

Thus, inhale by speaking the mantra inwardly, smoothly, rhythmically and non-violently, the breath moving alongwith our thought as we breathe in. Inhale/exhale with the help of the above mantra for atleast 5 to 10 minutes in the morning as well as in the evening and slowly and **steadily** we will start feeling totally rejuvenated with a glow on our face. And soon in a year or so, it will help us to look 15 to 20 years younger than our chronological age, and lighter in weight by about five kg. Thus, Hurray, we have won the battle of the bulge. We can also substitute another breathing mantra with good benefits.

2. Exhale with   =   PHROOOOÑ
    Inhale with   =   PHRAAÑ

We should first exhale with above mantra 'phroooñ', by keeping half the mouth open. This will exhale out the accumulated gas in our stomach/ abdomen, thus cleansing the abdomen before it is, filled in by inhaling with 'Phraaaañ'. While exhaling with the mantra 'phrooooñ', we simultaniously shrink in the abdomen to help the collected abdominal gases to get phrooed out plus it gives exercise to all the abdominal organs including the pancreas, the liver and the spleen and the intestines - the total abdomen getting to and fro vibratory exercise, because the abdomen returns to normal when we inhale with the word phraaaañ. The word 'PHR' is the combined seed word for the lungs (PH) and abdomen (R) and is thus very helpful in energizing our lungs/abdomen system. Do it for 10 to 30 times as convenient. We can do phrooooñ/ phraaaañ quickly in rapid succession. Though this is some- what violent, but some violence becomes necessary to shed off the fat from the abdomen.

3. Another very suggestive inhale/exhale mantra is given to improve the action of the liver to fight obesity

<pre>
Exhale with   =   IMPROVE LIVER
Inhale with   =   LAVARA — PRAMMA
</pre>

We can supplement the above breathing regime with the following steps necesary for achieving quicker results in fighting the battle of the bulge.

a) Have a sun-bath daily for about 10 minutes or so as it suits you.

This will improve the metabolism and absorption of calcium in the body. If you are near the sea-beach, roll yourself on the hot sun-baked sand for some time, playfully and then have a dip in the sea with the sea waves splashing against your body to charge it up and massage it lovingly.

b) When stressed, warm your both feet in luke-warm water for about 10 minutes. This will improve circulation in the body and melt away the fat, this is particularly good in winter season.

c) Take a hot/cold bath daily, It will improve circulation of blood.

d) Enjoy your daily walk for 45 minutes or so, there is no better natural aerobic exercise than walking. It will also help to shed the extra fat from the abdomen.

e) In an office with sedentary type of job, it would

be good practice to stand up and to move around for a minute or two every one hour to give movement to our legs/mind system. This re-establishes the communication between the legs and the brain through the spine and also gives a dynamism to the sleeping metabolism.

f) If you can make the habit of dancing regularly in the evening with 2 to 4 dance nos; this is the best method to shed extra weight. Besides giving movement to the whole body, it elevates our spirits. you can also dance with the musical cha-cha breathing mantra given in this book. This dance mantra can be called the capsule of obesity reduction.

g) Another easy way to increase the heat to digest food and thereby shed body fat/weight is to sleep for about first twenty minutes by lying on the left side of the abdomen, in order to make the right nostil open up for breathing. This right nostril breath is called the sun (hot) breath which heats the body to digest the food.

h) For similar purpose, we can drink a glass of very luke-warm water every two hours in a cold season. This boosts metabolism and helps to reduce the weight/fat in our body.

Recently, there is a good news for obese people, that scientists in USA have discovered the protein called Leptin which helps to reduce about 30% of body-fat but it is yet to be proved that this hormone is safe.

Let me stress here, like Leptin, all other hormones, secreted by various glands in our body are all one type of the protein or the other. Similarly, the hormone 'Thyroxine' secreted by

Thyroid, useful for Fat & Carbohydrate metabolism is a protein containing iodine in its structure, and hence the great importance of providing balanced nutrition of proteins, fats, carbohydrates, vitamins and minerals in their proper quantities within the bio-logical needs of our body. Thus, we are now well prepared and equipped to fight this most difficult battle of the obesity. Buck up.

OM — TAT — SAT

Chapter - 51

REMOVE CONSTIPATION
MANTRA
MOVE - WELL

If our bowels move well, that is the greatest feeling of well being for us. It is the best Good Morning to us, from Nature, otherwise the whole day is miserable. Some people get habituated to take chemical laxatives which, though work fast, but ultimately weaken the intestines, resulting in chronic constipation.

Why the constipation results? because the linings of the intestines become dry and inelastic and are not properly irrigated with water and also the intestines are not getting the pranic life energy to carry on the life processes in the cells of the intestines. Each cell of our body contains water-both inside and outside that cell structure separated by a membrane and the ionic concentrations of sodium, potassium, magnesium and calcium in the cell electrolytes maintain a potential gradient of ionic currents for life processes to carry on. (See Chapter on water).

Thus, the first and the foremost method to remove constipation is to take plenty of water daily i.e., 5 to 6 glasses of water, about 1.5 litres of water daily. Start your day with a glass of water or take a glass of luke warm water with juice of one lemon and one spoon-ful of honey. This will greatly help in easing out stool from the bowels and remove constipation. If it does not work, we can stimulate

241

the lower intestines with its seed word 'V'.

1.	Exhale with	MOVE WELL
	Inhale with	LAVVAM
2.	Exhale with	MOVE — OUT
	Inhale with	VAMANT
3.	Exhale with	PUSH — IT/ PUSH — SHIT
	Inhale with	SHAPANT

Instead of using the inhale mantra, we can exhale rapidly with any one of the above three exhale mantras silently and then inhale deeply. Rapid exhalation with the mantra and inhalation will also give physical movements at the site of bowels with 'V' and also activate it with pranic life energy.

Also, walking is the most natural way to give movement to the lower intestines. Make walking a habit. Atleast walk for 30 minutes in the morning and go for slow walk for five to ten minutes after dinner, if possible, and if you continue to take six glasses of water daily, it will help greatly in removing constipation.

To provide the salts of sodium and potassium, calcium and magnesium and sulphur etc. to nourish the dead cells of the intestines, we must take fresh seasonal fruits and vegetable salad at lunch time consisting of i) Lettuce, ii) Tomato iii) Cabbage iv) Raw Onion, alongwith lemon sprinkled with comon salt (iodised), black pepper and cumin

Also take two slices of washed dried figs with a glass of water. This will enliven the intestines by providing the proper nutrients and fibre; and help to remove constipation.

Take a spoonful of triphla powder with slighly

luke warm water while going to bed. You can also take it with a glass of hot milk. This will enliven the intestines by providing alkanity and the proper nutrients. In case of obstinate constipation, take a table spoonful of wheat bran to provide the fibre. This is a sure physical treatment to shield the intestines from the acids/irritants etc. Alcoholic drinks cause irritation and dryness in the intestines. Fibre-the outer skin of grains, though not digestible but protects the intestines and helps in elimination of stool. Taking two oranges a day will also help in removing the constipation and last, but not the least the surest way to remove constipation is to take two bananas dipped in olive oil, which will surely help to remove constipation.

Chapter - 52

CURE BRONCHIAL ASTHMA

In bronchial asthma, there is spasmodic inflammation of airways in the lungs, the air passages get narrowed and thereby cause choking sensation alongwith wheezing and cough. When the attack is severe, immediately call a doctor. The treatment usually given by doctors consists in administering bronchodilators either by mouth or inhalation (ii) and using antibiotics and corticosteroids to subdue the inflamation in the lung linings. Care should be taken to keep the living environment pollution free.

But to cure asthmatic patients permanently, we have to fortify his/ her immune system and this is quite possible to achieve by using breathing with the healing words as follows :-

(1) The first breathing mantra is BRONCH (BRANK) and the word BRONK can be spoken both as inhale as well as exhale Mantra as follows :-

Inhale with   =   BRANK
Exhale with   =   BROONK

The speciality of this breathing Mantra is that the word 'BR' helps to breath from the lungs with 'B' and also from the abdomen with 'R' which is indeed very desirable for the asthmatic patients because the lungs airways being inflammed and narrow, we must supplement breathing from the abdomen.

The word 'R' is the seed word for Navel chakra/ Solar plexus, it strengthens the liver, the abdominal

244

glands and the Pancreas for proper digestion of food and assimilation of glycogen to give FIRE to our body. The word 'R' also stimulates the adrenal gland which is our body's emergency gland to meet the demand of Asthmatic patients. Other body glands which need to be stimulated for the asthmatic patients are Thyroid and Parathyroid glands which are strengthened by the seed word 'H' and above all the pituitary gland which is the master gland controlling the total glandular activity of our body, that is why pituitary gland is called "The master of the endocrine orchestra : and the pituitary gland is stimulated by 'N' - the seed word of Brow Chakra. Thus, the words R, H, N and any one of the words which help breathing apparatus are B, BH, P, PH, etc.

Thus, the simplest Mantra for asthmatic patient is :

(2) Inhale with   =   BRAHAN
    Exhale with   =   NIHIBREE

(3) Inhale with   =   BRAHANANTH
    Exhale with   =   NEEHI — BREATHE

In the breathing Mantra no 3, only the word TH has been added which helps in the mouth action of breathing, plus also strengthens the taste gland to help in the digestion of starches etc. and also stimulates the sense endings of our brain to develop control over the mind and breathing action.

(4) And a sure - shot breathing Mantra to cure asthmatic patients is :-

Inhale with   =   SHFA — BRAHAMAN
Exhale with   =   MIBHI — FRESHEN

The word 'BRAHAMAN' in Sanskrit/ Hindi language means God and the word 'SHFA' means health-giving. Thus in the Inhale Mantra, we are invoking the God to heal us.

In this inhale mantra, the breathing apparatus is supplemented in a three-fold manner :

(i) The word Sh helps to breathe, from the origin of the breath about 7 cm below navel. The word 'SH' also kindles the divine 'Kundalini' energy to move upward to illuminate and cure our body/mind system.

(ii) The word Ph or 'F' is the seed word for breathing from the lungs, it stimulates the lungs to breathe more efficiently.

(iii) The action of the word BRA & H has already been explained The word BRA helps to breathe both from the abdomen and the lungs.

(iv) And the word H also helps to breathe from the lungs/throat besides stimulating the Thyroid & Parathyroid glands.

(v) The word 'M' is the seed word of Crown Chakra, it strengthens the right-brain, the mind and the pineal gland, which is a pacifying gland.

(vi) And the word 'N' is the seed word for Brow Chakra which by it resonant sonic energy strengthens the left brain, the eye sight and the pituitary gland to boost our immune system so that we can fight the invading infection. Thus, it is a complete body/mind rejuvenating mantra to boost our total body immune system.

Inhale/exhale with any of the above mantras, by speaking the breathing mantra inwardly, silently, smoothly, slowly and rhythmically, to simulate the natural breathing without causing any violence to the already strained breathing system of asthmatic patient. Since the breathing mantras help us to breathe totally and efficiently, these fulfil our BEING with oxygen/pranic life energy besides stimulating various endocrine glands in our body to strengthen our total immune system. Thus, inhale/exhale with above breathing mantras for five to ten minutes in the morning and five to ten minutes in the evening but convenience is the watch word. Slowly, the time of breathing with the mantras can be increased but take care to select a pollution free environment for breathing with these mantras. This is an essential condition. This is to be supplemented by light nourishing diet suitable for asthmatic patient like tomato/vegetable/chicken soups and boiled/steamed vegetables etc as advised by the doctor.

So doing, slowly and steadily, the frequency of asthmatic attacks will become much less and then ultimately you will be able to completely get rid of bronchial asthma. So powerful and potent are these healing breathing mantras.

Last but not the least, gargling with a dilute luke warm solution of potash alum ($K_2 So_4 Al_2 So_4$ 24 H_2O) will help to subdue inflammation and hoarseness in the throat, thus giving great relief to asthmatic patients. Potash alum also helps to form new tissues to cure asthmatic patients.

Smoking and alcoholic drinks should be avoided alongwith fried and greasy foods. The stomach should always be kept at least 1/3rd empty, for that, we must never resort to over-eating. Honey is soothing for the asthmatic patients and one spoon of honey mixed with one spoonful of ginger juice is good expectorant and helps to relieve cough.

Chapter - 53

CURE CERVICAL SPONDYLITIS
THE MANTRA
'SAHAM'

Cervical spondylitis is a common ailment these days particularly amongst desk workers i.e. persons working for long hours on computer screens, typing machines, reading for long hours with neck bent. Also with age, the neck blood arteries get semi-clogged with waxy matter and other salt deposits, thus decreasing the supply of blood to the brain; which results in the development of pain in the cervical region of the spine and upwards in the brain. In acute stage of spondylitis pain, one must consult the personal physician. Once the disease has been diagnosed and the acute pain stage relieved, one can get rid of cervical spondylitis permanently by inhaling/exhaling with the breathing mantras as follows, mounting a two fold attack on the disease in the most natural fashion (i) to provide pranic life energy to the neck muscles by proper breathing (ii) To strengthen the glandular system of our body, with the resonant sonic vibration of certain healing words, And the word 'H' is the cure Word for cervical spondylitis as it is the seed word for Vishudha/ Throat Chakra and it helps to strengthen the Thyroid gland which in turn helps the carbohydrates and fat metabolism in our body and thus also helping to remove fatty deposits from the cervical region and the oxygenated blood replete with pranic life energy scavenges the salty deposits away.

1) Thus Inhale with = AAHHAAÑ
   Exhale with = OOHHOOÑ

The word H also helps to re-establish the communication link between the lower body and the brain, through the cervical region of the spine. That is why, the thyroid gland is called the watchman between the brain and the lower body.

2) And we can move the pranic life energy through the throat (H) to the crown of the Head with its seed word M, thus strengthening the right brain and the soothing pineal gland.

Inhale with = AAHHAAMMMM
Exhale with = MIHHOOO or MEEHHEEE

The word 'Ahham' in Sanskrit language- the mother of Hindi language means - I AM

3) In order to make the breath start from its natural origin in our body, we make use of the seed word S or SH for breath start. Both the words S, and the breath originate about 7 cms below Navel in our body.

Thus Inhale with = SAHHAMMMM
Exhale with = MIHHISH

4) We can fortify the healing effect of the above mantra, by including in it word Y or J- the seed words for Heart chakra. It strengthens the heart as well as imparts compassion to the Heart, the main characteristic of a Human Kind. Also, we can include the word R, which is the seed word for Manipur/ Navel Chakra or Solar Plexus. It represents Fire principle and helps to release the proper digestive juices, enzymes and hormones for proper assimilation of food.

Thus Inhale with =   SARA-YAH-HAM
Exhale with   =   MIHI-JEE-RISHI

This mantra will also benefit obese persons to shed their fat and extra weight with the help of healing words H & R.

5) In the above mantra, we have forgotten to energize the left brain and the eyes and the conscious sense organs for which the seed word is N.

Thus Inhale with =   SAHHAN

Exhale with   =   NIHHEESH

Thus, inhale/exhale with the above five mantras for one minute each, by speaking the mantra inwardly, softly and rhythmically, and as non-violently as possible to simulate the natural breathing as nearly as possible, and repeat it for five minutes in the evening daily, then I am sure, persons will never suffer from spondylitis and those suffering from this ailment will also benefit from it greatly but they should also supplement it with some neck exercises as follows:

(i) Move neck slowly without any jerk to the extreme right while inhaling with the mantra PAHAÑ and exhale with HIPPIEÑ, while bringing the neck back to middle position. Now move your neck to the extreme left, while inhaling with PAHAÑ & then exhaling with HIPPEEÑ, while bringing the neck from extreme left position back to the middle normal position. Do it for ten times or as convenient.

ii) Similarly lower your neck to its lowest position in the front, then move up your neck while inhaling with the mantra PAHAÑ and exhale with HIPPEEÑ while bringing the neck down.

Do it ten times or as convenient. After the exercise, stop and watch the movement of the on-rush of bio-energy currents in the neck and the brain and the hands. This will open up the partial cloggings in the neck blood arteries, thus alleviating the spondylitis problem.

(iii) Another beautiful exercise which can benefit greatly the spondylitis patients is to raise up and bring down the hands alternately as in natural walking, with this precaution. First observe, which one of your noses is breathing better. If the right nose (sun or hot breath) is flowing more easily, then raise your right hand up first. This will help to breathe from the right nostirl better, so as to be in tune with Nature.

(iv) Doctors usually advise the patient suffering from cervical spondylitis to sleep on the hard bed, with very thin pillow or no pillow at all, in order to facilitate the blood flow to the brain.

Breathing with the above mantras is the most natural method to re-establish the communication channels in the cervical spine region, thus affecting a permanent and lasting cure for cervical spondylitis.

OM TAT SAT (AMEEN)

Chapter - 54

MANAGEMENT OF BACK ACHE

Backache is one of the most common ailments these days. This is due to over-stressing the back due to bad posture, car driving for long hours and in the women due to child birth and associated infection in the uterus, causing strain on the muscles and ligaments of the lumbar region of the spine

In case of acute pain, bed rest alongwith pain killers/anti inflammatory drugs is a must (consult your physician) for a few days and then we can use the power of healing words to start curing the backache problem permanently. The word V is the seed word for lumbar region of the spine and the ovary and the lower intestines which help in the assimilation of digested food in the blood as well as in the elimination processes of the stool, etc. :-

1. Exhale with   =   JUVENATE
    Inhale with   =   VAJATAN

The above mantra rejuvenates the lumbar region with 'V' and the heart with the word 'J' and the word N - the seed word for brow chakra strengthens the left brain; and pituitary gland which is known to be the Director of total endocrine activity in our body to boost our total immune system against infection thus saving us against. repeated backache on the slightest cause.

2. In order to strengthen the total spine, we stimulate the thoracic region of the spine with

'Y' & 'R' and the cervical region of the spine with 'H' - this re-establishes the communion between the brain and the total spine.

(2) Inhale with   =   VARAYAHAN
    Exhale with   =   NIHI — YOUREEV

This mantra will completely rejuventate the total spine. If alongwith backache, there is also sciatica pain extending upto the thighs, then we strengthen the legs with L the seed word for MULADHARA CHAKRA.

3.   Exhale with   =   IMPROVE — LEG — COM MUNION
     Inhale with   =   LAVAPRAGA — KAMMANAN

                  OR

4.   Exhale with   =   IMPROVE ILLIAC — COM MUNION
     Inhale with   =   ALLA — VAPRA KAMANAN

The above two mantras are indeed very very potent to rejuvenate the total body/mind system and to cure us of backache as well as sciatica problem. This mantra helps to re-establish the supremacy of our mind over body by setting up communications between various parts of our brain.

In case of slipped disc, physio-therapy or surgical intervention may become necessary.

Last but not the least, the mantra - 'Improving' is very effective in improving backache problems :-

5.   Exhale with   =   IMPROVING
     Inhale with   =   VAPRAMMANG

This very suggestive mantra is indeed very very helpful in removing the backache.

Chapter - 55

CURE DIABETES

MANTRA
INTERIOR/ARRADHNA

'R' is the seed word for curing diabetes, because it stimulates the pancreas, with its resonant sonic vibrations, and the common word, MIRROR gives double stress on the word 'R' and is thus aptly suited for stimulating the pancreas

1. Exhale with   =   MIRROR
    Inhale with   =   ARRAM

And the word 'M' is the seed word for crown chakra which stimulates the right brain and the pineal gland. But to control diabetes, we require to stimulate with N - the seed word of brow chakra, which strengthens the pituitary gland which directs and controls the secretions of all other body glands including the pancreas, therefore, a more suitable breathing mantra for controlling diabetes is NIRROR.

2. Exhale with   =   NIRROR
    Inhale with   =   ARRAN

Also, let us stimulate the salivary glands with its seed word T which help in predigestion of food, this is necessary so that, pancreas don't get overloaded. Since the word T stimulates the soft palate in the mouth which because of its proximity to pituitary gland is able to stimulate it with the resonant sonic vibrations of T.

3. Thus exhale with =   TIRROR
    Inhale with   =   ARRANT

Also let us stimulate the Thyroid gland which helps in fats/carbohydrate metabolism to help the pancreas.

4. Thus exhale with = HIRROR
    Inhale with   = ARRAHHAÑ

Just as overdrinking of alcoholic drinks damages the liver, similarly overconsumption of white sugar and over-eating beyond the caloric needs of our body damages the pancreas, because of its over activity. The pancreas secrete the hormone insulin which helps to assimilate glycogen in our body. When the pancreas get some-what damaged and don't secrete the hormone insulin in sufficient quantity, sugar is eliminated in the urine when its level rises in blood to 180 mg / 100 cc while the normal level of sugar in blood is 80 - 120 mg/100 cc of blood. The diabetes can cause many complications like the hardening of blood arteries of heart/brain/kidneys/retina of the eye etc. and also it impairs circulation of blood to the extent that it may cause gangrene in the feet and fingers. Such are the horrible effects of diabetes, if not treated in time. Too less/much of sugar in the blood can also result in diabetic coma. Therefore, we must take steps to prevent diabetes, by restricting the intake of sugars, and too much calories in foods and instead take more of fresh seasonal fruits and raw vegetables in salads and also lead a less sedentary life by making it a habit to walk at least 40 minutes every day and after the walk, give physical exercise to the pancreas with the following breathing mantra :-

5. Exhale with   = PHROOÑ
    Inhale with   = PHRAAÑ

We have to inhale/exhale with the above mantra by keeping the mouth half open. While exhaling with the mantra 'phrooñ', contract the abdominal muscles inside towards the spine and exhale out completely from the lungs and the abdomen forcefully; as if you are flushing out completely the abdomen. Then inhale deeply with half mouth open with 'Phraañ' and also simultaneously bring back the abdominal muscles back to normal position. Thus, inhaling/exhaling with the above mantra rapidly will give exercise to the total abdominal muscles including the pancreas to give them aerobic movement. Do it as long as it is convenient. Then, rest a while and re-do the above breathing mantra exercise but convenience is the watch word, And ultimately this breathing mantra will bring a new shine on the face, by yoking us with Infinity with 'Ñ' and also fulfilling the lungs with PH. Thus, we shall also provide pranic life energy to the pancreas to restore them to normal healthy action.

6. The mantra which combines all the above healing words is :-

Inhale with = SHRAPHAN
Exhale with = FREESH — SHEEN

This mantra will indeed a give fresh shine on our face, by rejuvenating the pancreas, the liver, the lungs, the pituitary gland and above all by kindling the divine kundalini energy with the seed word-SH.

Herbal Treatment

1. The seeds of fruit of SYZYGIUM Jambolanum tree, grown in India (Jamun Tree) which has an edible blue juicy fruit, the powdered stone seeds of which is a sure remedy to cure diabetes, taking one tea spoonful, three times

a day. Also a homoeopathic tincture of this seed is available as SYZYGIUM IX which definitely helps to remove sugar from the urine.

2. Juice of Bitter gourd (Momordica Charantia) is also very helpful in the management of Diabetes.

3. Also Fenugreek seeds (Hindi, name Methi) are very useful in the management of Diabetes. A spoonful of powdered fenugreek seeds or Syzygium seeds will help a great deal to provide the necessary nutrients to the pancreas.

4. The Biochemic salts useful for helping diabetic patient are (i) Natrum Sulph 6x (ii) Natrum Phos 6x to metabolise lactic acid and Schussler also suggests calcarea sulph 6x alongwith kalisulph 6x for further remedial action.

Management of Diabetes with Combination Therapy

I myself belong to a diabetic family and I have sweet teeth, I am fond of sweets and my usual blood sugar level is 160 mg/100cc. which is on the higher side, but during Mango season, it shoots upto 250 mg/100cc and I usually bring it down by taking one seed of fresh Syzygium along with the 20 or 30 of these juicy fruits.

Also when I am mentally tired and stressed, after long sessions of intensive study or writing this book, I feed myself with plentiful honey or glucose or raisins/mangoes if in season etc; this brings about a spurt in sugar level, because during stress, the sympathetic nervous system directs the oxygen supply to the brain to save itself, while it makes the digestive system, the sex organs and the pancreas to wait. As a result, the pancreas are starved of oxygen, the sugar level rises; I control it judiciously by :-

I. Restricting the balanced diet to 1800 K Calories at my present age of 66½ years, dividing these calories as follows :-

(i)   Bed Tea + Evening Tea with = 150K calories with one/two biscuits or one banana etc.

(ii) Breakfast   =   450 K calories

(iii) Lunch   =   600 K calories

(iv) Evening Snack   =   300 K calories

(v)   A light Dinner   =   300 K calories

Now I shall throw some light on a typical evening snack I take to give a balanced variety to it during the week :-

(a) A bowl of mixed seasonal fruits plus 200 CC of milk - 2 days

(b) An omellette (two eggs Omellette size) made out of black gram flour made spicy and tasty by adding one little green chilly, onion, corriander leaves etc. followed by hot 200 CC of milk — 2 days. As for eggs, I consume three eggs a week only at breakfast with two cloves of garlic to look after the naughty cholesterol.

(c) A mixture of 50 gms of popped whole grains mixed as follows :-

    (i)   Popcorns popped up by popping them without butter or fat   -   15 gms

    (ii) Black grams popped up   -   15 gms

    (iii) Whole rice popped up   -   10 gms

    (iv) Pea nuts   -   10 gms

Sprinkled with about a few drops of mustard oil or olive oil, green chillies, finely chopped onion, assorted salts etc. followed by a hot cup of 200 CC of Milk - 2 days.

(d) A freelance evening snack on sunday.

II. Controlling diabetes by walking and exercise regime.

(i) I enjoy to go for a walk for about 40 minutes in the morning and then do assorted exercises for 10 minutes to give movement to various parts alongwith breathing mantras.

III. Controlling Diabetes by Mantric breathing

I use the following seed mantra for controlling diabetes by smooth and non-violent inhaling/ exhaling silently for 10 minutes :-

Inhale with	=	ARRAYAHAN
Exhale with	=	NIHI YOURIR

I focus my thought on the Navel/pancreas at the word 'R' in the above inhale/exhale mantra. Double stress has been given on the word 'R' for making it an effective mantra for diabetic control. On certain days, for a change, I use the equally effective seed mantra for eradicating the diabetes.

Inhale with	=	ARRADHNA
Exhale with	=	INTERIOR

IV. I take a spoonful of herbal powder of Fenugreek seeds etc. as given above; after breakfast, along with water.

Thus, I am able to control the diabetes and bring its level down to 140 mg/100 CC and as we know, life is a judicious combination of variety to make it spicy and enjoyable and even to control the diabetes or any other disease, we need to combine herbal/medicinal treatment, alongwith nutritious diet plus a dose of mantric breathing for 10 minutes to stimulate the Endocrine hormonal system of our body. As correctly said by Hippocrates long back "Food is our Medicine". This combination therapy brings about much quicker recovery.

Chapter - 56

MANAGEMENT OF PARKINSON'S AND ALZHEIMER'S DISEASES

MANTRA
"HEY! YOU WILL RECOMMUNICATE"

How sad we feel when the first wrinkles appear on our face. These wrinkles indirectly indicate the development of many more wrinkles in our brain's intercommunication channels. It also indicates the inadequate supply of oxygen/glycogen/nutrients to our brain/memory system. Our brain's demand on oxygen is about nine fold more than other organ of the body. Though, we take immediate steps to apply anti wrinkles cream on our face and also get face lifts done through Beauticians, but we totally ignore to feed or care for the brain. Instead, we continue to overload our eyes/brain system. And, this ultimately over-stretches our brains's neurological system, resulting in the depletion of neuron density in our brain, which, if continued over long periods, without proper nutrition and rest, starts disrupting the communication links in the brain/memory system. This is the beginning of old age diseases like Parkinson's disease and Alzheimer's disease.

PARKINSON'S DISEASE :- Slow gait in old people is a common sight. This is the beginning of the Parkinson's disease, which, if not arrested well in time, progresses slowly to cause tremors in hands/ legs and it further leads to the rigidity of leg muscles, with complete disability in walking. Then,

261

the Doctors describe it a neurological disorder when the motor control in the brain gets particularly affected and the production of a chemical called dopamin stops or becomes less in the brain. This dopamin helps to transmit nerve messages.

But, do not despair - our body/mind system has the infinite capacity to repair itself provided we re-link our brain/body system with the superconsciousness through the medium of breath by supplying the required pranic life energy.

Another ray of hope comes from the findings of enlightened Hindu sages who observed conglomerates of seven energy centres called chakras or wheels of Energy Flow which control and stimulate the action of various body glands. These glands secrete various hormones in the blood stream to boost our immune system and help in body's metabolism, growth. In our body, each of this energy centre gets resonated with the sound energy of certain seed words given a little later here.

Some of the simple breathing healing mantras to stimulate various sections of the brain are given below using seed words K, KH, G, N, M, T, D & Ñ :-

Inhale with

1. SAHANK
2. SAHANKH
3. SAHANG
4. SAHHAN
5. SAHHAM
6. SAHHANT
7. SAHHAND
8. SAHHAÑ

Exhale with

1. KIHHISH
2. KHIHHISH
3. GIHHISH
4. NIHHISH
5. MIHHISH
6. TIHHISH
7. DIHHISH
8. HOOSHIEÑ

And a total body/brain/memory rejuvenating mantra is given below.

9. Exhale with = Hey! You will Recommunicate.
   Inhale with = Alla- Vara-Yaha-Kamanakant.

This inhale mantra is the mirror image of the very suggestive exhale mantra and this inhale mantra is so heal - some, because it traverses and gives resonant sonic energy to all the seven chakras or conglomerates of energy centres as follows :-

(i) 'L' is the seed word for Basic/sex/muladhara chakra, located between the bottom of the spine and the genital organ. It represents earth principle, strengthens sex organ and the legs. The word 'L' also helps to illuminate our mind, as the word 'L' helps to kindle the kundalini to move up to the crown chakra.

(ii) 'V' is the seed word for ovary/swadhishtana chakra, it represents water principle, strengthens the ovaries and helps the lower intestines to absorb the digested food in the blood stream etc.

(iii) 'R' is the seed word for Navel/ Manipur chakra/ solar plexus which represents the Fire principle and helps in the assimilation of food. It stimulates the liver, the pancreas and all the abdominal secretions for proper digestion of food. It also stimulates the life saving Adrenal gland.

(iv) 'Y' is the seed word for heart chakra, it helps to strengthen the heart's action and also helps in optimal breathing through the lungs alongwith the word 'H'.

(v) 'H' is the seed word for Throat/ Vishudha

chakra which helps to control the carbohydrate/ fat metabolism by strengthening the thyroid gland. The word 'H' also helps to improve the communication in the cervical region.

(vi) The word 'N' is the seed word for "Brow Chakra". It strengthens the left brain and the pituitary master gland.

(vii) The word 'M' is the seed word for the Crown Chakra, it strengthens the right brain and the pineal gland which releases the brain soothing hormone called Melatonin.

(viii) And the words K, KH, G, help to strengthen various sense endings in the brain and the word T strengthens the taste glands and the gums of the teeth. as well as it stimulates the pituitary gland to some extent

Here, I salute the Linguists of English language, who knew the power and origin of the words as seen from the word - COMMUNICATE spoken as KOMMUNIKATE. This is a beautiful word which helps to re-establish communication between various conscious sense endings in the brain/memory system. These words i.e. (a) COMMUNICATE (b) COMMUNION and (c) COMMUNICATING used below in breathing mantras is my greatest discovery to treat people suffering from Parkinson's and Alzheimer's diseases.

First, the mantra no. 9 cures by it hypnotic suggestive power (2) Secondly, this inhale mantra - helps to breathe in right from the legs upto the crown of our head, because, it traverses all the seven energy chakras as given above i.e. L, V, R, Y, H, N, M and more than that (3) It sets up communication between various SENSE ENDINGS in the brain by the words i.e. K, M, T, N by the inhale word KAMANAKANT and its exhale counterpart - Kummunikate supplying pranic life energy **TO AND FRO** in various Brain Sections.

Thus, this breathing mantra is our ultimate weapon in curing the chronic old age diseases like Parkinson's and Alzheimer's diseases. The use of the above breathing mantra will first stop the progression of the disease and then slowly and steadily over a period of a few months, it will bring about reversal of the disease, by fortifying our immune system by strengthening our total glandular activity in our body/mind system.

It also helps to re-establish communication links in the brain/memory system to put the mind in a commanding position as originally ordained by God. Of course, a balanced Nutrition alongwith un-polluted environment is a must.

Inhale/exhale with the above mantra, by speaking the mantra inwardly, smoothly, rhythmically and as non-violently as possible, so as to simulate the natural breathing as nearly as possible. Do it for ten minutes in the morning as well as for ten minutes in the evening and in a few weeks time, one will start experiencing the on-rush of bio-energy blissful currents in the brain/hands etc. But for first one week, let us inhale/exhale with simple breathing mantras no 1 to 8, ten times each and then use the very potent mantra no 9 and, this breathing mantra no 9 is the Fountain of our Health and the Foundation to re-build the shattered immune system of an ailing person who will definitely recover provided he/she has the DESIRE TO LIVE ON and CURE HIM/HERSELF.

The above breathing mantra no 9 is however a

multi-stage breathing mantra and may not be easy to breathe with, particularly for a beginner. I have formulated a set of simpler but very suggestive mantras both for benefiting the hands and the legs separately as given below :-

MANTRAS FOR HANDS COMMUNION

10. Exhale with   = MOVE HAND SPOKEN AS Moovvihhand for continuous exhalation.

    Inhale with   = VAHHAMMAND

11. Exhale with   = IMPROVE HAND spoken as Improvih-hand.

    Inhale with   = VAPRAHAMAND

12. Exhale with   = IMPROVE HAND COMMUNION

and then inhale deeply making your thought move alongwith your breath as it starts from the bottom of the spine upwards into the crown of the head, OR

    Inhale with   = VAPRA-HA-KAMANAKAND

MANTRAS FOR LEGS COMMUNION :-

13. Exhale with   MOVE-LEG

    Inhale with   LAVAGGAM

14. Exhale with   IMPROVE LEG

    Inhale with   LAVA-PRAMMANG

15. Exhale with   IMPROVE LEG COMMUNION

    Then inhale deeply OR

    Inhale with   ALLAVA-PRAGA-KAMANAN

The inhale Mantra is a mirror image of the exhale Mantra.

16. Exhale with   IMPROVE-ILLIAC-COMMUNION
      Inhale with   ALLAVA-PRA-KAMANAN

ALZHEIMER'S Disease Now, we turn our attention to special mantras for the first stage of the Alzheimer's disease in which there is a steady loss of memory, particularly recent memory and then progresses to degenerate the memory /brain system that one is not able to recognise people - even close relatives. Then the afflicted person becomes a complete burden on society and hence we must find its cure. This happens because our human memory has a finite capacity to store and every moment, except during sleep, new data are being poured in by our various sense organs, the old data has to yield place to new, plus the total neuron population also declines with age as said earlier, thus, decreasing our total memory storage capacity. This affects the permanence of our recent memory. Just like Parkinson's disease, in Alzhiemer's disease also, the interneuron transmission between various sense endings in the brain and the memory gets impaired and partially snapped with time as the disease progresses. This also happens because brain has no reserve stock of energy like some other parts of our body, particularly muscles, which store fat as alternative stock of energy for emergency use. And the demand of brain for glycogen/oxygen/nutrients is nine fold more as said earlier. Thus, Alzhiemer's disease sets in when there is a total degeneration in our body - mind system and thus we have to regenerate the complete body/brain/memory system. For this :-

17. Exhale with   MEMORY-RELINK
      Inhale with   LARRAMAMANK

18. Exhale with   MEMORY-REALIZING
     Inhale with   LARAZAMMANG-MOM

19. Exhale with   MEMORY BRIGHTENING
     Inhale with   BRAHMA-NAMMANG

20. Exhale with   MEMORY WILL REZOOM
     Inhale with   LAVARA-ZA-MAMAM

21. Exhale with   COMMENDABLE
     Inhale with   LABA-KAMMAND (COMMAND)

22. Exhale with   MEMORY-WILL-LINK
     Enhale with   ALLAVARA-MAMMANK

23. Exhale with   MEMORY-REGAINED
     Inhale with   ARRAGA-NAMMAND

24. Exhale with   MEMORY-RE-AWAKENED
     Inhale with   AVARRA-KAMMAND (COMMAND)

25. Exhale with   YOU-RE- ILLUMINATE
     Inhale with   ALLA-RA-YA-NAMMANT

26. Exhale with   YOU-WILL-BE-COMMUNICATING
     Inhale with   LAVA-YA-BTA-KAMANAKANG

And the best of all Mantras is the 9th Mantra given earlier.

9. Exhale with   HEY-YOU WILL-RE-COMMUNI CATE OR
                  HI-YOU WILL RE-COMMUNICATE

    Inhale with   ALLAVARA-YAHA-KAMANAKANT

This Mantra No. 9 is a sure shot Mantra, what we in India call 'RAMBAN' which means an arrow shot by Lord Ram (An Incarnation of God) which can never fail and miss its target. Here our enemy is Alzhiemier's disease and Parkinson's disease and this Mantra, because of its all round rejuvenating effect on the total body/mind/memory/brain system to re-establish the communication links in the brain/memory system is our ultimate saviour.

But, these breathing Mantras can help only those persons where the senile symptoms have not advanced to such an extent that the patient can use these breathing Mantras. A large list of breathing Mantras has been coined/given to combat both the above diseases. One can use first simple mantras and then slowly practice multi-stage breathing mantras and finally the ultimate mantra at serial No. 9. This breathing Mantra because of its powerful healsome effects, will regenerate the hope to live a decent, independent, zestful life.

However, before I end this chapter I recommend the following mild exercises, which simulate our most natural walking.

a) Sit comfortably in chair or stand up, preferably with spine in an erect position. Move your right and left hands up and down alternately as in walking, when the right hand goes up, the left hand goes down and vice-versa. This will physically help to re-establish the link between the upper part of the body and the brain through the neck. After you stop the exercise, you will notice the on-rush of bioenergy blissful currents in the head and the hands. It will be, of course, better, if we first notice which one of our nose is breathing more easily. Suppose it is the right nose, then we raise the right hand first - this way, we will be in tune with Nature.

b) Sit in a chair or lie on your bed on your back and raise up the right and left legs alternately, as in walking or raise first right leg and then bring the right leg down, then raise your left leg up and bring it down. Do it alternately for

10 to 15 times as conveient. This will re-establish the spinal link in the lower end of spine.

c) Lie down on the back on a cushioned sofa. Softly give a to and fro rubbing to your total spine by rubbing it against the cushioned bed. This will strenghen the total spinal column.

d) Clap your both hands by pressing them as lovingly as possible against each other without making any sound so as not to disturb people around. Do it for 10 to 20 times as convenient. This will press and activate all the body/mind bio-energy switches present in our both hands, what is now well known all over the world as Accupressure therapy.

Exhale while folding the hands and inhale while out-stretching the hands.

PROVIDING CONGENIAL COMPANY :-

So, let us not despair. Cheer up. There is great Hope well in sight for those who can commit themselves to self cure through the above system of breathing with power of the healing words which has all the potential to cure us surely and steadily to ultimately enable us to re-enjoy life in its full splendour, because various sections of the brain will be strengthened, as memory retrieval is activated by the combined action of the same sensory route which formed it, and all the brain senses become dull and less sensitive with age including the eye-sight, hence the need to stimulate all the sense organs by the healing breathing mantras given above. Also, I must stress that some of the old persons who suffer from Alzheimer's disease shut their MIND to outside world and the corresponding stimuli. This forms the greatest impediment in memory retrieval. Thus, this negative emotional response of older people is the most difficult to correct. For that, their interest in life and the outside world has to be re-generated by very congenial and friendly company. They must regenerate HOPE to LIVE on independently, which the above breathing healing mantras will re-invoke by showing progress in the rejuvenation of all sense organs. i.e. eye sight, taste sense and above all the hunger and lust for good food - thus, proper nutrition will provide the necessary fillup to regain taste for life.

The following herbs are also very useful for management of Parkinson's and Alzheimer's diseases.

1. The herb Brahmi (Centella asiatica) enhances the memory, because it revitalises the brain cells, by increasing the protein kinase activity and new protein synthesis.

2. The herb Shankhapushpi (Convolvulus pluricaulis) is very effective brain tonic and enhances the memory and promotes deep soothing sleep.

3. Another herb called VACHA (Acorus Calamus) sharpens the memory. In fact, the powders of all the above three herbs can be mixed and a tea spoonful dose can be taken with water or mixed with honey, daily for a period of one month or so.

4. Another herbal medicine - the seeds of Kaunch (Mucuna Pruriens) is a nerve tonic. Recent research has shown that it is very effective in the treatment of Parkinson's disease.

This combination herbal therapy and breathing with healing mantras given above alongwith balanced nutritious food will definitely help the patient to live a decent independent life, without becoming a Burden on Society.

OM — TAT — SAT/AMEEN.

Chapter - 57

DEVELOP IMMUNITY AGAINST CANCER AND AIDS

Immunity is like the God in the healing process of our body. A constant war is waging between the everpresent or invading disease germs / viruses and the Immune system. As soon as our immune system becomes weak, the disease germs multiply at a fast rate to make us ill. The four mantras given below are complementary.

1. Exhale with   =   IMMUNITY — PRESERVING
   Inhale with   =   VARAZA PRATANAMMANG
2. Exhale with   =   IMMUNITY — HEALING
   Inhale with   =   LAHATA NAMMANG
3. Exhale with   =   IMMUNITY-RE-ZOOM
   Inhale with   =   RAZATANAMMAÑ
4. Exhale with   =   IMMUNITY-DEVELOPING
   Inhale with   =   LAVA-PATA-NAMMANG

Now the exhale mantra IMMUNITY and its inhale counterpart TANAMMA is constituted of words T, N and M and we know by now that :

(i) The word 'N' which is the seed word for brow chakra strengthens the left brain, the eyesight and the pituitary gland which is the master gland and the director of total endocrine glandular activity of our body, and is thus the BEHOLDER of our body.

(ii) The word 'M' is the seed word for crown chakra which strengthens the right-brain, the mind and the pineal gland.

273

(iii) The word 'T' is the seed word for Taste glands as well as for the sense endings in the brain.

Thus, the words M, N & T (D) strengthen the mind and the yogis say, it is the mind which falls prey to the disease first and then body falls prey in unison. In order to strengthen the BRAIN, we stimulate the total glandular activity in the head, with the exhale mantra IMMUNITY and its counter part inhale mantra. Thus truly, the word/mantra IMMUNITY is like the God in self healing.

(iv) The word 'L' in mantra No. 2, is the seed word for basic sex chakra, it strengthens the legs, boosts sex power and illuminates the mind when the divine kundalini energy, thus kindled with the resonant sonic vibrations of L, reaches the crown chakra (M).

(v) The word 'V' in mantra No.1 is the seed word for ovary chakra, it strengthens the ovary and the lower intestines for proper water absorption, elimination and assimilation processes occuring in the lower intestines.

(vi) The word 'R' is the seed word for Navel Chakra/ solar plexus. It stimulates liver action, pancreas glands and all the glandular secretions in the abdomen to properly digest balanced food which acts as the medicine to protect us against diseases.

(vii) The word 'Z' helps the cardio-vascular system for proper circulation of blood/nutrients/oxygen in the body.

(viii)The word 'P' also helps the lungs to breathe to its optimum capacity and the word PRA helps to breathe totally from the abdomen (R) and from the lungs (P).

(ix) The word 'H' is the seed word for Vishudha/ Throat Chakra to strengthen the Thyroid gland for proper carbohydrate/fat metabolism in our body and to properly establish the communication link between the body and brain.

(x) And the word 'MAÑ yokes us with Infinity - the super consciousness to draw in as much pranic life energy as possible and then deposits it on 'G', another seed word for left brain.

Thus, the above four breathing mantras are very very powerful indeed to fortify our immune system to keep us healthy and I am sure that these mantras can help even patients suffering from AIDS and CANCER, in the first stage of the disease when the Cancer patients have not been yet exposed to the radiation therapy or chemo-therapy and if these patients have the WILL power to live on, they will be able to recover slowly and steadily, first the progression of the disease will stop and then slowly they will be able to over-come the disease with proper NUTRITION. The hypnotic suggestive effect of IMMUNITY PRESERVING/ HEALING will also go a long way to have the desired effect to cure. And exhaling/inhaling with above four mantras silently for five minutes each for a total of 20 minutes in the morning and 20 minutes in the evening will indeed be very helpful to cure such patients, supplemented with balanced nutrition.

OM — TAT — SAT/AMEEN

SECRET OF SUCCESS

WHEN I PLAY

I BECOME THE PLAY

WHEN I DANCE

I BECOME THE DANCE

WHEN I KISS

I BECOME THE KISS

THIS IS HOW

I ATTAIN THE BLISS

WHEN I READ A BOOK

I BECOME THE BOOK

THIS IS HOW

I TOPPED THE LIST

THIS IS THE SECRET

OF ANYBODY'S SUCCESS

DR. L. R. CHOWDHRY

SECTION - VI

STRESS MANAGEMENT

Chapter - 58

STRESS AND ITS MANAGEMENT SEED MANTRA

SACHA - ANAND — NEESHCHINT

Life is a struggle, Stress is its consequence, and Progress is its outcome. But, whenever, our body/mind system is worked beyond its natural Biological Limits, it generates ABNORMAL STRESS which we denote in this chapter as "stress" by eliminating the word abnormal from it. This stress has many dimensions. It can be due to the sudden emotional shock, like the death of a very dear relative which time alone can heal or crying soon after the Sad Event may somewhat lessen the shock stress. The stress can also be caused by over-using our body/mind system again and again without giving enough rest in between for the body/mind system to recuperate itself. Have you not seen the rubber band being stretched? If you stretch it slightly, it will return to its original shape, and if we stretch it again and again or stretch it beyond its elastic limits, the rubber will get permanently deshaped and not return to its original shape and if we stretch the rubber too far, the rubber band can break. The same thing happens with human beings also, though we are not exactly like rubber or the rubber stamps, because human beings have been endowed by God with will-power to repair themselves infinitely by connecting themselves with the greatest healer - The Almighty; unless one has stretched oneself to the Impossible Beyond, from where no one returns.

And these biological limits for stress are not only widely different for different persons and races, but these limits change with age. A simple example of stress will illustrate it. If after running for a while, we start panting for breath, and are not able to speak properly, we have caused stress to our body because we have run beyond the aerobic capacity of our lungs/heart system which gives a feeling of tiredness to our muscles; because we have accumulated lactic acid in our muscles due to the paucity of oxygen. For this, we need rest. And this capacity to run long distances is different for the different persons and can, however, be developed/increased with daily practice as in the case of fast or long Distance Runners, but this capacity to run diminishes with age. In fact, running can become hazardous for older persons unless they are used to running daily.

Anger is another common example of stress. Talking is natural to man, but talking continuously for many hours can cause hoarseness and stress, but so called ANGER is an extreme form of stress, when we shout at the top of our voice all sorts of hotch potch; this throws our natural breathig out of phase/gear, thus our heart starts beating faster in order to help reach the oxygen/glucose/nutrients to the brain, because the requirement of brain is almost nine times larger than any other part of our body, the adrenal glands release the chemical-adrenalin in the blood stream to help the liver to release more glycogen in the blood to tide over this emergency. In youth, we have full blooded veins and it is somewhat possible to withstand certain amount of anger, but in old age, Anger can stress the heart and even prove fatal.

But there is another form of anger - suppressed

anger in which we are constrained by our civil behaviour not to shout, but we suppress our anger which we may feel over the wrong decisions of our office bosses. And even at home; we suppress our anger at the behaviour of our wife and children. Such suppressed anger also releases and triggers the same emergency hormonal secretions though not on the same scale as the expressed anger. While, our expressed anger happens once in a blue moon unless one is Angry Type, but suppressed anger is like repeated stress and thus, it slowly deranges our body/mind system.

Similarly, our capacity to withstand extreme heat/cold diminishes with age, inspite of the fact that our body provides itself the best stable temperature system by keeping our body temperature around 98.6□F, inspite of large fluctuations in atmospheric temperature during the year, during our normal health. And our hair turn grey when we grow old in order to reflect the extra sunshine away from our head, otherwise the oxidants created by the sun-shine will damage the brain neurons. This happens, because in old age, the Semi Clogged Blood arteries are not able to give full blooded nutrition to the brain as in youth to metabolise the sun rays effectively but some of the over-zealous persons will dye their grey hair to black again in order to look younger but such persons carry extra risk to themselves when the atmospheric temperature shoots upto 105□ F and beyond, in tropical climate; thus they need to take greater precautions from bright sun-shine.

And further I must assert that our modern technology has been very unkind to our delicate eyes, exposing the eyes to bright flash lights or long bright exposures during television photo-sessions or having to read voluminous newspapers/ journals/office work/working on computer screens/ watching home television for long hours and that too with semi-bent forward neck position which impedes the supply of blood to the brain, thus further enhancing the strain on our eyes. Such excessiveness is beautifully described by Lao Tse thus :-

"Continuing to fill a pail, after it is full, the water will be wasted, continuing to grind an axe, after it is sharp will wear it away. Excess of light blinds the eyes, excess of sound deafens the ears, excess of condiments deadens the taste. He who possesses moderation is lasting and enduring. Too much is always a curse; most of all in Wealth."

There is another great cause of emotional stress, particularly in our old age, when our near kith and kins - our own sons and daughters far-sake us and admit us in Help Age homes and rarely visit us - that feeling that I am no longer needed becomes a source of great stress. And I quote Shakespeare in "As You Like It" when the King in Exile in the forest laments thus :-

"Blow, Blow Thou Winter Winds
Thy Sting is not so sharp
As that of Ingratitude;"

Similarly, Raj Kapoor - a great Actor and Film Maker of India sings in one of his pictures

"Dost, Dost Na Raha
Pyar Pyar Na Raha
Ai Zindgi
Tumahara Aitbar Naa Raha"

Another very great cause of stress is some kind of lurking 'FEAR' over-shadowing us, which hangs like a Sword of Democles on our head and is a continous stress. Such type of stress is also faced by Soldiers on the War Front under Cannon Fire - Cannons to the left of me, Cannons to the right of me and Cannons everywhere.

Such type of Continuous stress slowly eats like white ants the immune structure of our body and if not attended to in time, the body will one day collapse like a dead wood. But much before that, stress shows itself in various related symptoms like tiredness, restlessness, sleeplessness, Nausea, Diarrhoea, high Blood Pressure leadinng to Angina and aggravations of all sorts of body pains and headaches etc. with bouts of depression which makes us age faster with early appearance of wrinkles on the face which further aggravates the state of depression.

The Anatomy of Stress Response in Our Body

Thus, when a stress causing event occurs, the sense endings in the hypothalamus region of the brain actuate an alarm signal which stimulates the autonomic nervous system and endocrinal activity directed by the Pituitary gland - the Director of our body's Endocrine Orchestra, which thus directs the adrenal gland to secrete Andrenalin and nor-Andrenalin hormones in the blood stream to cope up with stress, resulting in increase in the strength and rate of heart beat, constriction of blood vessels and consequent rise in blood pressure, eye pupils dilate, blood glucose level inceases, blood circulation is shifted to the brain and the heart; while depleting its flow to the digestive system. Glycogen is released from the liver to meet the brain's increased demand, the spleen contracts, releasing blood cells, all this is done by the Hypothalamus region in the brain to save itself from the ravages of stress and when the stressful event is over, it is followed by exhaustion due to lactic acid build-up in the muscles due to inadequate Oxygen supply and if we can give enough rest to our body/mind system, our body returns more or less to its normal position, but not without causing its shadow on our brain/body.

But, if the stressful conditions continue to bog the mind again & again, the sympathetic nervous system as outlined above itself gets over burdened with neural & endocrine activity beyond its natural limits, resulting ultimately in the appearance of neurological disorders with time.

Stress Management

Man is a dynamic potentiality and has thus the innate capacity to charge one's life battery through the seven Energy Chakras of the Astral body which surrounds our gross body with which it is connected with vital life energy, as known by our sages after intensive meditation. There is potential divine Kundalini energy which is normally lying dormant, but can be made kinetic and kindled by the seed words V, S, & L of Swadhishtana and Mooladhara Chakras respectively. The kindled divine kundalini Energy can move to the crown Chakra to illumine our Total BEING, to dissolve our stress totally. The stimulation of Astral Chakras with the following words can strengthen our body alongwith rejuvenating the total endocrine activity of our body/mind system.

(i)   The word 'L' gives strength to our legs to walk & walking is one of the best yogic aerobic exercise for our body (see chapter on Walking). The word 'L' by its resonont sonic vibrations boosts our sex power and kindles the divine kundalini.

(ii) The word V is the seed word of Swadhishtana/ Ovary Chakra. It helps to irrigate all the cells of our body with water/blood/nutrients thus strengthening the cellular life processes.

(iii) The Word 'R' the seed word for Navel/Manipur Chakra stimulates by its resonant sonic energy the Adrenal gland - the emergency saviour gland to keep it in full preparedness to meet the challenge of stress. The word 'R' also strengthens the liver, the Pancreas & the other abdominal secretions to help restore the disturbed digestion on account of stress.

(iv) The word 'Y' helps the heart for better circulation to meet the challenge of stress.

(v) The word 'H' - the seed word for Vishudha/ Throat Chakra strengthens the Thyroid/ Parathyroid glands, for better fat/Carbohydrates metabolism & to re-establish the connection between the body and the brain.

(vi) The word 'N' - the seed word for Brow chakra, helps to strengthen the left brain - the sympathetic nervous system to keep its vigilance and alertness to cope with stress. This also stimulates the pituitary gland - the master gland. Since pituitary gland is the Director of all glandular activity in our body, it has to be kept in its optimum condition to cope with stress.

(vii) The word 'M' is the seed word for crown chakra, it strengthens the right brain and pineal gland. Because crown chakra is a higher chakra than Brow chakra, it comes to the rescue of sympathetic nervous system when it is over-worked by repeated stress. This crown chakra is a chakra of illumination of our mind & also helps to develop control over our mind. The more we stimulate this chakra, the more of brain's spatial capacity is expanded, because normally a limited brain capacity is utilised and when we yoke our Crown Chakra with the Super - consciousness with the inhale mantras like AUÑM & AHAÑM, we fulfill our total Being with the effulgence of pranic life energy, and this gets amplified thousand fold when the kindled divine Kundilini energy reaches this chakra - Sahasrara chakra of thousand fold potentiality to blossom and illumine our mind. The pineal gland produces the hormone Melatonin to soothe and calm our stressed mind.

2.   We are yoked with God - the Super consciousness, through the medium of breath every moment of our life. But, when we fall ill, our breath becomes shallow & erratic. Thus, our first attempt is to restore our natural sequence of breathing. The word SAÑ or SHAÑ helps us to start our breath about 7 cms below our Navel Chakra, and the words S & SH also originate from the same place where our breath originates. And the word SAÑ yokes us with INFINITY - the superconsciousness to draw in as much pranic life energy as possible to fulfill our BEING. The well known words LONG, SONG, and MONK etc. also yoke us with the Superconsciousness with the word AÑ to re-charge our life battery and to get rid of the stressful condition of our mind.

3.   Another approach of using suggestive healing breathing mantras has been adopted, like "IMPROVING' which Goads us to think that continuous

improvement in my body is happening. It has a hypnotic influence to cure, because thought is the finest & concentrated form of Pranic Energy and as also told by Swami Vivekanand," Matter is Mighty but Thought is Almighty". The suggestive healing Mantras are so chosen i.e. IMPROVE or BRILLIANT, HEALING which are in consonance with natural sequence of breathing or the sequence of location of astral chakras.

IMPROVE YOUR BODY AND MIND

| Exhale with | = | IMPROVEMENT |
| Inhale with | = | VAPRAMMANT |

(i) It is a total body/mind rejuvenating breathing mantra. The word MANT or MENT stimulates the memory/brain/mind with M (Crown chakra), N (BROW chakra) & T (Taste Endings in the brain) and also Yokes us with superconsciousness with MAÑ.

(ii) And the word 'PR' helps us to breathe both from the abdomen with 'R' and from the lungs with 'P', thus helping us to breathe totally. Also the word 'R' helps to strengthen the shattered digesation due to stress, by stimulating the liver, the pancreas, the abdominal secretions and above all the over-used, Adrenal gland.

(iii) The word 'V' helps to irrigate our total life cellular processes through blood/water circulation with nutrients, thus augmenting the healthy process of repair of our body/mind system.

The above mantra however does not contain the word 'H' - the seed word for Vishudha/Thyroid chakra.

Strengthen the thyroid and the mind

The word 'AHAÑM' which means' Myself' is one of the simplest stress dissolving breathing mantra. Also, it re-establishes the dignity of self esteem/ self healing in us, because we love ourselves the most.

Thus inhale with = AHHAÑM
Exhale with = OOHHOOÑM OR MIHHIEÑ.

(i) The word 'A' in AHANM constitutes inhalation

(ii) the word 'H' strengthens the Thyroid gland and it also helps to re-establish the communication between the body and the brain.

(iii) The word AÑ yokes us with Infinity-the superconsciousness to fulfil us with pranic life energy to recoup from stress.

(iv) And the inhale breath ends at 'M' - th seed word for crown chakra - the crowned healer in stress.

2. **Strengthen the Heart** - Heart is one of the most harassed organ in stressed condition as it has to beat faster to cope with stress. In order to strengthen the heart, we add Y-the seed word of Heart chakra

(i) Inhale with = YA+AHANM = YAHHANM
Exhale with = OOHHOOYOUM OR
MEHE YOU
OR MIHHIYYOUÑ

(ii) Another very suggestive mantra for strengthening the heart with its seed words Y and J is ENJOY or INNIJOY. This is indeed a stress dissolving mantra

Exhale with = ENJOY or INNIJOY

Inhale with	=	YAJANNAÑ
Also Exhale with	=	I AM JOYOUS
Inhale with	=	SAYAJAMMAÑ

3. Strengthen the Digestion

As already said, during stressful condition, the sympathetic endocrine system diverts the blood from the digestive organs to save the brain, thus starving the digestive organs of oxygen and nutrients. In order to restore the digestive processes to normalcy.

Inhale with	=	BRAHAMMAND
Exhale with	=	MIHI - BREATHE

(The word Th is almost equivalent to D).

or

Inhale with	=	RAHHANM
Exhale with	=	MIHHEER.

4. Strengthen Swasdhishtana chakra.

Exhale with	=	VA-BRAHANM
Inhalw with	=	MIHI-BRAVE

This mantra strengthens the assimilative and eliminative processes occuring in lower intestines.

Bliss Endowing Suggestive Mantras

You will get engulfed in bliss and dissolve all your stress; if you make bliss your breath

(i)	Exhale with	=	I AM BLISS
	Inhale with	=	BLOSSOM
			(SPOKEN AS BLASSAM).

This mantra helps us to re-blossom.

(ii) Another similar suggestive and very effective peace giving breathing **mantra** is :-

Exhale with	=	I AM IN PEACE
	OR	OOMNI PEACE
Inhale with	=	SAPANAMMAÑ

(iii) A very powerful Hindi peace endowing mantra which is chanted daily is 'SHANTI' which is complete inhale/exhale mantra. The word 'Shant means PEACE, Make 'Shanti' as your breath.

| Inhale with | = | SHANT |
| Exhale with | = | TI or TEESH. |

This mantra helps us to take the breath from its centre in the body, about 7 cms below the Navel - exactly the place where the sound 'S' or 'Sh' originates in our body. The mantra 'Shañ' yokes the breath with Infiinity with the help of word (ñ) which unites us with the super consciousness and the breath ends with 'T', one of the seed word for stimulating the taste glands endings in the brain and to boost our taste for life.

A very useful modification of the above mantra is :

| Inhale with | = | 'SHANTTAM' |
| Exhale with | = | 'MINTEESH/MINDEESH/ MENDEESH |

The word 'AM' has been suffixed to Shant to make it SHANTTAM so as to make the breath reach the crown chakra which strengthens right brain with its seed word 'M' which also helps to stimulate the pineal gland. This pineal gland comes to the rescue of much harassed pituitary gland which is everytime called upon when - ever a stressful situation arises. The pineal gland also releases the hormone Melatonin to give peace (Shanti) to our Mind.

The inhale mantra 'Shantam' means that I am at peace.

The exhale mantra - 'Mendeesh' may be thought to mean that God is mending my stress-torn body because I am yoked with my source of life-the God.

Another suggestive happiness endowing breathing mantra is :-

Exhale with   =   I AM HAPPY
Inhale with   =   APPAHHANM.

This mantra strengthens the lungs/heart with 'P' and Thyroid gland with 'H' and the crown chakra with M.

Boost Your Immunity

Immunity is like the God of healing in our body. Make Immunity your breath.

(i) Exhale with   =   IMMUNITY HEALING.
     Inhale with   =   LAHATANAMMAÑG

(ii) Exhale with   =   IMMUNITY BOOSTING.
      Inhale with   =   SABATANAMMONG.

(iii) Exhale with   =   IMMUNITY PRESERVING.
      Inhale with   =   VAZA-PRATA NAMMONG.

The mantra 'Immunity' - strengthens the total mind with words M, N and T. and boosts our Immune system by stimulating Pituitary & pineal glands.

Life Style Changes

In order to cope up with daily stress, we have to make life style changes in our life and rise above 'FEAR', so that no stress arises. For this, we have to lead a life of Sat, Chit and Anand i.e. a path of truth and blissful existence i.e. to live a life of

Satyam (Truth), Shivam (Godliness) and Sunderam (Beauty) and as the poet Keats has said "A thing of beauty is a joy for ever" and if you are healthy, joyful and stress free, you are the most beautiful person for yourself to enjoy this beautiful world.

For this

Inhale with   =   SACHA-ANAND
Exhale with   =   NEESH-CHINT.

The inhale mantra - 'Sancha Anand' means pure bliss and it strengthens eyes with the help of seed word 'N' - our eyes being the most harassed sense organ of our body. This mantra also strengthens the brow chakra and the pituitary gland with its seed word 'N'.

The exhale mantra 'Neesh-Chint' means that now I am absolutely carefree and stress-free and fearless and the above suggestive mantra thus goads us to live a truthful, stress-free life without any anxiety.

This is the seed mantra for endowing BLISS

Restore Equilibrium Of Mind

Nothing in this world is in perfect equilibrium or moves in perfect circle. Even the earth moves around the sun in an elliptical path like the electrons moving around the nucleus of an Atom. Thus, we should accept the slight craziness or disequilibrium of other person. Make 'equilibrium' your breath.

Exhale with   =   I AM IN - EQUILIBRIUM
Inhale with   =   LA BRAYAKA-NAMMAÑ

This is also a complete body/mind rejuvenating mantra and will thus help to restore equilibrium in our body/mind system.

This is the seed mantra for Management of stress.

Another suggestive breathing mantra to quieten the mind is :-

Exhale with	=	I AM QUIET
Inhale with	=	YATA KAMMAÑ

The inhale mantra, with the resonant sonic vibration of M stimulates the pineal gland to calm our mind and also by yoking us with superconsciousness with the word MAÑ

Mantra to Remove Depression

To remove depression and bring about brilliance in your mind :-

Exhale with	=	I AM BRILLIANT
		or
		IMMI-BRILIANT.
Inhale with	=	ALLA BRAMMANT.

In the above mantra, the word 'L' helps to illumine our BEING by kindling the divine kundalini and the word M,N & T help to strengthen the MIND and remove depression. The word 'BR' plays it big part in removing depression by helping to breathe fully from both abdomen with R and lungs with B and experiments have confirmed that total breathing from abdomen and the lungs helps to dissolve depression, because it fulfills our abdomen with pranic energy, because abdomen is called the second brain of our body.

Enjoy Yourself

We should make every moment of our life full of joy, so that stress can not come near us, but if we exceed our body limit in sense enjoyments or in sexual enjoyment or even by dancing in discos for long hours, even this can become tiresome and painful, and this is particularly so in old age, when any excess enjoyment can turn into sadness. Thus enjoy within your body limit and make "Enjoy yourself "your breath", & not enjoy beyond yourself.

Exhale with	=	ENJOY YOURSELF
Inhale with	=	LA-SARAFA-YAUJNA

Inhale mantra stimulates the sex glands with L & S, the liver, the pancreas and the emergency adrenal glands with R, the lungs with F, the heart with Y & J and the pituitary master gland with N, thus this mantra strengthens almost our entire glandular system to give us protection against stress and disease. Besides this exhale mantra is very very suggestive to remove depression.

Mantra to Bring About Cohesion

It is the lack of cohesion between the different parts of the mind which is aggravated by the process of ageing and stress. This can be brought back into coherence with the following suggestive mantra :-

Exhale with	=	I AM COHERENT
		or
		IMMIK -KOOHHERENT
Inhale with	=	RAHA-KAMMANT.

(i) The word 'R' brings about coherence in digestive system,

(ii) The word 'H' helps to restore coherence between body and brain and restore communication in the cervical region of the spine, while the words T, K, N & M stimulate and strengthen the whole mind. to bring coherence in the

MIND/BRAIN system.

Meditation : Meditation is the ultimate method to still our agitated mind and thus get rid of stress when we focus our thought on a single object so that the thought becomes mono-directional, and coherent and ultimately we can silence our mind. For meditation, we can also make our thought move alongwith the breath, as it traverses various chakras. Make the thought move alongwith the breath as it starts from the bottom of spine with the word SH and take your thought to the crown chakra with M. It is called Vipasana Meditation, as advocated by Lord Budha. For this,

Exhale with   =   MEDITATION SPOKEN AS MEDITAISHUN.

Inhale with   =   SHTA-NAMMAND

The inhale mantra means - I salute the person who can complete healthy hundred years and we can achieve this, with the help of this mantra, because the word 'SH' kindles the divine kundalini, the word 'N' stimulates the left brain and the brow chakra and the pituitary master gland and the word 'M' stimulates the right brain and the crown chakra and the total word MAND stimulates the total mind and the word MAÑ yokes us with the infinity - the superconsciousness to draw in as much pranic life energy as possible to fulfill our BEING to live stress-free 100 years. The word MAÑ opens the sushumna opening and makes the kundalini energy move upto the crown chakra 'M' to illuminate our BEING. The word Mañ also helps to stimulate the total brain and forms the communication bridge - between the left brain and the right brain. The word AÑ is the Transducer of Super Conscious Field.

Control Your Anger

In order to control your anger, if you are angry type, use a suggestive mantra.

Exhale with   =   I AM ANGERLESS
Inhale with   =   ALLA-SARAGA-MAÑ

The word 'L' helps to illuminate our mind while the word Sa, Ra, Ga, Ma give musical harmony to our body/MIND system, thus helping to remove anger from our mind.

Relationship problems in office and home

Since we spend most of the day either at office or at home, our relationship with the people we meet plays the most important part in making us happy or depressed. In our work-place, we should make the motto-"Work is worship" and also respect our office boss, then things will be smooth sailing. But inspite of that, if one is so placed that the office job is found to be boring and routine and does not provide job satisfaction, or self esteem, this may lead to cause stress in the work place.

For this, either one should change one's job to one's satisfaction or accept it and make the work place as happy a place as possible, by changing one's attitude to life. If we develop the optimistic attitude of seeing the **HALF GLASS EMPTY AS HALF GLASS FULL**, then much of the stress can be dissolved.

Similarly, unhappy conjugal relationships can become the continuous cause of stress at home. They say that behind every successful man - there is a woman, but the reverse is equally true, that behind many unsuccessful men, there is also a woman, because daily nagging at home can make life a hell.

I am myself a fast turbulent husband and my wife is a very beautiful lady who can throb the heart of one and all and I being a jealous husband thus, on certain occasions, we will quarrel during the day and at night of course we both will swear love for each other, but my neighbour is a very quiet person, and would never quarrel with his wife, inspite of his wife being a very nagging type. I once complimented my neighbour by saying 'you are calm like the river Ganges near Delhi, where it comes down to the plains with no turbulence on the surface of water and I also added that while my life is like a turbulent river flowing down in the hills with all its turbulence and noise. Upon this, my neighbour quipped, "Dr. Chowdhry, my life may look quiet to you but how much agitation is going on under the surface of my mind, you cannot imagine." Thus, this type of suppressed anger slowly can also lead to the build up of the stress and damages the immune system ultimately, and this constant tug of war between the husband and wife goes on and on in life and in some 20% cases, this ends in divorce, while 60% live on enjoying this daily push and pull, while the other 20% live on happily fully adjusted to each other. Thus, to sublimate the negative reactions, use the breathing mantra 'MOVE ALONG'.

| Exhale with | = | MOVE |
| Inhale with | = | ALONG |

This mantra besides providing sonic energy to combat stress, suggests to be in tune with nature or be in tune with your boss in office or be in tune with your wife at home or be in tune with your own self and hear to your body limits, which we should not exceed. Thus, be in tune with the whole world so that there is no opposition to our existence in the environment. We have surrendered to God completely. This is indeed a very beneficial mantra to succeed in this tough world 'Move Along'.

Stress And Digestion

Stress can disturb our digestion while impending danger can cause diarrhea is well known and can become the cause of stomach ulcers. Even normally, the oxygen/glucose demand of brain is about nine fold more than other parts of the body but in stressful condition, the sympathetic brain system immediately orders to divert the blood supply to heart and the brain in order to save itself from damage, while the digestive system is asked to wait till the stressful situation is over. The use of word 'R' in any one of the above breathing mantras helps to strengthen the Abdominal secretions, the liver, the pancreas and the adrenal glands to restore them to their normal state. A very suggestive and potent breathing mantra to restore digestion is :-

Exhale with   =   INCREASE - APPETITE
Inhale with   =   SAKRA PTANANT.

The word Appetite is really appetising because it sets up 'to and for 'resonant sonic vibrations in the taste endings in the brain to stimulate the hunger while the word 'R' as said above strengthens digestion, the word 'P' helps optimal breathing, the words N & K help the hypothalamous region of the brain to regain its control over itself, because the word 'N' stimulates the pituitary gland to regain its control over other glands in our body. Similarly, the following mantra rejuvenates the total body and total digestive system. The word 'H' helps to stimulate the thyriod gland and to help in fat and carbohydrates metabolism.

Exhale with = HEAL - LIVER
Inhale with = LAVARAHHAÑ

Also the word 'H' re-establishes the communion between the body and the brain to bring about normalcy in body/mind system.

Invoke Divinity

And when everything else fails, we turn to the Divine, because man has been made in the image of God, and is constantly seeking divinity. Thus let us make - 'I AM DIVINE' as our breath.

Exhale with = I AM DIVINE
Inhale with = VADA - NAMMAÑ

The words 'N, M &D strengthen the total brain and mind and the word MAÑ yokes us with DIVINITY to fulfill our total BEING with God's effulgence, to make us stress-free and the word 'V' helps also to kindle the divine kundalini and helps to move it upto pituitary and pineal gland and the crown chakra.

There is another very potent breathing mantra given by our sages to their disciples "SOHAM' which means that I AM LIKE THAT - I am like the God, cast in ITS GLORY. For this :-

Inhale with = SOHAM PRONOUNCED
AS SAUHHAMM
Exhale with = MIHHISH.

This mantra helps to kindle the divine kundalini energy with the word S or Sh, 'H' restores the communication between our body and the mind for which the seed word is M. Thus this mantra infuses divinity in our mind. So let us start the day with divinity by inhaling/exhaling with the above two breathing mantras and then live in divinity throughout the day and fulfill our evening with divinity by using the above suggestive breathing mantras "I AM DIVINE or Soham and you will then never be afflicted with stress.

Communicate with the superconsciousness

And last but not the least, I must point out that there is a constant, communion going on between our gross body and the Superconscious Energy field, that is how we keep our life battery charged with pranic life energy and that is how we often get the power of Intuition and clairvoyance to see into the future.

Thus inhale with =   RAHA-KAMANAKANT
Exhale with   =   HI, RECOMMUNICATE.

The word 'RAHA' means I am on the path of Kamanakant which means- full with the desire of Effulgence to evolve into better species i.e. to grow daily into a better and better personality and if we continue to communicate with the universal superconscious field, we can continue to evolve every day and for this the word AÑ is contained in the inhale mantra - KAMANAKANT. The word AÑ yokes us with the superconscious field to draw in as much pranic life energy as possible to fulfill our total BEING to recharge our life battery, thus rejuvenating us to face the challenges of our modern world which is highly demanding. And the suggestive mantra re-communicate helps to communicate between various parts of the brain as well as with the superconsciousness as said above. Another similar mantra is :-

Exhale with   =   IMPROVE COMMUNION.

Inhale with   =   VAPRAMAKAMANAN

(9) A Life Saving MANTRA

If the person is ill and bedridden with a chronic disease and if he has the desire to live on and cure himself then he/she should use the mantra "Want to Live"

Inhale deeply with   =   WAANT
and exhale with   =   TO LIVE

and believe me if he wishes to live and breathes with the above mantra he will be cured and will live on, because our thought is our BEING and as beautifully told by Swami Vivekanand "Matter is mighty but Thought is Almighty".

For those persons who love their mother very dearly and whenever, they are in distress or down with illness, they call out - O, Mañ, which means- O, Mother because no body on earth can equal the love and affection of our mother except the God - Incarnate. They should use the breathing mantra- "Motherly Warmth".

(10) Exhale with   =   MOTHERLY
     Inhale with   =   WARMTH

And believe me, the healthy warmth will engulf your being as if you are well protected and safe in your mother's lap.

Prayer to God/Devotional Music :

Prayer to God and Devotional Music are the best antidote to stress. There is a famous Bhagti Cult all over the world who sing the devotional song" Hare Rama, Hare Rama, Rama Rama, Hare Hare, Hare Krishna, Hare Krishna, Krishna, Krishna, Hare Hare." Instead one can also use a very simple mantra - MERE RAMA

(11) Exhale with   =   MERE

      Inhale with   =   RAMA

We can sing as well as clap with this mantra and it has the advantage that we can go on breathing and singing with it, because we are exhaling with 'MERE' and latter inhaling with 'RAMA', thus we are in phase with breathing & hence do not get tired in the process. The devotee can get so much absorbed in the Mantra "MERE RAMA", as if Lord Ram has decended to come alive in the Devotee's Being. This is possible because after exhaling with Mere, one is thus able   to prolong the godly name of RAM as Sweetly or as Devotedly as possible to BECOME ONE WITH RAM.

Another beautiful way for some persons to destress is to put on some lively music of one's choice, it could be soft enchanting waltz music, to dance with one's partner, or a more vibrant variety of dance music or classical English Music, or classical Indian Music.

I have coined a dance mantra to dance when alone (Me with Me) to the tune of Cha-Cha Music, a pranic life giving dance Mantra;

(12) Inhale with   =   SA, RA, YAHAM, MAÑ

      Exhale. with   =   ME YOU RISHIH - HOOÑ

This dance mantra dissolves the stress surely in a Jiffy. They say that while Bank moves the money, the dance moves the Soul' to dissolve the stress. To some I recommend a popular song "Take It Easy, Urvshi" The contents of the song are quite hilarious and make us Laugh and laughter they say is the best medicine, to destress.

(13) I recommend the shorter form of this mantra **"Take it Easy"** as an exhale mantra and then

inhale deeply. Besides, this mantra instills in us the feeling to take things easy and face life as it comes and the circumstances will soon take a happy turn.

Laugh Away Your Stress

Another beautiful way to destress is to cultivate a group of friends who are good conversationists who can make us laugh by laughing over trifles, that is their style of talking and laughing. Seek the company of such joyful persons. The latest research shows that after laughter, levels of Immuno-globin A increase in the Mucus lining of the nasal cavity, and this Immunoglobin A helps people to fight illness by marking out invading bacteria and viruses for destruction by white blood cells, other wise when, we are over stressed, these lurking around bacteria/viruses can attack furiously and make us fall ill. There is a famous saying - "Laughter is the best Medicine".

Now, if our eyes are feeling tired due to their over-use, another thing I recommend is to "Palm The Eyes", a technique advocated by W.H. Bates in his famous book "Better Eye Sight Without Glasses". In this, we close our both eyes and then cover the right eye with the help of cupped right palm and left eye with the left cupped palm, without, putting any pressure on our eyeballs or obstructing the flow of breath from the nose. Look into this darkness as long as convenient, then remove the palms from the eyes and then open the eyes slowly. This is a sort of silencing meditation which relaxes the eyes and hence repairs them.

The simplest breathing mantra to provide succour to the tired eyes is :-

Inhale with = SHAFFAN
Exhale with = NOOFFESH.

Another suggestive mantra to give pranic life energy to the eyes, the pituitary gland and the left brain (the brow chakra) is :-

Exhale with = NUTRITION
Inhale with = SHATRANNAÑ

This mantra also reminds us to give proper balanced nutrition to our eyes/brain and the body in general to bring about quicker normalisation of the eyesight (See Chapter on Eye Sight Improvement).

Enjoy Blissful Walking

Any brisk activity like brisk walking, playing tennis, Badminton, table tennis, swimming and dancing etc. will stop the process of thought getting hooked to stressful event. But in ordinary walking, stressful thoughts can still accompany us to torture our mind, but how to help a person who cannot walk fast or run due to ageing process. Also not much energy is left, when a person is stressed. So, Walking is the most acceptable aerobic exercise. Walk with a breathing mantra.

Blissful Walking with Mantra

Walking is the most natural aerobic movement, in fact it is the best yogic exercise, because it provides aerobic movement to all parts of the body, the total spine and the brain with movement of legs and the hands. And in order to dissolve the stress, walk with a breathing mantra. For that, notice which one of your nostrils is breathing more easily. Suppose, it is the right nostril, then start walking with the right foot forward first, inhaling with the mantra - 'Shfaañ and exhaling with the mantra -

BLISS or INS with the left foot forward. After walking for some time, you can change over. Now, inhale with the left foot forward with inhale mantra - Shfañ and exhale with right foot forward with the mantra - BLISS or INS. This will bring about equilibrium in breathing by breathing from both the right and left nostrils, because the breathing mantra - Shfañ/ INS or BLISS is neutral and it does neither prefer left brain nor right brain and the mantra Shfañ enables us to open our Sushumna opening in the spine for the divine kundalini energy to move up with the sonic resonant energy of word S or Sh. The word 'F' helps to fill our lungs to their optimum capacity and the word Fañ yokes us with infinity - the superconsciousness to draw in as much pranic life energy as possible, and to dissolve our stress completely. Thus, I call it the blissful walking, because the above walking mantra, besides fulfilling our total Being with pranic life energy, it is very suggestive - the inhale mantra Shfañ in Urdu language means Health giving and the exhale mantra - Bliss besides helping us to exhale completely upto the breath centre'S', gives us the hypnotic blissful feelings.

Best Stress Dissolving Exercise

For those persons, who due to ageing or otherwise can not even walk, for them, I advocate stationary walking i.e. sit comfortably in a chair or stand comfortably with spine erect, move up your hands alternately as in natural walking. If the right nostril is more open for breathing, start with the right hand up first. Thus, we will be in tune with nature. Then after 10 to 20 movements of hands as convenient, rest for a while and then start with the left hand up first, it will now open up the left nostril for breathing. Thus, it will bring about - Equilibrium in breathing, restoring equilibrium in our Mind to dissolve stress completely. Do it for 10 to 20 times as convenient. Convenience should be the watch-word in all our doings. This exercise re-establishes the communication between the heart and the brain, through the cervical region of the spine by these alternate hand movements. Thus, I call it one of the best Anti-Stress Exercise. After a few days of this exercise you will start experiencing the on-rush of bio-energy blissful currents in the neck, in the brain and in the hands, after you finish the exercise and watch what is happening in the mind.

Symphony of Body, Brain and Soul

An ultimate breathing mantra to bring about symphony of body, brain and soul to absolve a person of stressful conditions is :-

Inhale with = ASHA - BRA - HA - ATMAÑ
Exhale with = IMTI - HOO - BROO - SHEEÑ

1. With the word ASHA which means hope, we stimulate both the Muladhara (Basic) and Swadhistana (ovary) chakras. With the word BRA, we cover the Navel and the heart Chakras, thus with Asha - Bra, we breathe totally and cover the whole lower body.

2. With word 'HA' we re-establish the communication link between the body and the brain besides stimulating the Thyroid gland.

3. The right brain is stimulated with M.

4. And the word 'ATMAÑ' (which means soul) yokes our total BEING with Infinity - the superconsciousness - the super soul to fulfill our total BEING with pranic life energy.

Thus, truly this breathing mantra brings about the symphony between our Body, Brain and the Soul. Another breathing mantra to achieve this Harmony is

Exhale with   =   HI, YOU - RE - ILLUMINATE
Inhale with   =   ALLARA - YAHA- NAMANT

This mantra includes N to stimulate the left brain and pituitary gland and thus illuminates the total brain/body system.

Sleep and Rest :

Deep sleep is the best tranquiliser and dissolver of stress. It is during this deep sleep period that there is a rise in the output of the growth hormone and protein production is stepped up. The body repairs itself and the dead cells are replaced. All the healing breathing mantras which contain the word 'M' - the seed word for crown chakra are very helpful in endowing deep sleep.

Similarly during the working period also, after any brisk activity of body or mind, proper rest is a must, for which we should lie down on the back in a completely relaxed state with arms lying comfortably along the body. During the rest period, if we can watch the flow of breath at the tip of our nose or the rise and fall of navel point as we breathe, it will relax us completely in 10 minutes or so. This relaxation restores the harmony between our body and mind.

Also, while lying down, we can inhale with - SMAÑ - and exhale with MSIEÑ -. This mantra yokes us with Infinity - the super consciousness with the word MAÑ and supplies the required pranic life energy to the stressed mind and the word 'M' stimulates the crown chakra and the pineal gland which releases the tranquility endowing hormone - Melatonin to give us also a restful sleep, thus this Mantra restores the harmony between our body (S), mind (M) and the soul (AÑ) -

Congenial Company And Honey :

You can pleasantly, play with your sons/ daughters or grand children, kiss them affectionately to completely dissolve depression. Or enjoy a love play with your own wife- a few warm embraces will completely evaporate the depression or let some one massage & rub the shoulders, arms/spine to restore the blocked flow, or enjoy a hot or cold bath depending upon the season, a cold bath in the hot season & a hot bath in the cold season. This will freshen us up & thus destress us.

Another very useful method to destress in cold season is to warm your both feet in a luke warm water, your feet dipped beyond the ankles for ten minutes or so; and then dry up your feet with a hand towel. This will warm your feet and your spine and re-establish the communication along the blocked spine, because spine blocking is the first casualty due to acute stress.

And above all, let us not forget the role a nourishing balanced food can play to dissolve the stress, and for quick relief to stressed mind, take a spoonful of Honey on the tongue; I also take about 60 pieces of raisins (dried grapes) taking 20 pieces at one time, in three lots so as to feel their luscious taste on the tongue by keeping them in the mouth for as long as possible for •the fructose to be absorbed in the brain directly from the soft palate of the mouth or a good quality chocolate of my taste or one tea spoonful of glucose, taken on tongue in 4 lots of quarter spoons, so as to be absorbed directly on the tongue. Afterwards, take a glass of water, just plain water which in itself is a great tranquiliser and the heat equaliser in the body and is also the integral part of each cell of our body with glucose and hence its great utility in drowning the stress, particularly in conjunction with something naturally sweet like honey on the tongue or five or six dates taken slowly by enjoying the taste of dates as much as possible. Of course, incidently if you can date with a friend, there is nothing better to dissolve the stress or instead enjoy a ripe luscious mango, if in season, by keeping the luscious mango in the mouth for as long as possible & top it with a cold milk to dissolve the stress or enjoy taking a few oranges (not their extracted juice) so as to absorb yourself in the act of eating deliciously for as long as possible, to divert the attention from the cause of stress which constantly weighs upon the mind or one can munch any other seasonal fruit like Apple, Banana etc. or a bowl of mixed fruits or coconut water which is very nourishing and stress relieving. The roughage of the fruits also protects the stomach linings against agonising stress secretions which irritate the stomach linings. Follow it up with a hot cup of tea/coffee or a glass of hot/cold milk as it suits you.

All these natural multifarious ways to drown the stress are also being suggested to suit different persons' temperament.

But, there are others who because of stress, cannot eat anything because they get a feeling of nausea or vomiting sensation. This could be either due to consuming large amount of alcoholic drinks overnight which damages the liver and irritates the linings of the stomach (see chapter on alcoholism) or a some people also suffer from nausea/vomiting due to the complete restriction of common salt from food as advised to high blood pressure patients, they are advised not to completely stop taking common salt but rather reduce its in-take, after consultation with the physician.

This vomiting or nausea feeling could also arise from too much smoking or taking lot of cups of coffee or tea etc. or this nausea could be the result of overwork or over-exposure to strong lights as in film shooting for very long hours.

This nausea feeling can be got over by exhaling deeply from the stomach while keeping the mouth half open, so that toxic vapours piled up in the stomach are exhaled out completely from the stomach. Using the following mantra for inhaling/exhaling will definitely be of help.

Exhale with   =   PHROOÑ
Inhale with   =   PHRAAÑ

Inhale/exhale with mantra given above for ten to twenty times as convenient.

Mantra for Headache Relief :

As headache is the first symptom of stress, this can be alleviated by all the previous mantras, however a special suggestve mantra but also very effective for giving relief from headaches is :-

16) Exhale with   =   IMPROVIH - HEADACHE

And then inhale deeply or

Inhale with   =   VARA-PAHA-KAMMAND

Inhale/exhale silently as above for a few minutes and the headache will slowly ease out. All types of headache whether caused by stress, or congestive type or other type are ameliorated with this mantra definitely except the headache initiated by the approaching weather storm, when due to the ingestion of higher ionic presence in the stormy air, due to Radon or other-wise can initiate headache in certain persons for which the author has discovered a special medicine which immediately cures the weather struck headaches or headaches caused by watching television which emits high energy x-rays to cause damage to the eyes directly plus due to ingestion of ionised air caused by x-rays. This medicine is given to the patient on personal consultation and cannot be sent by post, as it is spot prepared.

It is interesting to note that the word Headache is constituted of three seed words H, D & K (CH) - all these words are specific to Head and hence this mantra - IMPROVIH - HEADACHE is very very efficacious. Besides, the word Improve includes the seed word 'M' for strengthening the mind and the pineal gland to release the pacifying homone melatonin to relieve headache and the word 'H' helps to improve the communion between the body & the brain and the word 'K' strengthens the left brain and pituitary gland. Besides this mantra improves circulation with the word V which helps to remove all congestive headaches.

Re-establish Connection With Six Life Principles

And all these headaches and other stress symptoms will never bother us, if we re-establish our body/mind connection with the basic six principles of nature - Earth, Water, Fire, Air and Ether principle and the sixth being the OMNI - principle-the God almighty and even God will not help us, if we continue to exceed our body/mind biological limits agains & again.

Proper intake of balanced nutritious food is a must because our health is another name of - what we eat, what we drink, what we breathe and above all what we think. And our food should mostly include milk, curd, fresh fruits/vegetables/grains or the enlivened sprouted grains, etc. without too much of fats, or condiments, and the food quantity to be taken should be just sufficient to keep us alive and one fourth of the stomach should be kept empty for air/ether to act, taking only a small quantity of water alongwith the meals, but one should take a glass full of water about half an hour after the meals and we must take atleast 6-8 glasses of water everyday to keep ourselves healthy (See chapter on Water).

Also, one should avoid taking too hot/too cold food stuff. Too hot food can cause blisters in the mouth, as well as toothache in case of loose teeth. Similarly, too cold foods like very cold icecreams can make the throat feel numb and can initiate a headache or a toothache.

Sunbathing for 5 minutes to half an hour can rejuvenate the body but those suffering from sarcoma of the skin should avoid direct sunbathing. Similarly, we must re-establish our connection with the earth by walking bare footed, particularly in our lawn for sometimes daily.

Mantra for Stressed Politicians :

Last, but not the least, I must give a soothing mantra for stressed politicians who in democratic countries often get displaced after four or five years term, because people get fed up with the party in power and people want to try the other political party for a change. The deposed party politicians feel ill at ease, like a fish out of water, but what cannot be cured or procured must be endured. This interval should be used for self analysis, rest and Hibernation, to recoup health so as to capture power again with renewed zeal, when the next opportunity comes, because as they say, politicians have nine lives of a cat and thus, those who survive this stressfull period, can hope to capture power again and you can surely survive using the following mantra:-

17) Inhale with   =   SWA-RAJA MHAN
      Exhale with   =   MIHI - JEESHWERIEN

The inhale mantra Swa-RAJA-Mhan, means that I am the great king of myself and one who can become the king of the self or the master of one's desires, has achieved all. He is now a king of the whole universe. And the Exhale Mantra-Mihi-Jeshwerien means that "I will live on and on."

This mantra prescribed for politicians is for one and all and is the universal mantra to help us to rejuvenate and recuperate ourselves completely.

Now the beneficial action of the above healing mantras as help in breathing is six fold:

1) These help to re-establish the shallow and erratic breathing disturbed by stress to its normal pattern.

2) The above mantras have been so formulated by proper selection of healing words as to provide pranic life energy to the stressed sense organs like eyes and the total mind which receives and co-ordinates and interprets the sense signals, so that mind can re-establish its supremacy in controlling the body, by bringing about Harmony between the Body, Brain and Soul.

3) These breathing mantras help to restore the digestive as well as waste elimination system in the body to its peak performance again; the pores of the skin reopen to cool by perspiration; the action of kidneys/intestines is improved. All blockages are dissolved.

4) These breathing mantras also help to scavenge the blood veins/arteries of fatty cholesterol and other salt deposits by optimal oxygenation of the blood, thus decreasing the blood pressure raised by stress. These mantras also help to rid us of stress by the Vipasna Meditation effect of the mantric Breathing because in this, our thought also moves alongwith the breath, thus quietening our agitated mind. The Vipasna Meditation is a famous one advocated by Lord Buddha. If our thought is fixed on breathing, all stress is dissolved.

5) All the breathing mantras have been so formulated that they have also a psychological hypnotic effect on our mind by being very suggestive in nature i.e. Inner-equilibrium, I am in bliss, Omni-Peace, Take it easy, Motherly warmth etc., thus psychologically goading us back to bliss/equilibrium state of mind.

6) These mantras, because of their sonic resonant vibrations, activate our various body glands to secrete their normal hormonal secretions, to boost our immune system back to normal, thus restoring our vigour & energy so that we are able to say yes to the new Day, with the New Zest and with the new Vision-O, Blossom.

Chapter - 59

SAY, YES TO LIFE

MANTRA
HAÑ/HOOÑ

The inhale mantra HAÑ in our Hindustani language means - 'YES' i.e. Yes to life and yes to our own existence and yes to God which means, we have surrendered to God completely i.e. I have become a valley to be fulfilled by the grace of God, the pranic life energy of God - the Effulgence of God - the superconscious field of God's presence everywhere. And accordingly, the mantra HAÑ helps us to yoke with AAÑ with Infinity - the Superconsciousness to draw in as much pranic life energy as possible to fulfill our Being. The word 'N' in HAÑ is like 'N' in LONG which can be stretched far and far i.e. as long as we like; with the Ñ. And its exhale mantra - HOOÑ means - I exist - I am very much there and thus the inhale/exhale mantra HAÑ/HOOÑ can make us live for ever, as long as we desire, because the word 'H' helps our body to communicate with the brain through the cervical region of the spine through the resonant sonic vibrations of the word 'H' which is the seed word of Vishudha/throat chakra. It stimulates the Thyroid and para-thyroid glands. The thyroid is our body's gland of growth and vitality. It helps to metabolise fats and carbohydrates in our body and it is also called the watchman between our physical and mental body. This gland constantly secretes the above hormones into the blood stream to give

315

us our youthfulness, sex drive and virility but we have to feed it with its necessary nutrients i.e. Iodine and good quality proteins and Vitamin 'B$_1$' which are its help mate to carry out its assigned role.

1. Thus inhale with = HAÑ SPOKEN AS HAAA
   ÑÑÑÑÑ

   Exhale with = HOOOO Ñ Ñ Ñ Ñ

It is a neutral breathing mantra, it neither prefers the right brain nor the left brain, rather it helps to strengthen both the left brain/pituitary gland and also the right brain/pineal gland, thus stimulating the total brain. Pineal gland is the transducer of superconscious field, we can stimulate the 3rd eye with this neutral mantra, and also store pranic life into the 3rd eye, by taking our thought focussed between the two eye brows, slightly above, at the location of 3rd eye. Thus, give a covenient pause in breathing at the end of the mantras HAÑ & HOOÑ. and thus activate the 3rd eye with your thought. Within a few days practice of ten minutes breathing both morning and evening with this mantra by speaking it silently and deeply, one will start experiencing the on rush of bio-energy currents in the location of 3rd eye. And these blissful bio-currents will goad us to continue on this journey of self healing.

2. Strengthen Your Heart

We can strengthen our heart by adding Y-the seed word of Heart chakra to the above mantra.

Inhale with = YA + HAÑ = YAHHAÑ
Exhale with = HOOY-YEEÑ

3. Strengthen Liver and Digestion

We can strengthen the liver, the digestion, the

pancreas and the life saving adrenal gland by adding 'R' to the first mantra.

Inhale with	=	RA + HAÑ = RAHHAÑ
Exhale with	=	HOORRIEÑ

4. **Strengthen Lower Intestines** for proper assimilation of digested food into the blood stream and other life eliminative processes occuring in the lower intestines.

Inhale with	=	VA + HAÑ = VAHHAÑ
Exhale with	=	HOOVVIEÑ

5. We can boost our sex power, strengthen our legs and kindle our divine kundalini energy to illuminate our mind by adding the word 'L', the seed word of Muladhara /basic chakra.

Inhale with	=	LAH + HAÑ = LAHHAÑ
Exhale with	=	HOOLLIEÑ or HEALLEEÑ

6. **Fulfil with maximum possible pranic energy**

If we add the seed word 'PH' (F) of lungs and 'R' the seed word of abdominal breathing, this will help us to draw in as much oxygen/air, pranic life energy as possible.

Inhale with	=	PHRAHHAÑ
Exhale with	=	HOOF - FREEÑ

7. **Generate Hope in Life**

For that, we add the word ASHA (HOPE) to Mantra No. 6. The word SH is the seed word of both Muladhara/and Swadhistana Chakras and thus stimulates both the chakras. Also the word 'ASHA' helps us to breathe from the bottom of the legs upwards.

Thus inhale with	=	ASHA FRAHHAÑ
Exhale with	=	HOO FREESH SOOÑ

This is a complete body/mind rejuvenating breathing mantra, as it stimulates all the chakras of our body and mind system to generate the lamp of hope to live on, in a person suffering from any disease whatsoever, because it energises the total endocrine hormonal system to boost our immune system to help us recover from any disease, supplemented with balanced nutrition and above all the DESIRE TO LIVE ON & ON.

"A person who has Health has Hope
And who has Hope, has Everything."

An Arabian Proverb.

Chapter - 60

I AM INTERESTED IN ME

The more interest we develop in our-self, more healthy and all round fit we will become. It is infact the lack of interest in our own self that we fall prey to disease; because we don't pay attention to the early symptoms of the incoming disease, that is why, we must show sensitivity towards our own self. Make 'I am interested in me' as your breath and you shall never fall ill.

Exhale with = I AM INTERESTED IN ME
Inhale with = SARA - TANAMMAND

This mantra gives treble importance at T & D (T, T & D) and double importance to M and also N which are the seed words of MIND to develop full control over it. In this breathing mantra :-

i) The word helps S kindles the divine kundalini energy and boosts sex power.

ii) The word R - the seed word of Manipur/Navel Chakra helps in the assimilation of food, because it stimulates liver, pancreas and all the abdominal secretions. It also stimulates the life saving adrenal gland.

iii) It stimulates the left brain and the master pituitary gland with N; to boost our Immune system.

iv) It stimulates the right brain and the pineal gland with M.

v) It stimulates taste/salivary glands with T & D.

Thus, it is a rejuvenating mantra for our total body/mind system and goads us to develop interest in ourself by its hypnotic suggestive power.

Chapter - 61

THE SOUL SEARCHING MANTRA
ATMAÑ/ATMAN

Just as the Sun, though one, appears as many when reflected in many vessels of water, so does the one Atmañ, reflected in many individuals, appears to be manifold.

— *Srimad Bhagavatam. xi.iii.*

When the Atmañ - (Soul) gets embodied, it becomes ATMAN - the self, and this gives foundation to my concept of mantric breathing i.e. the word AÑ as inhale breath helps us to yoke with the super-consciousess because AÑ constitutes inhaling into Infinitum - the God, while the word AN helps us to inhale finitely into the brow chakra because N is the seed word for Brow chakra and the conscious organs in the brain.

And it is the soul (Atmañ) which enlivens the body through the medium of breath, commanding the senses to perceive, the brain to integrate the sense perceptions and the memory to store these perceptions, while soul acting as the charioteer of our body vehicle. The Soul - ATMAÑ, thus embodied, becomes ATMAN - the SELF, but when the Soul leaves the body chariot, it again becomes free and is again ATMAÑ, and moves about as a separate entity, till it takes rebirth. Of course, some of the enlightened souls merge after liberation from the confines of the body, into super consciousness (super soul) and thus get spared from the cycle of birth/rebirth - this is how the Hindu thought is revealed in their religious texts.

The word Atmañ is a very good mantra to yoke us with the infintiy, to recharge our body battery continuously.

1.Thus inhale as deeply as possible with = ATMAÑ
   Exhale with   = IMTIEÑ

Now in order to help our breath arise from its seat of origin i.e. about 7 cm below the navel, we take the help of the word SA, or Sha because the word 'S' or SH also originates in our body from the same point as the breath.

Our Atmañ (Soul) is beyond all illness but our Atman, because of our delinking with Atmañ and due to mal - nutrition and environmental pollution, can fall prey to diseases. In order to restore proper health.

2. Inhale with   =   SHFA + ATMAN

The word 'SHFA' means - healthy in Hindi/ Urdu language and it also helps the lungs to breathe to its full optimum capacity, thus keeping us fit and healthy.

    Exhale with   =   OOMNEESH FIT

The Exhale Mantra "Omni" conveying that I am as fit as the God.

3. Another rejuvenating mantra using the word Atman which benefits the total body/mind system is

    Inhale with =   ALLA-RAJA-ATMAN which means that Atman (SELF) is the King (RAJA) of our whole body/mind system.

Exhale with= YOU -RE-ILLUMINATE

This mantra, because of the power of the words L,R, Y,M,N,T can re-illuminate and rejuvenate our BEING., by stimulating the total endocrinal orchestra of our body.

Thus with the help of above mantras, we link our body/mind system with the super consciousness to breathe in as much pranic life energy as possible to make us fit and strong and thus feel blissful, because BLISS is the ultimate reality of Soul.

Chapter - 62

"I AM IN EQUILIBRIUM"

Life is a process of pulsating equilibrium, all the stress agents causing some sort of disequilibrium in our body/mind system but rest and our immune system again restores it to its equilibrium and that is how the life asserts itself.

And each individual human being has its own equilibrium trait, its own setting which may be some-what different from the other individual. Thus, all human beings appear to each other somewhat eccentric and hence we develop a bias against each other. Some persons are too talkative, others are some- what shy and too quiet. Some persons are too sexy and are always running after women. Some others hate women and so on. That is why, nothing in this world appears to be in perfect equilibrium.

Even the earth/moon/sun do not revolve around in perfect circles, but in elliptical orbits. Hence, some sort of dis-equilibrium is a natural phenomenon and we should accept it as an individual trait or its speciality or its beauty and never hate the other person for its dis-equilibrium or its craziness. Let us accept the God's creation as a variety of alive flowers, with their own colour, their own characteristic fragrance, their own personality, a slight different embodiment of God's Qualities. Then alone, we can develop the real compassion, and also develop our own inner equilibrium. For this, make the word inner equilibrium as your breath.

1. Exhale with   =   INNI-EQUILIBRIUM

And then Inhale deeply from the bottom of the spine or

    Inhale with   =   LA-BRA-YA-KANNAM

2. or Exhale with   =   EQUILLIBRIUM
   Inhale with   =   LA-BRA-YAK KAM

3. or Exhale with   =   I AM IN EQUILIBRIUM
   Inhale with   =   LA-BRA-YAKA-NAMMA

Inhale/Exhale with any of the above mantra speaking it inwardly, rhythmically, deeply and as softly as possible to simulate the natural breathing. Do it for five minutes in the morning and five minutes in the evening by sitting in a chair, with the spine kept in its erect position.

This breathing mantra helps to breathe from the bottom of the spine (L) - the seed word for basic sex Muladhara Chakra upto the crown of the head, for which the seed word is M, and in between, it resonates with Manipur/Navel chakra with R to improve the fire action of our body. And it strengthens the heart by its seed word Y and the combined word BR helps the lungs/bronchial tubes to breathe in to their full optimum capacity besides helping to breathe in also from the abdomen with the power of the word R. The word N is the seed word for Brow Chakra and strengthens the eyes and the left brain. The word K also supplements this action and above all the word M helps to improve our right brain. And the words N & M combine to strengthen both the pituitary and the pineal glands, which together control the total glandular activity of our body/mind system. Thus, this mantra boosts our total immune system; While the pituitary gland meets the challenge of stress, the pineal gland brings about Tranquillity

As we exhale with these very suggestive mantras which give a hypnotic healing effect on our mind to always remain in equilibrium, besides providing pranic life energy to our total body/mind system, to rejuvenate it and also boost our immune system, thus dissolving our stressful condition completely to restore our equilibrium.

OM-TAT-SAT (AMEEN)

Chapter - 63

A FRIENDLY MANTRA

Our mind is always seeking a friendly union, it always likes the company of those things it can merge itself or immerse itself i.e. become one with it i.e. a good delicious food in which it can absorb itself tastefully, seeks a good conversationist who can make the person laugh and converse on mutually acceptable topics, and the mind likes to see the beautiful girls go past a fashion cat-walk in all their beautiful and most fashionable dresses and above all a heart throb with which it can enjoy ecstastic sex or see a good cinema picture or a television play or reading a good novel or story book, or just walk hand in hand with a girl friend. As soon as the mind feels tired and bored, the mind says full-stop to all this activity. Thus, when you are not doing anything, make your breath your best companion there is no better friend. And Inhale/ Exhale with the following mantra.

(1) Inhale with   =   SKHA-NAMMA
    Exhale with   =   OOMNEESH - SUKHI

   Or - OOMNI - KHUSHI (This mantra means TRANSCENDENTAL HAPPINESS or Bliss)

(2) Exhale with   =   FRIENDLY BREATH
    Then inhale deep or inhale with AU, BLASSAM
                              (O, BLOSSOM)

These are indeed blissful mantras. With age, all the sense endings become dull after enjoying all sorts of sense pleasures. Then, the mind can turn to God Almighty to seek the bliss. Thus, this is a stress relieving mantra because our mind has made breath as its friend, and it is the breath, which is the link between our BEING and GOD and GOD is the Fountain of ALL BLISS.

Chapter - 64

BECOME AN ANGEL
MANTRA
I AM AN ANGEL

All of us aspire to become an angel and for that let us make 'ANGEL' as our breath. There is a beautiful song:-

> "Walk like an Angel
> Look Like an Angel"

(1) Thus exhale with = **ANGEL - LOOK**
    Inhale with = LAJJANK

(2) Exhale with = I AM ANGELIC
    Inhale with = LAJA-MANK

The exhale mantra I am Angelic is very suggestive indeed and it inspires us to become angelic and the word 'ANGEL' really stimulates us to become an angel because the word 'J' is the seed word for Heart. It strengthens our heart for better circulation of blood in our body and it also endows compassion to our heart to develop angelic qualities.

(ii) The word 'L' is the seed word for Basic chakra. It helps to kindle the divine kundalini energy by the resonant sonic energy of word 'L' with which it illuminates our total BEING to develop the Angelic looks.

(iii) The word MAÑ in Mank Yokes us with infinity - the superconsciousness to draw in as much pranic life energy as possible to have enough strength to walk like an angel, because the word 'L' also gives strength to the legs.

(iv) The inhale mantra ends at 'K' the seed word for left brain to develop the sensitivity of an angel.

Thus, the above mantra is truly an angelic quality mantra. to bestow us good health and make us compassionate.

Chapter - 65

A SIMPLE MANTRA TO REACH THE SEASHORE OF LIFE SAFELY

'SAHHIL'

The word 'SAH' in Urdu means Breath and the complete word 'Sahhil means sea-shore. And truly so, the word/mantra 'Sahhil' helps the boat of our life breath to move to and from one bank to the other in this beautiful journey of breath and we can also accompany this journey by making our thought move alongwith the breath. Thus, we become a part of this inner breath journey, the inner bliss, dissolving any stress in the process. But, for that, we must know all about the words S, H and L, the consonants forming the word 'SAHHIL.

Both the word 'S' and the breath originate in our body, about mid-way between the bottom of our spine and the navel. Thus, the word 'S' is the seed word for breath and constitutes as one end of the breath and with the word 'SAH', we help the breath to move upto the throat and beyond into the brain somewhat, because 'H' is the seed word for Vishudha Chakra/throat chakra.

1) Thus Inhale with =   SAH
    Exhale with   =   HILL

We, should inhale with the help of the word 'SAH' by speaking it inwardly, smoothly, rhythmically and as deeply as possible and then similarly exhale with the word HILL. The word HILL is quite apt for exhale breath, as it is like a Down Hill Journey, effortless & more rapid, and takes less time than the Inhale breath, which is like an uphill journey requiring effort. In order to make the breath yoke with the super-consciousnes-the other Seashore of BLISS

| Inhale with | = | SAÑH |
| Exhale with | = | HILL |

Then, give a small pause at both H & L, where the boat of breath reverses at both the sea shores of breath journey. Thus, the word SANH-HIL comprises the complete breath journey from one end to the other end.

And the word 'L' is the seed word for the Muladhara Chakra - the basic sex chakra which is located between the genitals and the lowest end of the spine and Muladhara chakra also constitutes the bottom of the mysterious divine life energy called Kundalini which is normally lying dormant like a coiled serpent, but becomes kinetic and the energy starts moving up through the so called sushumna opening in the spine upto the head alongwith the breath (S), which starts from the top of this Kundalini. The sonic resonant power of the word L, sets up vibrations to Kindle the Kundalini which can now move up to throat chakra alongwith the breath with the help of inhale word 'SAH'.

The word 'H' as said earlier is the seed word for throat chakra, and with its resonant sonic energy,it strengthens and energizes the Thyroid gland located in the throat which secretes its hormone 'Thyroxine' etc which helps to regulate carbohydrate and fat metabolism in our body. Thus, breathing mantra SAH-HIL is the first arrow we shoot out, to fight the battle of bulge on our abdomen.

And, when we fall ill, our breath becomes shallow and erratic and this breathing mantra SAHHIL helps to restore our beath to its healthy normal pattern, burning the extra fat with the power of the word 'H' and bringing the shine of health - glow on our face, by kindling the Kundalini with the power of word L, thus making our life journey a blissful experience.

I remember an Urdu couplet which talks about this SAHIL thus :

"Jub Kishti Sabit Salim Thee
Sahil Kee Tamanna Kis Kau Thee
Ub Itni Khasta Halat Hai
Sahil Kee Tamanna Kaun Karai"

It means :- When I was young & my life boat was strong and firm, I was busy enjoying myself thoroughly. Then, who had the time to think of the ultimate goal of life. Now, my boat of life is in such a delibitated condition that I cannot even think of achieving the supreme goal of my life to reach the sea shore.

But, you need not despair, my friend, inhale/ exhale with this mantra SANH-HIL and it will repair your Life-Boat again, & you will be able to start your boat journey again to your new goal, with the new Zeal & the New Zest. Cheer Up!

OM-TAT-SAT (AMEEN)

This chapter is dedicated to my grandson
whose name is 'SAHIL GAUBA', for His Well
Being. He is a Student Millionaire
Businessman.

Chapter - 66

SLEEP INDUCING MANTRA

"WANT TO SLEEP"
SAUÑM/MEE

I believe the greatest asset a head of state can have is the ability to get a good night's sleep.

— Harold Wilson

As long as we are young and healthy, our sleep comes to us as soon as we lay our head in the pillow and that sleep is deep and heavenly and when we get up in the morning ,we feel so fresh to say 'yes' to the New Day. And sleep is as natural to man as breathing or eating and is the most restorative tonic when we are tired.

At my present age of 66 years, luckily I am able to get sound sleep for seven hours but, when ever I do not get sleep,I imagine myself lying in the lap of Heavenly Fairy of Sleep which lulls me to sleep. I invoke the goddess of sleep by seeing HER in between the two eye brows, by keeping the eyes closed, thus :-

O, sleep, O, my Sweet fairy of sleep
Take me into your bosom
And make me asleep
I beseech thee
O, heavenly sleep
Make me worry free
Want to sleep
Want to sleep
Lull me to sleep"
— Author

And so, I go to sleep. But sometimes, it so happens that more we think of sleep, more difficult it becomes for us to get into sleep. This happens when we are tense and sleeplessness makes us more tense. Take sleep as your friend as in the above poem, sweetly surrender into her lap and soon you will get into sleep.

Another ways is to take the help of a friendly thought which goads us to sleep i.e. the hypnotic sleep inducing mantra — "Want to sleep".

1) Inhale softly and inwardly with = WANT
   Exhale softly and inwardly with = TO SLEEP

Another mantra which simulates the natural breathing is SAUNM/MEE

2) Inhale with   =   SAUÑM by speaking inwardly.

   Exhale with   =   MEE by speaking inwardly.

This is simplest and best sleep inducing mantra. The word 'M' helps to produce the pacifying harmone-melatonin to give peace and induce sleep.

3) Another sleep inducing mantra is — SHANTEESH

   Inhale by inwardly speaking with = SHANT
   Exhale by inwardly speaking with = TEESH

4) Another breathing mantra which is very soft and gives the hypnotic effect to get us into sleep is :-

   Exhale softly with = 'I AM ASLEEP' by speaking inwardly.

Then inhale softly without any inhale mantra.

5) Another similar hypnotising mantra in Hindi for inducing sleep is :-

| Exhale with | = | DAI SOONIEND |
| Inhale with | = | SANAND or SDA-ANAND |

And if you are not getting sleep due to over-eating which happens some times, try to sleep on your left side. This will open up the right nostril, which is the hot (Sun) Breath. This gives heat to our body to digest the food.

| And also, Inhale with | = | WARRANT |
| Exhale with | = | TO SLEEP - by speaking inwardly. |

Normally we do not add the word R in any sleep inducing mantra, Because R increases the metabolic rate, but it helps when we have over - eaten. And if it is cold season, we should supplement it by covering our abdomen with a warm blanket, in order to retain the heat in the abdomen to digest the food. And a few inhalations and exhalations with the breathing mantra - 'Warrant to Sleep' will induce us to sleep, as if we have sent a warrant to the goddess of sleep, to invoke her benign presence.

7) And last, but not the least, the simplest breathing mantra which simulates the natural breathing and is the most non-violent to breathe is SAÑ- IÑS

| Inhale with | = | SAÑ or SMAÑ |
| Exhale with | = | IEÑS or MSEEÑ |

And while inhaling and exhaling with the above mantra, if we can watch our breath as it goes in and goes out either at the nose tip or at the abdomen's Navel point - its rise and fall with the breath, we will soon be overlapped in deep sleep. This mantra also stimulates the crown chakra and pineal gland with its seed word M & the pineal gland releases the pacifying Hormone-Melatonin for inducing sleep.

8) Another beautiful and easy method to get sleep
    without the mantra is to watch, while sleeping,
    into the darkness between the two eyebrows
    while our eyes are closed and lo!, you are
    already in deep sleep.

In order to get good sleep, we must not overload
our stomach at night and keep at least 1/3rd of our
stomach empty for the oxygen and the pranic life
energy to digest the food properly. Some persons
are habituated to take a glass of hot milk before
going to sleep. That helps because milk contains
Tryptophan- an amino acid needed to make serotonin
in the brain which brings about sleep.

On the other hand, alcohol, smoking, taking
lots of cups of tea/coffee will cause sleeplessness
as well as the quality of sleep will not be deep and
peaceful. The above breathing mantras will definitely
induce you to get into sleep. We have given eight
sleep inducing mantras; choose anyone which
suits your temperament.

Let the goddess of sleep be with you at night or
let it be the goddess of your Love- your Heart-Throb
- a dynamic Ecstatic love session is the most
natural way to get into the blissful kingdom of
sound sleep.

OM-TAT-SAT (AMEEN)

Chapter - 67

"STILL THE MIND"

A mind can make hell out of heaven and heaven out of hell. It is like an un-bridled horse. We have to bridle it, we have to still it and in order to still our mind, we have to still our breath momentarily by giving it a pause. Just try it for yourself. Give a convenient pause **after inhaling** the breath as well as **after exhaling** the breath, you have also given a pause to your thinking process. When we breathe naturally, there is a very short natural pause, before the breath reverses itself. And inhaling creates eddy currents and inhaling with a mantra, being more forceful, creates more eddy bio-currents and secondly using the mantra as help in breathing, the sonic vibrations also produce their sonic resonant vibrations which also take time to ebb out to smoothness. Thus, if we give a pause after breathing, the fusion of this male and female breath gives us a feeling of bliss. Enjoy this blissful pause - this is like the ecstasy of sex pleasure, but without draining our sex energy.

And notice the beauty of the words-Silent, Shanti, Bliss, Still (As in Still your mind), all these words are constituted of the common words S, T, & L. Thus, to obtain bliss, we must still our mind by i) stilling our sex (S), particularly after the age of 50 years, we should use sex only as a valve to release our over-brimming energy, then alone, we enjoy sex in its thoroughness and fullest ecstasy. If we indulge in sex too much, we drain out our vital energy too rapidly and for that we have to eat more, we have to digest more in order to replenish this lost-energy and this causes tumoil in our body/ mind system. Thus, enjoy sex in its moderation. ii) In fact, moderation should be the key word in all our activities, including eating, because, If we want to still our mind, we have also to still our tastes (T) and not use too much condiments to boost our eating. iii) We have also to still our talking (T), in order to conserve our energy and for that try to get into silence for some time during the day. iv) Still your mind by stilling your breath as said above, by giving a pause after each inhalation/ exhalation. Start with giving a pause of one second only, then slowly practice to increase this pause to two seconds, three seconds and so on but only for as long as convenient. Thus, during this convenient pause in breathing, you will soon enter into silence and experience the bliss and you will start enjoying these blissful moments.

In order to achieve it more rapidly, we can also exhale the breath with the mantra- "Still the Mind or I still the Mind" or Immi-still the Mind. With this mantra, we are addressing our intelligence to still the mind. It will have a hypnotic effect, repeat it a number of times while exhaling with it and soon you will get into silence of the Mind - the blissful state of the mind. After each exhalation, with the above mantra, inhale slowly and rhythmically and deeply. I am not advising any mantra for inhaling, because that will also be an effort on the part of the mind to remember the inhale mantra., or use the effortless mantra - SHANT-TEE to breathe with, and soon you will get into the desired stillness of your mind. You have thus entered the Kingdom of Bliss.

OM-TAT-SAT- AMEEN

Chapter - 68

I AM HOPEFUL

"Hope Springs Eternal in the Human Breast" — *A. Pope*

As long as there is life, there is Hope. Infact, it is the hope that sustains life and as said by O.S. Marden, "There is no medicine like Hope, no incentive so great, no Tonic so powerful, as expectation of something tomorrow." Thus, make "HOPE" your breath.

And Exhale with = I AM HOPEFUL
          or   IMMIH - HOOPEFUL
And Inhale with ≠ LAFAPAHHAM

The word hopeful should be spoken inwardly as 'HOOPEFUL' for exhalation purpose, as orginally designed by the linguists. As we grow old, we also grow less hopeful and slowly become pessimistic due to the stark realities of life interactions; while, in our youth time, we are always hopeful and optimistic and thus feel more happy. Do not we find the old people generally wearing a Sad Look. Thus, hope is the sign of youth. This breathing mantra will also generate hope in you, first by the hypnotic suggestive power of the word, 'I am hopeful' and secondly the (i) word L which is the seed word for basic sex muladhara chakra, being procreatve, gives hope particularly because the word L helps to Kindle the divine Kundalini - the divine battery of life energy to make its life currents move up alongwith breath to kindle and illuminate us. And the illumination on our face generates hope in us.

ii) And the word F helps the lungs to breathe upto its full optimum capacity.

339

iii) The word P helps in the Heart circulation.

iv) The word H - the seed word for Vishudha/ Throat Chakra helps to strengthen the Thyroid gland for better carbohydrate and fat metabolism. The word H also helps to re-establish the sagging communication in the cervical region of the spine; thus generating hope for patients suffering from cervical spondylitis.

v) The word M is the seed word for crown chakra and it helps to strengthen the right brain and control over the Mind when the Kindled Kundalini reaches the crown chakra (M), the person starts illuminating with God's Bliss and Effulgence. Thus, the above breathing mantra is indeed very healsome. Inhale/Exhale with the above mantra by speaking the mantra inwardly, smoothly and deeply and as non-violently as possible, to simulate the natural breathing. Do it for five minutes in the morning and five minutes in the evening and you can surely hope to increase your health span. The word 'M' also stimulates the pineal gland which generates Hope in an ailing person by secreting the tranquillity Hormone - Malatonin in the blood stream.

2) We can introduce the word R in the above inhale mantra to re-ignite the dwindling Fire in our abdomen with age, to get rejuvenated.

Thus inhale with =   LAFA-PRAHHAM
Exhale with   =   MIHI-PRE-FILL

vi) The word R is the seed word for Manipur/Navel Chakra, it represents the Fire principle and strengthens the total abdominal glandular system for better digestion & assimilation of food. including the pancreas and the Liver.

vii) The word PR helps us to breathe both from the lungs with P as well as from the abdomen by the power of the word R. This mantra is the most efficient mantra for breathing because, breathing is helped threefold by the words (a) FA, (b) PRA and (c) HA and helps to take the breath to M - the crown chakra - The Charioteer of our body/mind system.

This breathing mantra, along with the following mantra, are very helpful for Bronchial patients. We can also substitute the word BR instead of PR because both these words are almost equivalent.

3) Inhale with = LAFFA- BRAHHAM
   Exhale with = MIHI- BREEFFILL

4) Our Hindi language word for Hopeful is Ashawan. This is also a good inhale mantra. The word 'Asha' means Hope.

Inhale with = ASHAWANNAÑ
Exhale with = UNNESSWIEÑ

This breathing mantra particularly strengthens the left Brain and the eye sight with the help of the seed word N for Brow Chakra. This also strengthens the pituitary gland, which is the master gland directing the total immune system of our body. This is complementary to the above mantras. The Exhale mantra - 'UNNEESWIEÑ' means Nineteenth. Thus, with this mantra you will always be feeling young Hopeful Nineeteen. - yet in your Teens-Nineteen — the most youthful Nineteen.

I am dedicating this chapter to my middle son - Mr. Ashawan Chowdhry for His Future Well Being. He is a Commerce Graduate and a successful businessman, who has earned millions right in his youthful age.

Chapter - 69

THE MANTRA

I AM BRILLIANT

Who does not want to shine like a Brilliant Star on the life's Horizon? And those of us who succeed to do so have tremendous stamina/health to support us in our mission. For this :-

1. Exhale with   =   I AM BRILLIANT
                               or
                               IMMI — BRILLIANT

   Inhale with   =   ALLA — BRAMMANT

Another more useful mantra, which incorporates word 'H' for improving our Thyroid gland action is given below.

Inhale with   =   ALLA — BRAHAMAND
Exhale with   =   MIHI — BRILLIANT

This is indeed a brilliant mantra to make us brilliant in health and to possess brilliant memory to achieve brilliant results in life, because this mantra helps to kindle the kundalini with its seed word L, it also gives strength to the legs with inhale mantra Alla, it improves our digestion with the seed word of Solar Plexus-R to give us the necessary FIRE for dynamism. The word BR helps us to breathe from the lungs with B and the abdomen with R and then the word H- the seed word of throat Chakra also helps the Cardio-respiratory system to breathe better. The ward H also strengthens the Thyroid gland for better fat/Carbohydrate metabolism and also to improve the communication between the brain and heart through the cervical region of the spine. Since our stamina to work for long Hours is limited by the ability of our heart/lungs to supply blood/oxygen/glycogen and other nutrients to our body cells and brain neurons which this breathing mantra adequately achieves and prepares us, thus for brilliant performance in life. The word 'Mand' strengthens the righ-brain with word M, the word AÑ Yokes us with infinity to unite us with Superconsciousness to draw in as much pranic life energy as possible and then Inhale Mantra settles the pranic energy in the dome of our soft palate of mouth with the word D to help improve our all tastes in life. This is indeed a great rejuvenating mantra to make us brilliant.

3.   Another simpler mantra to practice before we use the above two breathing mantras is

Inhale with   =   BRAHAMAND
Exhale with   =   MIHI — BREATHE

The wrods T, TH & D are almost equivalent in their action.

The word Brahamand in our Sanskrit/Hindi language means universe and now we know that even the universe also breathes. It expands and contracts and also all the matter in it goes through Birth and Death Cycle, on an astronomical scale in billions of years-the energy/matter gets fused into a star which shines through the prime of its life and then slowly fades, like human ageing to become a cold star or Black Hole. The emitted energy/matter (both matter and energy being convertible into each other by famous Einstein's equation of mass/energy equivalence-$E=mc^2$) again gets fused into forming another star and so on -

the goody goody cycle of life/energy movement/
transformation of energy goes on and on.

And we human beings also go through our
brilliant youth and ultimately become COLD, but
these breathing mantras endow us the ability with
resonant sonic energy of the words used to prolong
our brilliant period of youth as long as we desire,
by strengthening our immune system as well as by
continuing to recharge our life battery with pranic
life energy.

OM — TAT — SAT — AMEEN

Chapter - 70

THE BHAKTI MANTRA

MERE RAMA

Bhakti yoga helps us to melt into dimensionless unity with God by our total surrender. In the bhakti song, the devotee's total Being dances with the bhakti song or mantra and thus experiences blissful union with super-consciousness.

There is a famous bhakti devotional song sung by the disciples of Hare Rama, Hare Krishna religious sect, now spread all over the world. The bhakti song is

Hare Rama, Hare Rama, Rama, Rama, Hare, Hare

Hare Krishna, Hare Krishna, Krishna, Krishna, Hare, Hare

This bhakti song is very aptly constructed so that one can breathe in-between properly; exhaling with Hare Krish and inhaling with Shna and similarly exhaling with Hare and inhaling with Rama.

Since this book is devoted more to exhale/inhale mantras, we usually start with a very simple Bhakti mantra :-

1. Exhale with   =   MERE
   Inhale with   =   RAMA

And we can fold and clap our hands while exhaling with 'Mere' and inhale with 'Rama', while outstretching the hands. So doing, Lord Rama becomes our breath and one gets so much submerged in Lord Rama (the God Incarnate) that Lord Rama starts flowing into the Devotee and the devotee starts merging into Lord Rama. Both, thus, become one i.e. merge into dimensionless unity, thus dissolving all stress in this total surrender.

2. Lord Krishna whose other name is SHAM, we can construct a simple Bhakti mantra for devotees of Lord Krishna.

Exhale with   =   MERE
Inhale with   =   SHAMA

Also we can combine devotional mantra No 1 and 2, on the pattern of Hare Krishna song :-

Mere, Rama, Mere, Rama, Rama-Rama,Mere-Mere

Mere, Shama, Mere, Shama, Shama-Shama, Mere-Mere.

Or simply Mere Rama, Mere Shama and repeat on, till one gets totaly unified with the super-consciousness.

The mantra-MERE-RAMA is also very healsome, because with the word 'R' - the seed word of Navel chakra, we stimulate the Liver, the pancreas and all abdominal secretions to boost our body's metabolism and digestion. And the word 'M' strengthens the Crown Chakra, and the right brain and also the pineal gland which releases the pacifying hormone Melatonin to soothe our shattered nerves due to daily stress and induce good sleep.

Besides, during clapping with the above mantra, we press the bio-energy switches in our both hands to heal us, as is now well known in Accupressure therapy. That is why I often say "Twenty claps a day keeps the Heart physician away".

Chapter - 71

THE MANTRA

I AM IN PRAYER

In prayer, we make a dedicated effort to communicate with God with hope for divine help. Thus, we completely surrender ourself unto God to become a vacuum, to be filled in by the Omni-grace, Omni Potency, Omni-Knowledge, and Omni-Bliss to illumine our total Being with His Glory and fill our heart with Omni-Compassion.

Sit in prayer and let us make the word 'PRAYER' as our exhale breath.

(1) Exhale with = PRAYYER
    Inhale with = RAYYAPRAÑ

While exhaling with the word 'Prayer' spoken inwardly, slowly evacuate your abdomen, to make it completely empty, then inhale with, by giving an emphasis to the inhale word - 'RA' to fill the abdomen, because it is the seed word for Navel/Solar Plexus/Abdomen/Liver/Pancreas.

ii) Then continue to inhale with 'YA' which helps the heart to improve circulation and then inhale with (ii) prañ, which helps the lungs to breathe in as much pranic life energy as possible and also Yokes us with the infinity - the super consciousness. The end of the mantra prañ sounds like pran which means life, Thus with this mantra, we are both in prayer as well as inhale the pranic life energy from cosmos.

Another similar prayer mantra with added benefits is

(2) Exhale with ═ I AM IN PRAYER or
                        OOMNI-PRAYER
    Inhale with ═ RA YA PRANAM

Another allotropic modification of the prayer mantra is

(3) Exhale with ═ I AM PRAYERFUL
    Inhale with ═ LA FRA YA PRAM

Inhale/ Exhale with all the three mantras for two minutes each for the total of 6 minutes both morning as well as evening. In the last mantra No (3), the basic Muladhara chakra gets resonated with the sonic energy of word 'L', the Solar plexus with 'R', the heart chakra with 'Y', the breathing lungs get fortified with both 'Fra' as well as with 'Pra', which ultimately breathe into the crown chakra, for which the seed word is 'M'. The words N & M strengthen the brain as well as the pituitary and pineal glands. Thus, it rejuvenates our total body/mind system, besides being prayerful which fills us with the effulgence of God's bliss and glory.

OM — TAT — SAT/ AMEEN

Chapter - 72

A ZERO GRAVITY SWIM
I AM FREELY - SWIMMING

If you are a swimmer, tie a 20 cms. x 20 cms foam enclosed in a cotton cloth around your waist, so that, you are able to float in the swimming pool without any effort, you are just able to float in equilibrium, without getting tilted, just sufficient to give you a floating feeling in the swimming pool or a small lake or a small canal. Just float around and feel as if you are swimming effort- lessly without the least effort on your part, of course, you turn about in the pool, by the proper movement of the legs. Then, the waves in the pool will move you, anywhere around and you enjoy this up and down and side way tossings effortlessly. It is indeed a great feeling of freely swimming, when even the gravity is not working. It is really an exhilarating feeling, an ethereal feeling, a great blissful feeling of being one with the universe floating effortlessly with zero gravity.

How nice it would be, if our journey through this universe is as effortless, as the above swim. We feel totally relaxed and thus blissful. You enjoy your this freely swimming feeling - this effortlessness. This also teaches us to enjoy our role in this world like a freely swimming person without any resistance, we have completely surendered to the will of God.

Then, when you come out of the pool and bask in the sun, to rest while lying down, exhale deeply with the words - "I AM FREELY SWIMMING"

By speaking the words inwardly and softly and then inhale deeply without any mantra. and with this mantra that feeling of freely swimming will linger on and on to make you stress free.

Chapter - 73

WEAR A COVETED SMILE

A Smile begets a Smile. Give a smile to a down trodden person and perceive the glow in his eyes and face, generating new life in his veins. I am talking of the downtrodden person because all successful persons are greeted with smiles where-ever they go - Genuine Smiles, artificial madeup smiles, but smiles all the way.

And a smile from a Nurse or a Doctor in the Hospital can enliven the patient and speed up his recovery. Thus let us greet every person with a smile because it puts the other person at ease and makes him/her happy to open the dialogue between the two. Thus a smiling person can win friends and influence persons and thus become a great success in his/her career. Sometimes a smile from a beautiful lady may also land her in trouble, because it can be misunderstood. Never mind, keep smiling and make smiling your breath.

1) Exhale with   =   SMILING
   Inhale with   =   LA — SMONG

Thus, this mantra will help us to illuminate our personality with the word L and take the kindled kundalini energy with breath (S) to the crown chakra (M) and the word 'ONG' yokes us with superconcious-ness and the inhale mantra ends with 'NG' which gives sonic energy to secrete immunoglobin hormone A in the Nasal Cavity to boost our immune system.

Also, the mantra smiling gives us the suggestive hypnotic influence to make us always wear a coveted smile on our face. It will help us and all others we meet.

Chapter - 74

REFRESH YOUR BODY/ MIND

THE MANTRA
I AM FRESHENED

How beautiful it would be to look as fresh as the newly bloomed flower. And the mantra "I am freshened" is a very potent rejuvenating breathing mantra, because it freshly strengthens all the glandular system of our body/mind system and also recharges our life battery with pranic life energy. Thus, look always fresh :-

Exhale with	=	I AM FRESHENED
		OR
		IMMIF — FRESHENED
Inhale with	=	SHRA — FAN — NAMAND

The word 'sh' kindles the divine kundalini and takes it alongwith the breath to the crown chakra (M), the word 'R' gives fire to our body, the word F helps the lungs to breathe to their optimum capacity. The word M also stimulates the right-brain. The word N improves the left brain and the eye-sight and the word 'Mand' yokes us with infinity with the breath and the word 'D' stimulates the dome of the soft palate in the mouth and it strengthens the gums of the teeth, and the total word 'NAMAND' helps to develop control over our mind. Also, the words M & N by their sonic resonant vibrations strengthen both the pineal and pituitary glands respectively which together control the total glandular activity in our body, thus boosting our total immune system, so as not to fall victim to any disease. Thus, it is a total body/mind rejuvenating mantra to make us look always fresh and smart. Also, we can use a slightly shorter breathing mantra.

2) Exhale with   =   YOU FRESHEN
   Inhale with   =   SHRAFAYAAN

The word 'Y' is the seed word for Heart Chakra for better blood circulation. So this breathing mantra will help us to look always fresh, brimming with energy.

Chapter - 75

THE MANTRA

"I AM IN HEAVEN"

"Earth has no sorrow that heaven cannot heal".
— *Moore*

If we are healthy and filled with the desire to enjoy life, we are as if living in heaven on earth, because health gives us cheers and these mutually beget each other. and it is our own cheerfulness which is heaven on earth, just-as the poet UMMARKHYAM sings thus :-

"A cup of wine
A book of verse
And she beside me singing
Then even wilderness
Is heaven for me"

And we can fortify our health by exhaling with the suggestive mantra "I AM IN HEAVEN"/OOMNI - HEAVEN

Inhale with   =   VAHANNAM

The word V is the seed word for Swadhistana Chakra, this represents water principle and strengthens the ovary and our assimilation/ elimination processes in lower intestines. And if our stool movement is easy and first class, our day has well started and in fact it is the best good morning, as it gives the heavenly feeling for the rest of the day.

The seed word H restores our health, restores

354

our communication link between the body and the brain and strengthens the thyroid gland which helps in the carbohydrates and fat metabolism in our body and thus gives us that perfect shape by dissolving the unnecessary fat which is the fashion of the day to look slim and trim.

The seed word N stimulates the Brow Chakra & improves our left brain and strengthens our master pituitary gland while the seed word M stimulates the Crown chakra & improves our right brain and strengthens the pacifying pineal gland. So, three cheers, we are feeling heavenly and psychologically, also, the mantra "I AM IN HEAVEN" transports us into that heavenly feeling because who said it, "All Heaven and Hell is in our Mind."

This chapter is dedicated to my wife
Mrs. Santosh Rai for HER WELL BEING.
She has indeed proved an ideal companion to
give that Heavenly feeling as stated in the
above VERSE.

Chapter - 76

LAUGHTER - THE BEST MEDICINE

There is a Japanese proverb that "Time spent laughing is time spent with the gods" and some persons are really gifted with pleasing laughter, they are able to laugh biosterously over trifles and also make others laugh. And there are others, who laugh rarely and are serene persons, always thinking and thinking and are therefore, more stress-prone. Such persons should seek the company of friends who are good conversationists and provoke laughter easily. Thus, laugh away your worries and try to cultivate the habit of laughing over your own small idiocracies alongwith your wife, to keep healthy.

There is a yogic exercise to laugh by laughing artificially by loudly speaking- Ha,Ha,Ha,Ha, by keeping the mouth open, as if to simulate the actual laughing process. After laughing with Ha,Ha,Ha,Ha for a minute or two, you will be tempted to laugh naturally over this idiocracy. Enjoy the laugh thus created. With laughter, we are able to exhale out toxic vapours from our stomach/body system and also activate the nasal glands to secrete immunity boosting secretions. This is supported by the recent work of Prof. Arthur Stone of the State University of New York, who has established the presence of increased levels of immunoglobin A-an antibody in the mucous lining of the nasal cavity of those persons who laughed more during the day, thus, also confirming that laughter is the best medicine.

And the seed word for activating the nasal cavity is NGH and please note that the word 'gh' is also contained in the word 'Laugh'

1) Thus Inhale with = LAFFANGH
  Exhale with = GHEEFFIL

Another breathing Mantra to activate the nasal cavity is

2) Inhale with = SO YOUNGH
  Exhale with = YOU SINGH OR YOU SING

        or/and

3) Inhale with = LAFA — YOUNGH/
         LAFAYOUNG
  Exhale with = YOU — FILLINGH/
         YOU — FILLING

        or/and

4) Inhale with = SARA YOUNGH/
         SARA YOUNG
  Exhale with = YOU RE — SINGH/
         YOU — RE — SING

And you always feel "Loftier", provided you laugh with the person and not at him. And to create this lofty feeling in your mind,

5) Inhale with = LOFT/ LAUGHT
  Exhale with = TIER/ TER

The whole mantra being Lofttier or Laughtter. Thus, this is a Mantra made out of words Loftier or Laughter.

Another breathing Mantra with similar effect is

6) Inhale with = SANGAM/ SANGHAM
  Exhale with = MINGEESH/ MINGHEESH

All the above mantras besides providing us with pranic life energy through breathing will also invoke the feelings of Song, laughter, Youngness, Union with friends (Sangam) and above all the lofty feelings, besides stimulating the Heart with 'Y', the right-brain, pineal gland with M, the liver and the pancreas with R, kindle the divine kundalini energy with L, S and fulfill the lungs and our BEING with pranic energy with its seed word F. And, above all, let us not forget that "Laughter is the best medicine".

Chapter -77

WALKING -
THE BEST HEALTH MANTRA

1. SAÑ/ IN S
2. LONG/ GLEE

Walking is as natural to Man as flying for the birds, since man has evolved into walking upright. And walking is the safest aerobic exercise which imparts movement to the total body/mind system, because our legs are connected through the thigh bone with the five lower vertebrae of the spinal column and the hands are connected to the seven vertebrae of the top of the spinal column in the cervical region of the neck and the neck is the communication link between the brain and the body/heart. Since during walking, legs well as hands move back and forth alternately, therefore the total body gets aerobic movement.

Thus, walking is the safest aerobic exercise, even recommended for heart patients to tone the heart. Thus, keep walking within your body limits. You should not get tired or become breathless, that is the limit. This is the greatest health mantra for all persons and Hippocrates told it so, long long ago, "Walking is the best medicine." However, I advise that you should also take a glass of water before you embark on your walking schedule. Also,

"Do not indulge in Talking
While you are Walking." Author

Because, talking superimposes haphazard breathing currents over the natural breathing pattern established during natural walking. Instead I recommend walking with a breathing mantra which is synchronous with natural breathing during walking. The breathing mantra is to be spoken inwardly.

WALKING MANTRA :- Those of us who can enjoy a fast walk, it will also help to dissolve the stress from the mind, because in running or fast walking, there is no time to think, thus, all thoughts vanish. But, as we age, our walking becomes slow and many stressful thoughts torment our mind during walking and to dissolve the stressful thoughts during walking, I recommend walking with a health imparting breathing mantra which you can choose from any one of the following mantras given below. It is preferable to walk with a neutral mantra. Enjoy walking without the mantra, if you are not stressed.

List Of A Few Walking Mantras

Table A :		Table B :	
Inhale Mantra	Exhale Mantra	Inhale Mantra	Exhale Mantra
SHFANG	GLEE	LFANM	MEEL
LONG	GLEE	SHFANM	MEESH
SONG	GEESH	SMART	TEE/TER/TEST
FRAN	FROON	FRAM	FROOM

Table C

Inhale with	Exhale with
Sañ	INS

Shfañ	FEEL/BLISS
Lfañ	FEEL
Vfañ	FEEL
Frañ	FROOÑ
Lanh	HEAL

Table A : Walking Mantras with right foot forward first when right nostril is more openly breathing.

Table B : Walking Mantras with left foot forward first, when left nostril is more openly breathing.

Table C : Neutral Breathing Mantras with any foot forward first.

We usually use single stage breathing mantra, starting the inhale mantra with words L, S, Sh and V because these words originate from the bottom of the spine particularly the words L, S, Sh which are the seed words for muladhara chakra and also give strength to the legs. The walking mantra - LONG-GLEE is also very gleeful mantra to dissolve stress; and the easiest mantra to walk with, with right foot forward first.

HOW TO USE WALKING MANTRA

Before starting the walk, first observe which one of the nostrils is flowing more easily with breath. Suppose it is the right nostril-that means that sun or hot breath is active, our body needs heat. Thus, we should also be in tune with nature while walking. For that, start walking first with the right foot forward while inhaling with the mantra LONG and then exhale with the exhale mantra GLEE with the left foot forward and so on. Then after a few minutes walk, you can interchange i.e. that is now you can inhale with left foot forward first with LAÑM and then exhale with MEEL with right foot forward. This will help to bring about the equilibrium in breathing pattern.

Thus, we can amplify the benefits of walking, with the power of healing words. We can also use the walking mantra - smart/ty, smart/ter and smart/test thus becoming smarty, smarter and smartest with every new day, developing trust in healing ourself with the power of healing words and also by the hypnotic effect of these suggestive mantras. And walking benefits will further multiply, if we can re-establish our connection with the Earth and the Sun, by walking barefooted in our lawn for some times during the day and also expose our total body to sunrays for about fifteen minutes everyday to impart strength to our bones and legs by proper absorption of solar energy to metabolise vitamin D in our body for proper calcium absorption and other manifold benefits.

WALKING IN BED

Those persons who are somewhat incapacitated to walk, they are advised to move their hands alternately up and down as in walking either by sitting in chair or lying in bed as convenient. Also they can move their legs alternately up and down as in natural walking. This will provide the most necessary movements for proper elimination and assimilation processes of our body. This can simulate the benefits of natural walking if we can repeat these bed walking excercises a number of times during the day, taking care to do these exercises atleast half an hour before breakfast/lunch/dinner i.e. that is only with the unloaded stomach. Keep it up, you are on the path of total recovery.

Chapter - 78

A LIFE SAVING MANTRA

WANT TO LIVE

'Want to live' is the most suggestive life saving breathing mantra, first because thought/desire is our being and thought is the finest form of pranic energy. As said by Swami Vivekanand, "Matter is Mighty, but Thought is Almighty", and secondly, the word 'Want' yokes us with infinity-the super-consciousness to fulfill our being with as much pranic life energy as possible, with WAÑ and then the mantra ends at T, the seed word for taste/ salivary glands. The word T also is able to stimulate the pituitary gland because of its proximity with the top palate of our mouth, with its resonant sonic vibrations. And thirdly, because the word W (V) is the seed word of Swadhishtana Chakra which stimulates the lower intestines for proper absorption of digested food into the blood stream so that it irrigates all the cells of our body/mind system. It is in the lower intestines where the Alcohol which is not able to be metabolised by Liver gets absorbed in the blood stream and if we inhale deeply and rapidly with WANT and exhale similarly with "TO LIVE" with half mouth open, when over-drunk, it can help us to save our life, because we flush out the abdomen and fill it with fresh oxygen/air/ pranic energy, besides stimulating the lower intestines with pranic energy by strengthening the Swadhishtana Chakra which energises the lower intestines through our Astral body.

And the exhale mantra 'TO LIVE' rapidly evacutes the lower intestines with exhale breath, besides stimulating the Muladhara Chakra with its seed word 'L' which gives us the WILL power to LIVE and also kindles the divine kundalini to energize our body. Thus, it is a very powerful breathing mantra to save our life while struggling against any type of disease. This mantra is our last ray of hope when everything else fails.

2. We can also add the word 'R' in the above mantra:

Inhale with   =   WARRANT
Exhale with   =   TO LIVE/ OR/ TRI-LIVE

This is a mantra which sends a warrant to the Goddess of Life to make us live on and on, because the word 'R' - the seed word of solar plexus/ Navel Chakra stimulates the life saving adrenal gland, also the pancreas, the liver and all the abdominal secretions for proper digestion and assimilation of food, to come to our succour.

3. Another similar life saving mantra is :-

Exhale with   YOU WILL LIVE
Inhale with   LAVAYAÑ

In this, we stimulate the heart chakra with its seed word 'Y' for better blood circulation and to give us the compassion to love and live, because without loving or being loved by some one, it is not worthwhile living in this world, full of tensions and stress.

The word YAÑ also yokes us with infinity - the superconsciousness to fill our MIND/heart with pranic life energy and God's effulgence because the mantra YAÑ is neutral, it stimulates the total brain and this mantra also stimulates the 3rd eye which is the transducer of superconscious field.

Also the words L & V help us to strengthen our WILL power to make the sex energy move upward to unite with superconsciousness so that our eyes begin to sparkle with bliss and thus we become a spiritual self so that we can live on and on and we leave this world with our own sweet-will.

OM — TAT — SAT / AMEEN

Chapter - 79

SILENCE -
THE GREAT TRANQUILLIZER

THE MANTRA
I AM SILENT

"A peaceful Mind is your most precious capital."
— *Swami Sivananda*

Silence comes to us from within, when we feel fully contented with life or detach ourselves from worldly attachments with full awareness.

This modern world is replete with all sorts of sounds-speech, soft music, high decibel music in discos, natural thunderstorm occasionally, but daily high pitch thunders of the air crafts, all sorts of noises from factories, motor vehicles, lound speakers etc, so much so that noise has become a major environmental pollution today, which deafens our hearing senses.

Also, there is a daily lively noise which arises out of married life, noise generated in the family due to mutual interactions of Husband/ wife/ children. In India, where wife takes some time to adjust to the new home after marriage, a popular saying usually describes the marriage life thus :- First ten years, the man speaks, the wife hears, next ten years, the wife speaks and the man hears and the next ten years, both husband and wife speak and the neighbours hear and then ultimataly, it all becomes Quiet, because, after that, some sort of un-easy mutual silence/understanding descends with age or we are naturally driven to seek silence by retiring to a recluse or a hermitage, particularly, as we advance in age, and even we get bored with the din of too much club life, as said by poet Sir Mohammed Iqbal:-

"Dunian Ki Mehfloon Se Ukta gya Hoon, Yarab Daman Main Kauh Kai, Aik Chotta Sa Jhoonpra Hau"

Now, to attain inner silence, retire to a particularly quiet corner of your home, if not to a hermitage, sit comfortably in a chair, in an erect spine position, with eyes closed and look into the darkness within, between the two eyebrows, feel as if complete silence is descending in you.

Exhale with   =   "I AM SILENT"
                        or
                        IMMEESH SILENT

Inhale with   =   LA — SHANTAM
                        (O, Bring silence).

Speak - Silent as sealent as exhale Mantra as if you have sealed your hearing ears to all sorts of external sounds.

Both exhale and inhale mantras mean silence and peace. The inhale mantra is the mirror image of the exhale mantra, "I AM SILENT".

Here, I recall Kipling proclaiming to the world that - East is East and the West is West & the Twain shall never meet, but here and now, the Twain have met in this Mantra to save this world from the Agony of Stress beautifully, and easily, as, this mantra is a great stress dissolver, because it brings about the Harmony of Body, Mind and the

Soul.

Inhale, Exhale softly with the above mantra by speaking inwardly, so as to simulate the natural breathing as nearly as possible, so as not to cause any further violence to our body/mind system. And at the end of the Mantra, get into complete silence with a convenient pause in breathing. Slowly, Slowly with this mantra - "I am Silent," you will move into complete silence, you have risen above the mantra. Mantra was necessary as a preparation, now you remain in silence by watching your natural breathing. Watch it at the tip of the nose, as the breath goes in and goes out, Thus, you have moved into the desired silence with your breath, I am saying-desired silence, because your mind will no longer be chaotically thinking or brooding over the past or building castles in the future or no more your energy is being wasted into thinking/ talking ill of others, throwing blame on others for all your own ills - the product of your own actions. Now, you, are at peace with the world, and with your own surroundings. The energy, thus, saved is being credited into your Bank Balance of life energy in the kundalini., because energy income is the same, either waste it or conserve it. This is the key to your healthy blissful living particularly in old age, when you need to conserve your energy the most, in order to fight out the infirmities of old age. And only in silence the divine energy can flow into our BEING.

This blissful silence is possible only, when we are completely non-violent in all our actions, even in our speaking, we have to be soft and affectionate to others because speech can hurt very deeply, conveyed beautifully in the following proverb :-

"A Bullet, an Arrow and a Word of Mouth, Once released, cannot be brought back".

In my mother tongue, it is conveyed similarly by a poet :-

*"Admi Jau Kehta Hai, Admi Jau Karta Hai
Zindgi Bher Voh sadain Piechha karti Hain".*

Thus, be at ease with the world and be at ease with yourself, then alone, you can attain the inner silence, though complete silence is a myth, because even in the State of Samadhi- the highest form of Meditation, the sages hear the all reverberating sound of AUM in the Ether environment from the Universe.

Thus, when I say, that I am Silent :- It means that all my way-ward thinking is now focussed on a single pleasant point, my brain wave pattern has assumed the more peaceful pattern as in sound sleep.

Here, I must say a word about anger which is the opposite of Silence in the mind. We should avoid anger particularly in old age, because anger can kill us. When we are angry, we speak all sorts of hotch potch and that too, at the top of our voice throwing our natural breathing out of gear/phase, we feel breathless, our heart starts beating faster to make the blood reach the brain, the adrenal glands release the chemical-adrenalin in the blood to tide over this emergency situation arising out of Anger.

Thus, when we are silent, we are not only saving energy by 'Not Speaking', but this way, we allow our natural breathing to proceed its natural course to sustain the body, because each spoken word can either aid or obstruct the breathing, depending upon whether the spoken word is in phase with natural breath or out of phase with it. It is true that normal speaking for short periods is within the bio-energy stress limits of our Body and is quickly repaired by our body, but speaking for long hours continuously can make our throat hoarse and is thus stressful but angry situation exceeds the stress limits of our body and reaches the agonising stage.

Thus, conserve your energy by remaining silent for some period during the day and if you close your eyes also, it will doubly benefit you:, to enter the inner silence. Then you will not only enjoy better health but also enter the much sought after kingdom of Divine Bliss.

And, we cannot enter into SILENCE unless we are FEARLESS (see next chapter).

Chapter - 80

BECOME FEARLESS

"All the negative thoughts and ideas that are in this world are produced from this evil spirit of fear. Therefore I say, be fearless, be fearless".

— *Swami Vivekananda*

The seed mantra for stress Management as already given is "SACHA - ANAND/NESHCHINT". The inhale mantra - Sacha - Anand means - Truthful Bliss, and the exhale Mantra-Neshchint means "CAREFREE and Fearless" and this can happen only if we lead a life of Satyam (Truth), Shivam (godliness) and Sundaram (Beautiful Existence).

And also I remember the closing lines of a famous novel - FORTITUDE in which the author says, "O God, make of me a man, to be afraid of nothing, to be ready for everything - Love, Friendship and Success - to take them, if they come and to care nothing if these things are not for me." Thus, let us make the word "fearless" as our breath.

Exhale with   =   I AM FEARLESS
                                or
                                IMMI - FEARLESS

Inhale with   =   ALLA-SARA-FAMMAÑ

This suggestive mantra besides goading us to become fearless, is indeed a very healsome breathing mantra, because it stimulates the Muladhara Chakra with 'L' to make us illuminate; because the

371

words L & S kindle the divine kundalini energy, the word 'R' makes us energetic and the word 'F' helps us to fill our lungs with oxygen and pranic life energy to their optimum capacity to make it reach all the cells of our body. And the word M by its resonant sonic energy stimulates the crown chakra and the pineal gland - the highest chakra which makes us know our right place in this universe and the word MAÑ yokes us with Infinity - the Super Conscious Field of Energy to fulfil our BEING with Divine Effulgence and Pranic Energy, since the word MAÑ acts - as the Transducer of Super-consciousness, thus making us divine and fearless in the process, besides helping us to enjoy the health in its full splendour.

Chapter - 81

I AM LIKE THAT

"SOHAM"

"Soham" pronounced as SAUHAM is a divine mantra, because in Sanskrit language, it means — 'I AM LIKE THAT', I am like the BRAHMAN — the God Almighty. I am cast in His Image, His divinity flows in me. The Soul which animates my body is a part of the SUPER - SOUL - the God Almighty and this divine thought — 'I AM LIKE THAT' is the greatest contribution of Hinduism to Mankind, because this infuses the feeling of divinity in human beings to become angelic and compassionate to love one and all — the whole humanity, without any discrimination of caste, creed, colour and Nationality.

Next to the Universal Hindu Mantra — 'AUM', Soham is the next best chanting mantra given by Hindu Sages to their disciples for their well being; but like AUM, Soham is also an inhale mantra, without its exhale counterpart. Its exhale mantra — its mirror image mantra is framed thus :

1. Inhale with   =   SAUHAM
    Exhale with   =   MIHISH

2. Its more beneficial allotropic modification which also yokes us with the Super-Conscious Energy field to draw life energy from the Infinitum Source is 'SAUHAÑM'. Thus :

    Inhale with   =   SAUHAÑM
    Exhale with   =   MIÑHISH

This is one of the best two stage breathing mantra, because it yokes the body's breath centre — with 'S', the crown chakra and the right brain with M through the cervical region of the spine with H, and it also mingles us with the Superconscious Energy Field with HAÑ, with which we can breathe as deeply as we like.

The word 'S' also kindles the divine kundalini energy which moves up alongwith the breath to the Vishudha Chakra — the seed word for which is H, which stimulates with its sonic energy the Thyroid gland — the gland of growth and virility which also helps in carbohydrate and fat metabolism in the body. The word 'H' also helps to re-establish the communication between the body and the brain through the cervical region of the spine. Hence, this mantra is the seed mantra for helping to cure the cervical spondylitis — a very prevalent disease amongst the desk workers. The word M is the seed word of the pineal gland which is a pacifying gland and is also the Transducer of Super-Conscious Energy field particularly with the help of the word 'HAÑ'. Thus this mantra illuminates our Being with God's Effulgence with the words S, H, AÑ & M.

3. The English meaning of the word 'SOHAM' — 'I AM LIKE THAT' is also a good healsome divine exhale breathing mantra :

Exhale with	=	I AM LIKE THAT/ IMMI-LIKE THAT
Inhale with	=	ALLA-CAMMAND
	=	ALLA-KAMMAND

This English version of Soham is indeed a very Commanding mantra because it also kindles the divine kundalini energy with the word 'L' then it stimulates the total brain — the left brain & the pituitary master gland with the word K, the right brain & the pineal gland with M, Yokes us with the Super-Consciousness with the word MAÑ and then it ends at D (T, TH) which stimulates the top soft palate in the mouth and the taste and salivary glands. The words K, M, D thus stimulate the TOTAL BRAIN. Thus, it is indeed a very healsome mantra to illuminate our body and mind and it is a useful mantra for persons suffering from Parkinson's & Alzheimer's diseases because it helps to put the brain again in a commanding position.

The above breathing mantras not only help us to inhale deeply but also help to stimulate the sex glands with S, L, the thyroid glands with H, the pituitary master gland with K & the pineal gland with M but also yoke us with Infinity — the God's effulgence as explained above. And above all, these suggestive breathing mantras infuse a sense of Divinity and hence help us to dissolve all stressful condition from our Mind.

And God said, Let us make man in Our image, after Our likeness: and let them have dominion over the fish of the sea, and over the fowl of the air, and over the cattle, and over all the earth, and over the creeping thing that creepeth upon the earth. So God created man in His own image.

Genesis 1:26

SECTION - VII

BECOME A SIDHA
AND
A PRANIC/REIKI LIKE HEALER

Chapter - 82

REMAIN ENERGETIC

ENERGIZE YOUR HANDS AND BECOME A REIKI /PRANIC HEALER

We, human beings, are a network of energy flow channels and any blockage in the harmonious flow of energy in our body becomes the cause of disease. And, above all, man is a dynamic potentiality and we have been endowed by God with the power to heal ourselves by restoring the harmony between our body, mind and soul by yoking our breath with the Super Conscious Energy Field and thus recharge our Life Battery with Pranic energy.

The brow chakra (Seed word 'N') is the chakra of energy, directing its distribution and channelising energy through the action of the heart (Seed word 'Y' or 'J') and through the digestion of the food in the stomach (Seed word 'R') and see how beautifully the word ENERGY is constituted of these very words, N, R & G (J). Thus, to remain energetic, bubbling and kicking:-

1. Exhale with   =   ENERGY
   Inhale with   =   RAJAN or RAJANNA

2. A better modification of the above mantra, add T & K in it.

   Exhale with   =   ENERGETIC
   Inhale with   =   RAJA - KANANT/RAJA-KA-ANNAD

3. Exhale with   =   I AM ENERGETIC or IMMI — ENERGETIC

379

Inhale with   =   RAJA— KAU—NAMMANT

The Inhale Mantra No. 3 is very suggestive and potent which means - Salutation to the KING of the LAND.

(i) The word 'R' stimulates the liver/ pancreas and all abdominal secretions to help digest food and assimilate it to give fire and ENERGY to our body.

(ii) It also helps to strengthen the heart with its seed word J for proper circulation of blood to supply oxygen / glycogen and other nutrients to each cell of our body to energize them to carry on various life processes. and to impart us the compassion.

(iii) The word 'N' the seed word for brow chakra stimulates the brain (left) the eye sight and also the pituitary gland to boost our immunity.

(iv) The word 'T' strengthens the taste glands.

(v) The word K also strengthens the left brain.

(vi) And the word 'M' stimulates the crown chakra, the right brain, and pineal gland.

Thus, it is a rejuvenating mantra to help us REMAIN ENERGETIC provided we take care to consume a balanced nutritious diet.

BECOME LIKE A REIKI HEALER

With the following simple mantra, we can also energize our hands to heal like the Reiki healer because Reiki - Universal Life Force is another name of PRANIC ENERGY.

(4) Exhale with   =   ENERGIZE HANDS

Inhale with   =   RAJA-HATHAN-NANZ

OR

(5) Inhale with   =   RA - JA - HATHAN - NAÑ

Exhale with   =   NEW-NEW-ENERGY-HAND

Both these mantras are very powerful to energize the hands quickly. With mantra no (5), we can also dance on CHA-CHA music as in chapter 41.

Another very suggestive and potent mantra to energize hands is :-

(6) Exhale with   =   ENERGIZE-HAND-TO HEAL

Inhale with   =   ALLA-RAJA-HATHAN-NANZ

However, in order to become a 'Reiki Healer', first, one has to become REIKI CHANNEL by learning from the competent REIKI master or become a Sidha (enlightened person) by stimulating each individual chakra as given in chapter 1, (Power of the Mantra) and the author of the book , being a PRANIC HEALER, can give a secret SIDHA MANTRA-a nine stage inhale/exhale mantra to stimulate all the nine astral body chakras simultaneously to become a Sidha, just in a short period of time, provided one leads a life of Satyam (Truth), Shivam (godliness) & Sunderam (beauty) in a pollution free environment with very keen and determined desire to become a Sidha. However, a Sidha mantra is being given in this book in the next chapter on (AUM), and another Sidha mantra has been given in chapter 41 to become a Healer.

However, with the simple mantras nos 4, 5 & 6 given above, with which if we breathe twenty times silently, this will energize the hands and you can yourself feel the pranic life energy outflowing in your hands and if you place your both hands on the ailing part, (See fig. 2) we can heal it just as in REIKI HEALING/ PRANIC HEALING/MANTRIC HEALING. And we can continuously recharge our hands with Pranic energy to heal ourself or others by recharging our hands with energy as above.

Also, we can move our hands up and down alternately to charge our hands with energy for healing, starting with the right hand up first. This is the easiest method to energize our hands for healing.

Here, I must also point out that the word REIKI spoken as "RAY-KEE" is in itself energy giving, exhale mantra because the word 'K' in it stimulates the left brain and the pituitary master gland and 'R' is the seed word of NAVEL CHAKRA to give FIRE to our body by digestion of food as said above.And we can also invoke this REIKI UNIVERSAL LIFE FORCE by the suggestive mantra -SAÑKRIY-REIKI which means - let REIKI ENERGY become active and move through me as channel. For this,

Inhale with　　=　SAÑK

Exhale with　　=　KRIY-REIKI

The word SANK yokes us with Super Conscious Energy Field to draw in the REIKI ENERGY. Thus you will now be able to heal yourself as well as others.

Healing the Knees
Fig. 2A

Healing Various Parts of the Body by Putting
Energized Hands on the Ailing Part.
Fig. 2A & 2B (P 384)

Healing Pancreas and Spleen
Fig. 2B

Chapter - 83

A SIDHA MANTRA

'AUM'

'Aum' spoken as 'AUÑM' is the most universally chanted mantra amongst Hindus from the ancient Vedic times. According to Hindu sages, they hear the all reverberating sound of 'AUNM' in the Ether Environment when they attain enlightenment. And according to Upanished TAITTIRYA, "AUM is our BEING - the sheath in which the Brahman (God) resides."

And, according to my breathing mantra concept, the word 'AU' denotes inhaling through the breath and this inhale breath denoted by (AU) connects us with Ñ which denotes superconsciousness- the infinite reserviour of life energy-The God Almighty, to which we are connected through breath, and this mantra ends with the word 'M', which is the seed word for the right brain and also for the Crown chakra. Thus, inhale breath denoted by (AU) is our link between our Being and the Super-consciousness (Ñ) and the mantra - 'AUÑM' establishes it firmly with the power of its words.

And you can yourself experience the 'resonance power' of the word 'M' in the crown of your head, as it beautifully resounds in the skull/dome of our brain as MMMM, the sound of M, slowly ebbing out. But, the word 'AUÑM' is only an inhale mantra and its exhale counter part in breathing is Mien. AUNM should be spoken silently by keeping the mouth closed. Then alone, it becomes an Inhale mantra.

1) Thus inhale with = AUÑM
   Exhale with   = MIEÑ

The total Inhale/ Exhale breathing mantra being AUÑM-MIEÑ. This sounds as if - 'I am the AUNM', and this is the greatest gift of Hinduism to mankind which proclaims in its upanishads (religious texts) - "Aham Brahmau - Asmi" - I am Brahman (God) - I am like THAT: I am born in the image of God. Thus, we all are the children of God.

Also, the mantra AUÑM-MIEN sounds similar to 'Ameen', an oft-repeated expression by devout Christians and Muslims all over the world; the word - Ameen means - Let God be with you in your endeavour.

But, only a trained Yogi can make the word AUNM arise from the base of the spine, from where the breath starts in our body almost 7 cm. below our Navel, which is denoted by the word 'S'/ Sh in our mantra breathing therapy. Thus, in order to help us breathe properly from its start point in our body, we add 'SA' to the mantra AUNM to make it 'SA-AUNM- a two stage breathing mantra. This means that my breath is Aunm, I am breathig with Aunm, because the word SAÑ denotes inhale breath.

2) Inhale with = SA-AUÑM
   Exhale with = MIEÑSH

The exhale mantra - 'Miensh' helps the exhale breath to complete its journey right upto its start point S/Sh.

The word S/Sh is very significant in our mantric breathing, first, as it denotes the normal start point of our breath in our body and secondly,

'S' also signifies the top of the vessel of divine life energy- so called kundalini by Hindu Sages, which is lying semidormant, like a coiled serpent, located about 7 cms. below the Navel chakra and this kundalini is bounded on the bottom by the Muladhara Chakra (L) the basic Sex Chakra which represents the earth principle and gives power to the legs to stand upon and the mind to illuminate when the kundalini life force becomes kinetic and starts moving up the spine, alongwith the breath, through the so called 'SUSHUMNA' opening in our spine. The Sushumna opens with the word AÑ/SAÑ.

The Muladhara Chakra is located between the base of spine and the genitals. Its seed word is L and the word 'All' helps us to breathe from below the Muladhara Chakra, i.e. from our legs. Thus the mantra "ALLA-YA-AUNM" helps the breath to arise from the bottom of the legs, takes it through the heart Chakra, represented by its seed word 'Y' and then connects it with "AUNM". With this breathing mantra, our whole being is thus connected with AUNM and the superconsciousness.

3) Thus, inhale with　　=　ALLA-YA-AUNM
   Exhale with　　　　=　YOU-ILLUMEEÑ

The above four stage breathing mantra not only helps to augment the heart's circulation for the blood to reach each and every cell of our body with the resonant sonic power of word 'Y', it also fills our heart with God's Compassion, while the word 'L' helps to move the stored divine energy in kundalini vessel upto the crown of our head, thus, filling our mind with God's GLORY, with which our whole body and mind can illumine. If we use the above breathing mantra, speaking it inwardly, smoothly and rhythmically for about 10 minutes both morning and evening as help in breathing, we will begin to notice in a month's time the sparkle of bliss in our eyes, spreading all around to become a Lamp to ourself and then to all others.

The word AUM is so much in the psyche of Hindus from generations that it is taken as the name of God. For them, AUM is both the inhale breath as well as the exhale breath, it is their total Being. With great diffidence and in great deference, I add the word SARA to AUM to give it the meaning that my whole being is AUM,

4) Inhale with   =   SARA — AUÑM

    Exhae with   =   MAIÑ — RISHI

This is indeed a very meaningful breathing mantra and the exhale mantra means - I am a sage. Also in the 3rd breathing mantra given above, - Alla-Ya-AUNM, we are also invoking by the word 'Ya' that all is AUM, which I hope, will be accepted by the enlightened Hindus and others, to breathe, 'AUNM' with their breath alongwith these useful additions, to give the users all the added health benefits, while simultaneously heightening the psyche of AUÑM. When I have traversed so far, I am further tempted to fortify mantra 'AUÑM' thus :-

5) Inhale with   =   SARA — JAHAN — AUÑM

                 or   SARA — YAHAN — AUÑM

    Exhale with   =   MIHI — JEE— RISHIEN

           or MUNI—YEE—RISHIH—HOOÑM

The word 'SARA' in Hindi/ Urdu also means All and Sara-JAHAN means — the whole universe which is filled with AUM as heard by our Rishis when they become enlightened. And the words 'S'/

SH are equivalent to 'L' and thus help to kindle the divine kundalini which moves to the Solar plexus (Navel chakra) with the power of its seed word 'R' which represents fire principle and improves digestion and assimilation of food by stimulating Liver and the pancreas; then the breath moves the heart chakra with the power of its seed word 'Y' or J to improve heart's circulation and to give compassion to our heart and then moves further to resonate with the throat/Vishudha chakra with the power of its seed word 'H' which aids in fat and carbohydrates metabolism by strengthening the Thyroid gland and then the word N stimulates the Brow chakra, the left brain and the eye sight and the pituitary gland which is the master gland controlling the total immune system of our body and then the breath ultimately joins with the Glory of AUNM to illuminate our total Being. This breathing mantra boosts our total immune system i.e. Pineal gland with M, the pituitary master gland with N, the Thyroid and Para-Thyroid glands with H, the Thymus gland with Y, the Liver and the pancreas and the emergency Adrenal glands with the word R and the sex glands with the words L & S/ SH. Thus, mantra No. 5 is a total body/mind rejuvenating breathing mantra to fortify our total immune system to fight any invading disease.That is why, I call it the Universal Healing Mantra.

This inhale mantra SARA-YAHAN-AUNM, though a five stages inhale mantra, but it resounds with all the seven astral Chakras surrounding our

---

For the benefit of Western readers, who are not used to chant the word 'Aunm' a separate chapter has been devoted in this book to the Mantra-"You-Re-Illuminate".

gross body. Thus, it is one of the most potent health mantra - it is so potent that it can even help a devotee to become a Sidha- a fully enlightened person, provided the devotee leads a stress free life of Satyam (Truth), Shivam (godliness) and Sunderum (Beauty), in a pollution free healthy environment.

Thus, with the power of AUNM in my breath, I hope to soon become a Rishi- a Sage with Capital 'S'.

OM — TAT — SAT (AMEEN)

Chapter - 34

THE PARTING SONG

The new generation thinks that they are different from their parents. They are! Because the children are usually more evolved genetic product of their parents. And the parents mostly want to cast their children so as to achieve their unfulfilled desires and Bob Dylon in one of his famous songs echoes the feelings of the new generation giving them a new entity thus :-

"Come mothers and fathers
Throughout the land.
Donot criticise what you donot understand.
Your sons and daughters are beyond your
command.
For the times, they are a changing".

But, my following poem echoes something unifying. Once I was invited in Calcutta by a large group of grown up boys and girls in our Belvedere Club to preside over their cultural function and to distribute the prizes and I addressed the young children with their parents at the end of the function thus :-

Dear friends, you have invited me to preside over this function because you think that I truly bridge the generation gap between you and your parents, because I think young, I act young and play and swim like all of you in the swiming pool as joyfully as you youngsters do. I have written a poem in blank verse entitled 'There is no generation gap' which I shall recite before you.

THERE IS NO GENERATION GAP

Life Moves
And time changeth.
But love is the same.
Lust is the same.
Is life not just a relay race?
Each generation carrying the race forward.
In its own beautiful way.
It has always been the same.
The tips of my fingers are aching.
From dialling the Telephone Number.
Of my girl friend again and again.
But my heart aches more.
From the lingering fear.
That my girl friend may be in conversation.
With some - one else
Who may be my rival in love.
My pain is no different.
From that of my mother.
Who during her youthful days.
Had also grown swollen finger tips.
From repeated servings of Musticated
Sweetened bread
To the Cawing Crow.
Who brought the message of love
Thus, time changeth
But pain in the fingers is the same
Love is the same
Lust is the same.
Pangs of separation are the same.
And Bliss in union is the same.
Where is then the Generation Gap?
It is nothing
But a growing and Gnawing Technical Gap.
Dancing on feverishly in this life's Relay Race
Non-stop, Faster and Faster.

And the whole audience of parents and the children gave a thunderous applause after I finished my above poem.

Is our life not a joyous but turbulent dance, going up and down through a vast spectrum of emotions, some times joyous, some times jealous. We need to summon tremendous fortitude and courage to face the hard realities of life; but those of us, who have a joyous heart and are hopeful will always remain young and thus age gracefully at a much slower pace, and will become ageless, if their heart is also full of compassion for one and all which the following mantra of the book stimulates in us abundantly.

Inhale with   =   JWAN (it means young)
Exhale with   =   JUVENATE

The exact mirror image of the inhale mantra JWAN should have been JUVEEN, but instead it is JUVENATE, like the new generation which possesses in them something evolutionary and is more tasteful with capital T. However, the inhale counterpart of 'JUVENATE' should be 'SDA-JWAN' which also means 'Ever-Young'. And indeed this doubly suggestive healing breathing mantra will help us to Bloom And Blossom At All Ages to remain full of youth.

BECOME A MAJESTIC KING OF YOURSELF

And youth is so majestic, we walk majestically, think majestically. Thus to remain majestic king of yourself and of all young hearts:

Exhale with   =   MAJESTIC KING

Inhale with   =   SAJATA-KAMAÑG

This breathing mantra helps us to kindle the

divine kundalini with 'S', strengthens the heart with 'J', improves our taste sense with 'T', and stimulates our hearing sensation with 'K', activates the smell sense with 'G', strengthens the left brain/the kingly pituitary gland with K&G, yokes us with Infinity- the Superconscious Energy Field with MAÑ and fortifies the right brain/the pacifying pineal gland with M - the seed word of crown / KINGLY CHAKRA which helps us to expand our right brain/ mind to discover something NEW, because man does not live by bread alone, he wants to satiate himself with the kingly taste of new discovery, i.e. to reach the moon/probe the mystery of atom and probe our true place in this universe- 'Who Am I'? This mantra will thus help us to fulfil THAT. And thus, let us part majestically, after our journey through this Temple of Self Healing.